IBERIAN AND LATIN AMERICAN STUDIES

# Carmen Martín Gaite

**Other titles in the series**

IBERIAN AND LATIN AMERICAN STUDIES

# *Carmen Martín Gaite*

## *Poetics, Visual Elements and Space*

ESTER BAUTISTA BOTELLO

UNIVERSITY OF WALES PRESS

2019

*www.uwp.co.uk*

*British Library CIP*
A catalogue record for this book is available from the British Library.


ISBN      978-1-78683-363-1
e-ISBN    978-1-78683-364-8

The right of Ester Bautista Botello to be identified as author of this work has been asserted in accordance with sections 77 and 79 of the Copyright, Designs and Patents Act 1988.

Typeset by Mark Heslington Ltd, Scarborough, North Yorkshire
Printed by CPI Antony Rowe, Melksham

# Contents

# Series Editors' Foreword

Over recent decades the traditional 'languages and literatures' model in Spanish departments in universities in the United Kingdom has been superseded by a contextual, interdisciplinary and 'area studies' approach to the study of the culture, history, society and politics of the Hispanic and Lusophone worlds – categories that extend far beyond the confines of the Iberian Peninsula, not only in Latin America but also to Spanish-speaking and Lusophone Africa.

In response to these dynamic trends in research priorities and curriculum development, this series is designed to present both disciplinary and interdisciplinary research within the general field of Iberian and Latin American Studies, particularly studies that explore all aspects of Cultural Production (inter alia literature, film, music, dance, sport) in Spanish, Portuguese, Basque, Catalan, Galician and indigenous languages of Latin America. The series also aims to publish research in the History and Politics of the Hispanic and Lusophone worlds, at the level of both the region and the nation-state, as well as on Cultural Studies that explore the shifting terrains of gender, sexual, racial and postcolonial identities in those same regions.

# List of Figures

# Acknowledgements

I would like to thank Professor Catherine Boyle, whose supervision, patience and encouragement were invaluable during my PhD studies, and Dr Luis Rebaza Soraluz for helping me with my studies and my life in London.

I am also very thankful for the conversations and support of all my friends, especially Jennifer Chambers, Alejandra López, Inés Alonso, Marisol de Lafuente and Marta Cocco.

My love for my mother and my father and all my family, specially my sisters, without whom this would not have been possible.

Thanks to my extended family in Spain for their support and love.

Thanks to Colin Brent for his translations and his readings.

Thanks to Ignacio and Daniel. Their love and understanding were the main ingredients that helped me throughout this project.

Carmen Martín Gaite, 1980

# Introduction

Carmen Martín Gaite, a Spanish writer from the *Generación de los 50,* was always interested in reflecting on her own writing process. Testament to this is *El cuento de nunca acabar. Apuntes sobre la narración, el amor y la mentira,* first published in 1983 but started in 1973. As well as exploring and questioning herself on the act of narrating, she also documents the process of writing this text. The author considers it to be like a 'diary [...] a kind of logbook'[1] in which to offload the vicissitudes through which she lived while writing these notes on narration and life. *El cuento de nunca acabar* enables us to understand writing as a process that privileges dialogue and brings the possibility of creating links with the words of others. The book was still unfinished when Martin Gaite went to the United States for the first time. This is why the way in which she wrote it and all the emotions that she went through to bring it to its conclusion are of such interest. The result was the creation of a poetics centred around the process of writing. But how can we reconstruct a complete image of that poetics, and of which elements is it is made up?

First we must note that poetics is Carmen Martín Gaite's idea of how her own narrative should be. Given that the writer reflected on this subject for several years, the revision of other texts is important, allowing us to reconstruct, reset, trace or develop a cartography with a whole range of elements that make up the posited narrative of Martín Gaite. For this, I will draw upon the analysis of *Agua pasada* (articles, prologues and lectures, 1993), *Pido la palabra* (2002) and *Cuadernos de todo* (2002). In these, we witness the journey as the fundamental principle with which Martín Gaite develops her narrative in the 1990s.

I have selected four novels published after the visit of the writer to New York: *Nubosidad variable* (1992), *La reina de las nieves* (1994), *Lo raro es vivir* (1996) and *Irse de casa* (1998). Given the constant role of travelling in these texts, I will analyse the journey as an aesthetic practice and identify a series of actions that allow the narrative to be linked with two essential elements of her work: the construction of space and the visual. To do this, I will use the theories of Francesco Careri and Michel de Certeau. The former understands walking as 'an aesthetic instrument capable of describing and modifying those metropolitan spaces that often present a nature that should be understood and filled with meanings, rather than projected and filled with things'.[2]

The poetics of Martín Gaite lies in the journey. Therefore, it will be necessary to identify and analyse a series of actions linked with that concept, such as *pasear* ('to stroll'), *desplazarse* ('to move around'), *orientarse* ('to get one's bearings'), *explorar* ('to explore') and *deambular* ('to wander'), among others. Through these actions, carried out in differing spaces, I identify different types of geographies in Martín Gaite's narrative: the domestic, the urban, the interior and the narrative. As well as explaining what each of these geographies consists of, I am interested in showing the view of the protagonists (in the writing of the 1990s) towards the diverse spaces that they passed through or inhabited. To do this, I will need to revise and analyse the function of the gaze in literature and in Martín Gaite's work in particular. I contend that actions such as *contemplar* ('to contemplate'), *mirar* ('to look'), *espiar* ('to spy') or *fisgar* ('to snoop') are the domain of the gaze and, taking into account the different meaning of each, Martín Gaite unites them to poeticise that a novel comes from all that which the eye contemplates, looks at, spies or snoops on. Let us look at the work of Mieke Bal on narratology and visuality. Bal discusses and analyses the way in which certain concepts – such as the gaze, the point of view, perspective and vision – shift or travel from one discipline to another.

The strategies identified in Martín Gaite's work correspond with the essential questions that will help to form her poetics. What is being looked at? How is it being looked at? Or, where is it being looked at from? It is important to observe how the objects and the gaze of the narrator are represented in relation to the space that they occupy, the characteristics of said space and the way in which this determines the actions of the characters – all seen through the notions of space and place. According to Mieke Bal in *Narratology: Introduction to the Theory of Narrative*, three senses are strongly linked with the perception of space: sight, hearing and touch. The images of space represented in the work of Martín Gaite are principally based around sight. In the writer's poetics, the *composición del lugar* ('composition of place') is a key and constant presence. The protagonists of her novels describe, and in some cases draw, the space they inhabit in detail. This entails a type of translation from the experience of walking – moving around those interior or urban spaces – to an aesthetic form. That is to say, the actions carried out in the space walked through are converted into a narrative and visual cartography.

The writer's poetics involved a process that continued to change over the years. The relationship between literature and painting was established in several lectures given by Martín Gaite in Spain in the 1990s. The Spanish Ministry of Culture organised an exhibition called '*El espacio privado. Cinco siglos en veinte palabras*', the aim of which was to reflect upon the way in which Spanish culture uses spaces and fills them with images. Carmen Martín Gaite took part in this exhibition, presenting an essay on the function of the window in the following works: *Figura en una ventana* by Salvador Dalí; *Gallegas a la ventana* by Murillo; *Sin tarea* by Maura Montaner; and *Horas de labor* by Salvador Tuset. Six years later, she wrote a lecture to present her point of view on *Hotel Room* by Edward Hopper. Martín Gaite's poetics continued to appropriate other discourses, while maintaining key elements such as the gaze. How does a writer look at a pictorial image? Why write about women looking out of a window? Why this interest in interior spaces? How does a writer create a spatial composition in her narrative, and how can we approach a spatial composition in painting?

Walking or strolling are aesthetic practices used by some artists to attribute an aesthetic value to a space. The act of walking is associated with creation. I will show how, using this, Martín Gaite builds a narrative and visual cartography in the process of her writing. By travelling through space, a transformation of this space, as well as of the person who crosses it, takes place. Narratives with different meanings are created. I will look at all the changes experienced by Martín Gaite during her multiple trips to the United States, and in particular to New York. Her narrative poetics developed in *El cuento de nunca acabar* change into the visual image in the collages that she made from the 1980s onwards. The union between literature and the visual can already be seen in the writer's first novels, but it becomes more accentuated after her trip to New York in 1979. That visit led to the creation of collages as a way to express what cannot be said only with wordsand requires images, too. These collages were published under the title *Visión de Nueva York*. What is the vision that Martín Gaite has of New York? What images does she show of this urban environment? What kind of elements does she use for the creation of her collages? How is the relation between these collages and her poetics established? What biographical traces can be found in these visual compositions? What does Martín Gaite express through images? These are some of the questions raised by an analysis of some of the writer's collages. The question of how to approach and work with the visual elements in Martín Gaite's work is based on the methodology proposed by Gillian Rose in *Visual Methodologies*, and principally in her chapter on the analysis of an image's composition.

Carmen Martín Gaite's poetics transcends writing. She builds bridges and dialogues with other disciplines. Her poetics is based on the aesthetic practice of working, of the journey, and of strolling around diverse geographies in which the gaze becomes a fundamental element. Everything that the eye lights upon becomes, later, narrative and visual material. In the work of Martín Gaite, literature, painting, collage and her interest in how to tell a story all converge. She is a writer who turns to the pictorial universe and whose tales contain a continual reference to painting and regularly even to particular paintings and painters – such as Edward Hopper – with whom she feels a deep affinity and who act as an inspiration for her narrative work.

The image of Carmen Martín Gaite that I propose is that of an artist who conceives of literary creation as a continual movement that produces a complex network of relations. This collection of intersections, charted in different ways in her novels of the 1990s, produces a reciprocal relation between literary language and visual elements – drawing, painting and collage. This is why the literature of Martín Gaite can be seen as a space of cohabitation and flow between literature and other disciplines.

# 1

# The Historical, Narrative and Poetic Path of Carmen Martín Gaite

Carmen Martín Gaite's narrative path dates back to the publication of *Entre visillos* (1958) and comes to a close with *Los parentescos* (2001), an unfinished novel published posthumously, a year after her death. The time gap between the two works represents the period, spanning more than forty years, in which the writer was actively productive. Many changes were to take place in this period, both socially and in literature, and the work of Carmen Martín Gaite was no exception.

I shall sketch the socio-political and cultural context to which Carmen Martín Gaite belonged, with a view to underlining the origins and development of the narrative elements employed by the writer in shaping her poetics, which is reflected in *El cuento de nunca acabar*, published in 1983, but the elaboration of which dates back to 1973. For this reason, I shall attempt to show that Martín Gaite's poetic concepts are already visible during those years in which she was classified as a writer belonging to the *Generación de los 50*.

I have divided this chapter into two sections that, in addition to revealing the socio-political and cultural context, highlight the persistent presence of the narrative elements with which the writer has worked during a period of more than forty years and which have contributed indisputably to the creation of a poetics in which writing is linked to visual elements such as drawing, painting and collage.

## The socio-political and cultural context

### The 1950s in retrospect

A glimpse at life in Spain in the 1950s necessarily implies a review of the Franco regime, which, by that time, had been shaping the way of life of Spanish people for over a decade. During the initial years, and particularly in the 1940s, economic politics and the general attitude of the government was characterised by interventionism and autarchy. Clear preference was given to economic self-sufficiency and total independence with respect to other countries. In addition to encouraging unforeseen circumstances, such as food shortage, the black market and rationing, such a political posture plunged Spain into a situation of total isolation vis-à-vis the international community. As we shall analyse further on, this isolated and stagnated society, much more apparent in the small cities and towns of the provinces, represents the backdrop against which Martín Gaite will sketch the conditions and concerns of her characters in *Entre visillos*.

In 'El franquismo: planteamiento general', Julio Montero Díaz points to the fact that the period from 1947 to 1951 revealed the beginning of a new stage in Spain's relationship with the outside world, symbolised in a series of key political events: Spain's entry into the United Nations Food and Agriculture Organization (FAO) in 1950, and the signing, in 1953, of an agreement with the United States, allowing the latter to instal military bases on Spanish soil in exchange for economic aid. Nonetheless, according to Montero Díaz, the dual basis on which the Franco regime continued to govern – namely, traditionalism and authoritarianism – did not alter. From this ideological point of view, Franco set out to obtain absolute control of Spanish society. In order to achieve this, it was necessary to build consolidated relations with the Church, the Spanish Falangist movement, the Army, the land-owning oligarchy and financial and industrial groups. An authoritarian, confessionalist and nationalist state was thus created in which political intransigence, multi-party representation and trade union diversity were prohibited and replaced by economic interventionism, press and radio-oriented propaganda, religious unity and the imposition of a national culture. This scenario endured until 1957, when a new political direction was ushered in with the presence in government of technocrats and certain Opus Dei members, according to information appearing in a monographic study in *Revista de Occidente* entitled 'Ideología y cultura en la España de los vencedores'.[1]

With respect to the way of life led by women, all laws passed during the Republic (1936–9), on matters such as divorce and abortion, were abolished. Marriage was for life and propaganda in favour of contraception forbidden. Francoist ideology extolled the traditional role of the mother and spouse confined to the home. This was carried out via the Sección Femenina, an organisation run by Pilar Primo de Rivera, sister of José Antonio Primo de Rivera, founder of the Spanish Falangist movement in 1933. The home was a woman's sole mission, according to the Sección Femenina. The most important thing was 'hacer agradable la vida a los hombres y educar a los hijos como siervos de Dios y futuros soldados de España' ('to make life pleasant for the men and bring up the children as God-fearing future soldiers for Spain'),[2] as stated by García Basauri in 'La Sección Femenina en la guerra civil española'.

The Sección Femenina reorganised the social services in 1940, with a view to disseminating Franco's ideology. For six months, young Spanish women received theoretical instruction and carried out active service at an officially approved centre. A woman's education was reduced to the domestic domain, the idea being to create the *mujer nueva* ('new woman'). In her book *La polémica feminista en la España contemporánea 1868–1974*, Scanlon reveals the characteristics of this *mujer nueva*, which 'sería una "mujer de su tiempo", feliz en la maternidad, educando a sus hijos, demostrando un interés femenino por los asuntos del marido y proporcionándole un refugio tranquilo contra los azares de la vida pública' ('would be a "woman for her times", content with her motherhood, bringing up her children, showing a feminine interest in her husband's affairs and providing him with a peaceful retreat from the travails of public life').[3]

In the era of Franco, the moral integrity required had a particular impact upon women who felt more acutely the pressures from without, both as potential mothers and as the cornerstone upon which the formation of future families was to rest. Molinero Carme underlines the fact that mixed education was forbidden in May 1939, so as to ensure correct upbringing from childhood. As a consequence, boys were pointed in the direction of a social life while the life of a girl was destined for the home. The end result was a society in which male and female roles were clearly defined and in which it was considered unbecoming to behave differently from the norms established by religion, the Spanish Falangist movement and the Sección Femenina. All action outside the stipulations set by religious dogma and social norms was frowned upon.

This aforementioned environment can be clearly seen in *Entre visillos* and *Ritmo lento*. In the former, for example, it is possible to observe that boys and girls study apart until it is time to go to university. The institute in which part of the action of the novel takes place is entirely female. The young girls in *Entre visillos* are educated with a view to being rescued and dependent, while the boys are brought up to be daring and autonomous. For this reason, the life of the female characters takes place inside the home, behind net curtains, and they feel inadequate and unprepared when their social life begins. An excellent example of this is when Natalia visits the casino for the first time.

### The *Generación del Medio Siglo*

If we leave to one side the poems published in the Salamanca review *Trabajos y días* at the end of the 1940s and, bearing in mind the fact that *El balneario* (1955), *Entre visillos* (1958) and *Las ataduras* (1960) were published in the 1950s, Carmen Martín Gaite can be included within the group of writers beginning to publish in that period and which has come to be known as *Generación del Medio Siglo* or *Generación de los 50*. José María Castellet in 'La novela española, quince años después, 1942–1975', Gonzalo Sobejano in *Novela española de nuestro tiempo* and Santos Sanz Villanueva in *Historia de la novela social española* (1942–75) refer to the *Generación de los 50* as that generation of writers who became known in the 1950s. Martín Gaite fulfils this characteristic, as mentioned above, and thus can be included within this classification.

The term '*Generación del Medio Siglo*' or '*Generación de los 50*' has been the motive for much discussion between critics and the writers included in the group, as I shall attempt to explain throughout this section. The actual formation and cohesion of this generation are due to a series of shared circumstances, as is so often the case when there exists the considered intention of grouping together a series of writers. For example, the dates of birth of the writers in question represent a criterion of selection. In this case, the critics referred to previously have singled out two periods. We witness the birth of Luis

Martín Santos, Alfonso Sastre, Ignacio Aldecoa, Ana María Matute, Jesús Fernández Santos, Josefina Rodríguez, Rafael Sánchez Ferlosio, Juan Benet and Carmen Martín Gaite in the 1920s, while, between 1930 and 1935, Juan Goytisolo, Juan Marsé, Luis Goytisolo-Gay and Gonzalo Torrente Malvido, among others, are born.

Another circumstance favouring such a grouping is the fact that they were eyewitnesses to the Spanish Civil War during their childhood. Josefina Rodríguez, Ignacio Aldecoa's widow, goes as far as to put together an anthology of short stories written by her friends, to whom she dedicates a brief biographical sketch, *Los niños de la guerra* (1983):

> El común denominador ... era que habíamos vivido la guerra de niños, con ocho, nueve y diez años, y que teníamos de aquella tragedia una experiencia desconcertante y bastante definitiva. Y así como nuestra infancia había transcurrido bajo el signo de la guerra civil, nuestra adolescencia amanece bajo el signo de la guerra mundial. Nuestro bachillerato se completó entre manifestaciones pro alemanas, desfiles, prensa y radio de un solo factor frente al conflicto ... llegamos a la Universidad, una Universidad empobrecida, censurada, mutilada ... sin otra experiencia de un país en guerra y posguerra.

> The common denominator ... was that we'd lived through the war as eight-, nine- or ten-year-olds, so we shared a significant and bewildering experience of that tragedy. And just as we had spent our childhood under the shadow of civil war, our adolescence dawned under the shadow of the First World War. We finished high school amid pro-German rallies, parades, biased press and radio war coverage ... we reached university – an impoverished, censured, mutilated university – ... with no other experience other than that of a war-torn or post-war country.[4]

Another factor is the proximity in dates of first editions, which, when added to the other two factors mentioned, contributes to the 'creación' of this generation of writers. Take a look, for example, at the chronological similarities in publication of the works of some of these writers – namely, Ignacio Aldecoa with *El fulgor y la sangre*, Jesús Fernández Santos with *Los bravos*, Juan Goytisolo with *Juegos de manos* and Ana María Matute with *Pequeño teatro*, all appearing in 1954. Two years later, Rafael Sánchez Ferlosio published *El Jarama* and in 1958 Luis Goytisolo presented *Las afueras* at the same time as

Carmen Martín Gaite received the news that she had won the 1957 Premio Eugenio Nadal for *Entre visillos*.

Grouped together on account of their dates of birth, as well as having the common denominator of having experienced the Spanish Civil War as children, the publication dates of their first works, not to mention belonging to and forming a circle of friends, as well as the much-disputed *conciencia generacional* ('generational conscience'), this 'Generación de los 50' is divided into two groups exhibiting different literary and narrative trends. For one, the meeting place was Madrid while, for the other, it was Barcelona. Aldecoa, Sánchez Ferlosio, Sastre, Josefina Rodríguez, Paso, Quinto, Fernández Santos and Carmen Martín Gaite all collaborate on the *Revista Española* under the guidance of the bibliophile Antonio Rodríguez Moñino. For their part, those pertaining to the Barcelona group published in the review *Laye* whose patron was José María Castellet. Included among its members were Jaime Gil de Biedma, the Goytisolo brothers, Juan Marsé and Carlos Barral. Given that Martín Gaite belonged to the Madrid group, I limit my analysis to what took place in that city.

The Madrid group was consolidated through the publication, between June 1953 and February 1955, of the *Revista Española*. In 'Poco más que anécdotas 'culturales' alrededor de quince años (1950–1965)', Alfonso Sastre has recalled those days in the following manner:

> Cuando, en 1953, Ignacio Aldecoa, Rafael Sánchez Ferlosio y yo visitamos a Pío Baroja, lo hicimos para pedirle algún trabajillo inédito. Se trataba de ponerlo en las primeras páginas de la *Revista Española*, que estábamos fundando por entonces con Antonio Rodríguez Moñino, el cual la ponía alegremente en nuestras manos.

> When, in 1950, Ignacio Aldecoa, Rafael Sánchez Ferlosio and I visited Pío Baroja, we did so to ask him for some piece of unpublished material. This was to be put in the first pages of the *Revista Española*, that we were then in the process of founding with Antonio Rodríguez Moñino, who was happy to place it in our hands.[5]

*Revista Española*, which appeared on a bi-monthly basis, was published under the directorship and editing supervision of Aldecoa, Sastre and Sánchez Ferlosio. Martín Gaite had met Aldecoa for the first time in 1943, when both were studying core units of the Bachelor of arts degree at the Palacio de Anaya. In

1945, Aldecoa left for Madrid and three years would go by before they met again, Martín Gaite having travelled to that city to begin a doctorate in romance literature. Aldecoa introduced the writer to his friends, including Sastre and Sánchez Ferlosio. In 1953, Martín Gaite and the author of *El Jarama* were married. That same year saw the foundation of the *Revista Española*.

In the review's second issue (July 1953), Martín Gaite published her first short story, entitled *Un día de libertad*. It should be mentioned, however, that she had previously published in other Madrid reviews such as *La Hora, Alcalá, Clavileño* and *La Estafeta Literaria*, as well as in the newspaper *ABC*. Her stories, like those of her fellow writers, were impregnated with new readings from abroad, which they eagerly passed around and exchanged, as Martín Gaite comments in her Prólogo to *Los bravos*:

> Por libre, por separado y casi siempre por casualidad, fuimos tomando contacto con los amigos de entonces, según iba pudiendo ser, con Sartre, con Hemingway, con Pavese, con Truman Capote, con Italo Calvino, con Tennessee Williams, con Dos Passos, con Kafka, con Priestley, con Joyce, con Ciro Alegría. Las voces desparejadas y lejanas de aquellos escritores eran como un rescoldo en torno al cual necesitábamos agruparnos para enlazar con algo, para no sentir que se partía de cero, y el hecho de pasarnos unos a otros, con los libros, la mención de sus autores, de si vivían acá o allá, de si habían muerto de tal o cual manera, fue lo que convirtió en un humus propio aquel montón de heterogéneas sugerencias.

> Singly, separately and almost always fortuitously, we regained contact with old friends such as Sartre, Hemingway, Pavese, Truman Capote, Italo Calvino, Tennessee Williams, Dos Passos, Kafka, Priestley, Joyce, and Ciro Alegría. The distant, mismatched voices of those writers were like a remnant around which we needed to gather to hook on to something, so as to not feel as if starting from scratch. The act of passing the books among us – mentioning their authors, whether they lived here or there, whether they had died in such or such a manner – was what turned that stack of heterogeneous inspiration into its own humus.[6]

In Jurado Morales' *La trayectoria narrativa de Martín Gaite*, Pilar de la Puente, María de los Ángeles Lluch and Carmen Alemany Bay, among others, point to the contact of these writers with other creative sources such as the *Generación del 98* (Baroja, Machado and Valle Inclán), the North American narrative of the 'lost generation'

(Dos Passos, Faulkner, Hemingway), French and Russian Realism and Naturalism (Zola, Verga, Gorki), the *nouveau roman* and, of greater relevance, Italian Neo-Realist cinema (Rosselini, De Sica and Cesare Zavattini), without forgetting the literary perspective of the same school (Pavese, Silone, Pratolini).

Belonging in the early years to the *Generación de los 50*, the narrative career of the Salamanca novelist is normally linked to the Neo-Realist postulates prevailing in post-war Spain and visible in *Entre visillos* (1958). In this book, Martín Gaite confirms the claustrophobic and oppressive environment of a provincial city in the 1950s. Pablo Klein is the stranger who arrives in that city to give classes for a year at the *Instituto de Enseñanza Media*. Through his story and that of other narrators, the routine and idle life of the city is gradually revealed, along with the personal paths pursued by certain young, middle-class individuals, the majority being girls. In *El neorrealismo en la narración española de los años cincuenta*, Fernández Fernández expresses the opinion that both Neo-Realist cinema and literature are rooted in the same assumptions: to reflect and, at times, condemn immediate reality. For this reason, preference is given to the description of the humble and forgotten, to their *predicamentello*, emphasising not only the sociological aspect of reality but also the repercussions of this reality on people's minds and hearts. In this sense, Neo-Realism produces a series of works characterised by an objective and humanitarian approach in which the exposition of the themes transcends the simple storyline so as to take on a general universal significance.

In 'Hilos, ataduras y ruinas en la novelística de Carmen Martín Gaite', Kathleen Glenn believes that when Pablo and Natalia narrate their experiences, use is being made of 'la técnica expositiva y no analítica, y la perspectiva, objetiva, al igual que la del narrador en tercera persona' ('a descriptive rather than analitical technique, and the objective perspective like that of the third-person narrator').[7] For his part, in *La trayectoria narrativa de Carmen Martín Gaite*, Jurado Morales finds 'acertado el juego de los narradores y la elección de los personajes encargados de narrar para el fin neorrealista de la novela: dar testimonio de la cotidianidad mediante la máxima fidelidad a la realidad circundante' ('both the narrators' recourse and the choice of narrator characters quite apt for the novel's Neo-Realist purposes: to attest to the everyday by means of maximum fidelity to the surrounding reality').[8]

According to Sanz Villanueva in *Historia de la novela social española*, 'hay que precisar [...] que el primer libro de Martín Gaite se publica en 1958, ya en pleno realismo crítico, por lo que esta escritora bien podría estimarse como una continuadora de la tendencia neorrealista' ('It must be pointed out [...] that Martín Gaite's first book was published in 1958, in the midst of critical realism, thus this author could well be considered a continuation of the Neo-Realist trend').[9] In my view, Martín Gaite takes part in this trend of the 1950s as a *de facto* member and not as a continuation of the work carried out by others. Regarding the chronological delay sustained by Sanz Villanueva, I believe it is not applicable when considering the writer's short story trajectory. At least six stories written between 1953 and 1958 slot into the Neo-Realist coordinates and testimonials of the 1950s in that they all reveal one or several of the following possibilities: they reflect a confrontation between different social classes; they denounce the social conditions of a certain reality; they recreate the circumstances that surround a character who has fallen victim to some social injustice; or they are focused on the labour context. In 'Un día de libertad' (1953), an office worker is dismissed by the boss. In 'La chica de abajo' (1953), two childhood friends drift apart on account of social differences. In 'Los informes' (1954), a girl who is prepared to serve as a maid is expelled by the owner even before she begins to work due to mistaken and maliciously distorted information. In 'La oficina' (1954), lack of communication between the characters results in the death of one and the possible life-long spinsterhood of the other. In 'La conciencia tranquila' (1956), the small girl dies because her mother does not have the necessary economic means. Finally, in 'La tata' (1958), a girl from a small town serves on a routine basis in a house in Madrid.

Unlike the combative attitude of the Social Realists, the Neo-Realists prefer to reflect the surrounding reality in a neutrally apparent manner, without adopting an openly denunciatory position. All in all, they coincide on two fronts. On the one hand, they reject the covering up of the truth by the official authorities through evasive action unrelated to the historical reality of the time. On the other, both seek the maximum degree of fidelity in their narrative goals and the events taken from real life. José Manuel Caballero Bonald reflects on this point in the following way:

Creo que hay una cosa, por lo menos, segura que nos unía, que era efectivamente dar una versión de la época del país en que vivíamos distinta a la versión de los estamentos oficiales, del régimen, es decir, describir una realidad cada cual a su manera, pero que era urgente que se ofreciera en términos verosímiles y verídicos … Lo que nos unía era, frente a la versión maquillada, falsa, de lo que estaba pasando en el país, ofrecer la verdad, eso por lo menos.

I think there's at least one certain element that united us: to offer a version of the times we lived in that differed from the version of the state, of the regime; to describe a reality our own way, but it was imperative that it should be in honest, truthful terms … Faced with the false, made-up version of what was happening in the country, what united us was the chance to at least offer the truth.[10]

This is Martín Gaite's attitude in *Entre visillos*. Through the story narrated in her novel she seeks to record the claustrophobic and oppressive atmosphere of a provincial city in the 1950s while, at the same time, revealing the consequences of a routine life and of a norm-oriented society on the individuals it affects, who are mainly women. The novel is structured around two narrative voices in the first person. One of these voices is that of Pablo Klein, a German teacher who arrives in the city to teach at the Instituto Femenino; the other point of view is that of Natalia, one of Klein's adolescent students who has always lived in the city. There is also Julia, one of Natalia's sisters, who becomes a narrator when the letters she writes to her boyfriend are introduced into the narrative. The boyfriend encourages her to leave the small city and go to live with him in Madrid. Julia, like Natalia, provides an inside view of the conflicts of life in the provinces. The final point of view employed in *Entre visillos* is that of the narrator in the third person, who opts for focusing on the narration of collective scenes in which dialogues occur between a considerable number of characters.

According to the widespread idea in the *Medio Siglo* that the writer should write about what he sees around him, the bases of Martín Gaite's narrative in giving shape to *Entre visillos* are her own experiences. In an interview with Celia Fernández, the writer says that '*Entre visillos* lo escribí como una especie de rechazo de ese mundo provinciano del que huía. Yo tenía veintitantos años y acababa de llegar a Madrid. Hay una crítica, aunque sin crueldad, de ese mundo pequeño y demasiado cerrado de mi infancia y juventud' ('I wrote *Entre visillos* as a kind of rejection of that provincial world I was fleeing. I was twenty-something and had just arrived in Madrid. It is a critique, though without cruelty, of this small and too closed world of my childhood and youth').[11] The first-hand testimony of the writer takes on relevance when the novel compensates for the lack of an objective press capable of transmitting the authentic reality of Spain under Franco. In *Entre visillos* it is possible to find a *bona fide* sociological document on life, particularly that of the young bourgeoisie, in a provincial capital of the 1950s. In this sense, it is a novel that helps us to get to know the 'intrahistoria' of the Spanish post-war period. Jurado Morales believes that 'lo narrado en la novela es extrapolable a cualquier otra ciudad española' ('what is narrated in the novel can be extrapolated to any other Spanish city'),[12] individual concerns thus becoming universal issues. In this way, Martín Gaite, in her novel *Entre visillos*, transcends and attains a much greater dimension.

Nevertheless, not all the critics consider Martín Gaite to be an important representative of Neo-Realist literature. *Entre visillos* is not entirely an objectivist novel, or obligatory paradigm of the Spanish novel of the 1960s, according to Adolfo Sotelo in his introduction to *Retahílas* (xxii–xxiii). The problem arising from all this controversy as to whether *Entre visillos* can be included or not within the Neo-Realist genre is that we are left with a somewhat obsolete classification that impedes the analysis of Martín Gaite's work from other perspectives. In my opinion, the writer borrows techniques from Neo-Realism and develops them in her own way throughout her narrative, as I shall discuss later. One of these is the use of the narrator as if he or she were a camera-novelist, in such a way that the knowledge that the reader might have of the characters will arise not from the description that the narrator provides of their inner world, but from the behaviour and conduct of what they say and do. Thus, Natalia's diary in *Entre visillos* will become the film script for Amparo Miranda's son in *Irse de casa*. In both stories, the reader will gradually shape the life of the characters throughout the novels. Characters themselves do not exist; they are in the process of being created. The inner changes are closely linked to the outer movements of the characters – that is to say, to the walks they take about the city (in the case of Natalia) or to the trips to other countries (in the case of Amparo Miranda).

The appearance of such a range of viewpoints helps show the sociological impact of the authoritarian and dogmatic discourse of

Catholic Nationalism on the lives of certain young, middle-class individuals in the post-war period. Martín Gaite does not judge that discourse directly. Her intention is to reflect on existential assumptions related to her historic moment – namely, the lack of communication, and the isolation, incomprehension and resignation, among others. In *Entre visillos*, the writer demystifies a series of conventionalisms that prevent women from fulfilling their full potential. Among such conventionalisms are differentiated education for men and women, the importance of marriage and the preservation of a heterosexual family structure with clearly defined roles. For example, the Instituto at which Pablo Klein works is strictly for young girls, the majority of whom have no intention of continuing their studies, their ultimate aim being to get married. The young girls in *Entre visillos* 'se veían del brazo de un chico maduro, pero juvenil, respetable, pero deportista, yendo a los estrenos de teatros y a los conciertos del Palacio de la Música, con abrigo de astracán legítimo; sombrerito pequeño. Teniendo un círculo; seguras y rodeadas de consideración' ('envisioned themselves escorted by a mature yet youthful, respectable yet sporty man, attending theatre premières and Palacio de la Música concerts, wearing a genuine lambswool coat and a pillbox hat. Belonging to a circle; confident and held in the highest esteem').[13] While not everyone is so fortunate, what is certain is that their only goal in life is to get married. Antonio Vilanova affirms that '*Entre visillos* nos ofrece una amarga radiografía moral del mundo expectante e ilusionado de las muchachas casaderas' ('*Entre visillos* offers us a bitter moral X-ray of the expectant, illusory world of young women of marriageable age').[14]

Fear of spinsterhood and provincial life form part of the reality of post-war Spain. The evidence can be read in *Entre visillos* and seen in Juan Antonio Bardem's film *Calle mayor* (1956). This correspondence has been pointed out in critical studies on Martín Gaite. Such is the case of the work of Pilar de la Puente Samaniego and of José Jurado Morales. Santos Sanz Villanueva underlines the fact that the relations that existed between cinema promoters and writers were decisive and profound.

The conclusion reached by Santos Sanz Villanueva in *Historia de la novela social española* merits special attention due to the relationship that the author establishes between cinema and literature, a relationship that characterises the novelists of the *Generación de los 50*:

Dos de los nombres más valiosos de la cinematografía española de aquellos años, Juan Antonio Bardem y Luis García Berlanga, son los correspondientes en el terreno del séptimo arte, de los escritores sociales en novela. Se trata de dos directores de una nueva generación que no han participado en la guerra (aquél nace en 1922; éste en 1921) y que pretenden, con vacilaciones y con sustanciosos cambios en su misma trayectoria, reflejar problemas y cuestiones de la España actual, *Muerte de un ciclista* es el equivalente en el celuloide de las novelas antiburguesas de los hermanos Goytisolo y guarda cierto parecido con los libros de García Hortelano. Bardem se enfrenta con otros aspectos de la realidad nacional y la crítica provinciana y el miedo a la soltería de *Calle mayor* (1956), recuerda el ambiente salmantino de *Entre visillos*, de Martín Gaite.

Two of the most renowned names in Spanish film-making of those times, Juan Antonio Bardem and Luis García Berlanga, are cinema correspondents and social novelists. They are two new-generation directors who did not participate in the war (the former was born in 1922; the latter in 1921) and who, with substantial wavering changes of course, try to reflect modern-day Spain's problems and issues. *Muerte de un ciclista* (*Death of a Cyclist*) is the film equivalent of the Goytisolo brothers' anti-bourgeoisie novels and somewhat resemble García Hortelano's books. Bardem deals with other aspects of Spain's reality; provincial criticism and the fears of remaining unwed in *Calle mayor* (*Main Street*) (1956) are reminiscent of Martín Gaite's Salamanca ambiance in *Entre visillos*.[15]

The fact that the critics compare *Calle mayor* with *Entre visillos* serves as the key to introducing the influences of Neo-Realist cinema on the writing of Martín Gaite. In 1950, the Instituto Italiano de Cultura de Madrid hosted a week of Neo-Realist cinema in which films by Antonioni, Zavatinni, Blasetti, De Sica, Fellini and Alberto Lattuada were projected. As a result of this week of Neo-Realist cinema, the first Spanish film with a testimonial perspective was *Surcos*, directed in 1951 by J. A. Nieves Conde, with a script by Torrente Ballester based on a Eugenio Montes plot. In *Esperando el porvenir*, Martín Gaite mentions that 'por primera vez, nuestro cine abandonaba los escenarios ostentosos para posar la cámara sobre lo que pasaba en la calle todos los días' ('for the first time our cinema abandoned flashy settings to fix cameras on what was happening in the streets every day').[16] In that same book, Martín Gaite recalls that the poster announcing the premiere at the Palacio de la Prensa carried the title *Surcos* in red, with a subtitle 'La lucha por la ciudad'

('The fight for the city'), an allusion to the life of immigrant workers who, at a later date, would be the inspirational subject matter for the stories of Ignacio Aldecoa. In Martín Gaite's opinion:

> El nuevo cine no sólo estaba proponiendo una denuncia y levantando un testimonio, sino sugiriendo a quienes buscábamos un cauce de expresión distinto para escapar de la mentira otro punto de vista. La cámara de cine se limitaba a enfocar las escenas desde el ángulo más idóneo, captarlas y mostrarlas, sin hacer comentarios ni meterse en juicios de valor.

> The new cinema was not just proposing accusations and testifying, but also suggesting another standpoint to those of us who were seeking different venues of expression to escape from the lies. Film cameras merely focused on scenes from the most advantageous angle, recording them and showing them without comments or judgement.[17]

If we think about it for a moment, in *Entre visillos* it is possible to ascertain that Pablo Klein and Natalia are narrators restricted to revealing how life evolves in a provincial city in the 1950s. In his role of visitor, Pablo observes from without and it is from this viewpoint exclusively that he attempts to glimpse the way in which the everyday life of the inhabitants transpires. However, his vision of what goes on indoors is extremely blurred, and all that he can do is to observe the outlines and imagine what is going on behind the lace curtains concealing the gaze of those inside. Natalia, for her part, provides her testimony from the point of view of someone living in the community and between those four walls of which which Pablo Klein is allowed only a glimpse from the outside. Through these two narrators, Martín Gaite reveals what life is like beyond the big cities, without seeking a solution to the conflicts presented.

In *Esperando el porvenir*, Martín Gaite confirms the influence of Neo-Realist cinema on the writers of her generation and, moreover, admits that it was necessary to have recourse to literary strategies and innovations to hoodwink the censors. In *Problemas de la novela*, Juan Goytisolo refers to the fact that, in Spain, the novel fulfils the role of eyewitness, which, in other democratic countries, corresponds to the press. Thus, 'el futuro historiador deberá apelar a ella si quiere reconstruir la vida cotidiana del país a través de la espesa cortina de humo y silencio de nuestros diarios' ('future historians may resort to it if they wish to reconstruct Spain's everyday life through the thick smokescreen and silence of our press').[18] On the other hand, José María Castellet notes that 'los jóvenes novelistas, entre el recuerdo de una guerra civil en la que no participaron y un incierto futuro político, intentan estudiar, analizar, descubrir y explicarse a ellos mismos la situación actual de su país, su estructura social' ('between the memories of a civil war they did not participate in and an uncertain political future, young novelists attempt to study, analyse, uncover and explain to themselves Spain's real situation, its social structure').[19]

In *Esperando el porvenir*, Martín Gaite also points out that, upon the conclusion of the Spanish Civil War, 'lo que más parecía preocuparle al gobierno español era mantener artificialmente en vigor una moral de triunfo, que cundiera el entusiasmo. La palabra entusiasmo era cimiento primordial de las consignas difundidas en himnos, discursos y artículos de prensa' ('what most seemed to worry the Spanish government was to artificially maintain a triumphant morale, to keep enthusiasm alive. The word "enthusiasm" was fundamental in slogans spread in anthems, speeches and press releases').[20] In the speeches of the Spanish Falangist movement and the Sección Femenina, it goes without saying that no emphasis was placed on the themes of Spanish underdevelopment and social injustice that inspired the films of Bardem and Berlanga, although caution continued to apply out of fear of censorship. In *Esperando el porvenir*, Martín Gaite points to the fact that 'también ellos, como el grupo de *Revista Española*, estaban influidos por el cine neorrealista italiano' ('they, like the *Revista Española* group, were also influenced by Italian Neo-Realist cinema').[21]

It is important to underline the fact that the 1950s in Spain witnessed a series of events of varying nature and composition that contributed to the resurgence of Spanish literature and cultural life that had begun in the 1940s. José Jurado Morales provides key data within a historical framework that had an impact upon the country's socio–cultural life. Spain's economy began to stabilise from 1963, when an agreement between Spain and the United States of America was signed, allowing the latter to set up military bases on Spanish soil in return for economic aid. According to research carried out by Jurado Morales, industrial production increased at an annual rate of 8 per cent. This fact, together with the Plan de Estabilización, generated fundamental changes in the economy and, subsequently, in society. Imports and exports increased, per capita income improved, there was greater control of public spending and Spain entered a decade of development. The Franco regime now allowed people to travel abroad and tourists to enter the country, and this gradually changed the way of life of the main cities. Martín Gaite was one of the few women who travelled outside Spain before the introduction of these changes. In 1946, at only 19 years old, she made her first journey, thanks to a two-month scholarship to study at the University of Coimbra. What is more, she went alone, 'cosa que me ilusionaba mucho' ('something I was very excited about'),[22] as she recalls in *Agua pasada*, it not being the custom for a young woman to travel unaccompanied. Beforehand, however, she was obliged to comply with a period of social service in which, in addition to having to listen to the teachings and sermons of the Sección Femenina, she spent time 'cosiendo dobladillos, haciendo gimnasia y jugando al baloncesto' ('sewing hems, doing gymnastics and playing basketball').[23] The teachings included accepting with 'alegría y orgullo ... nuestra condición de mujeres fuertes, complemento y espejo del varón' ('happiness and pride ... our condition of strong women, a complement and mirror to men').[24]

In 1948, having completed her degree in romance philology, she obtained a second scholarship to study at the Summer University of Cannes

> Entré en contacto durante aquellos cursos con muchos autores franceses que no había leído, Sartre, Camus, Saint-Exupéry, Gide, Proust, etc ... , perfeccioné mucho mi francés y, sobre todo, conocí por primera vez, a mis veintidós años, el sabor auténtico de la libertad ... y decidí que no quería seguir viviendo en Salamanca.

> During those courses I came into contact with many French authors I'd never read: Sartre, Camus, Saint-Exupéry, Gide, Proust, etc ... my French improved greatly and, above all, at age 22, I had my first taste of genuine freedom ... and I decided I didn't want to continue living in Salamanca.[25]

At the end of 1948, the writer moved to Madrid, where she met up again with Ignacio Aldecoa, who put her in contact with Medardo Fraile, Alfonso Sastre, Jesús Fernández Santos, Josefina Rodríguez and her future husband, Rafael Sánchez Ferlosio. In *Agua pasada*, Martín Gaite confesses that 'iba mucho al café, al teatro, a la taberna y de paseo con mis nuevos amigos, mucho menos universitarios que yo, mucho más bohemios, todos ellos buenos escritores' ('I would hang out at cafés, the theatre, in bars, and go on outings with my new friends, who were much less college-minded than me, much more bohemian, good writers all of them').[26] This circle widened with the addition of painters and theatre people such as José María del Quinto and Mayra O'Wisiedo.

In 'Carmen Martín Gaite: Reaffirming the Pact between Reader and Writer', Joan Lipman Brown has declared that the writer 'is most commonly introduced in histories of Spanish Literature as part of this almost exclusively male cohort, known to subsequent literary scholars as the Generation of Mid-Century'.[27] These writers shared the experience of the Spanish Civil War in their childhood and an interest in foreign literature and film.

In *Cuadernos de todo*, in the section entitled 'Fragmentos inéditos y notas fugaces', the writer jots down in 'un cuadernito azul de 1997' ('a little blue notepad from 1997'),[28] an outline or two for her novel, *Irse de casa* (1998) in which she states: 'hay una novela dentro de una ciudad (*tranche de vie*), la cuestión es enlazarla, ponerla en orden, ¿no crees? Lo pasado y lo de hoy mismo' ('there's a novel within a city (*tranche de vie*), the question is to link it, put it in order, don't you think? The past and what goes on this very day').[29] That *tranche de vie* ('slice of life') that the writer uses contains a fundamental part of her poetics, in that not only *Irse de casa* but also *La reina de las nieves* y *Nubosidad variable* are made up of fragments of stories, bits and pieces of life trapped by Martín Gaite's gaze in each of her walkabouts, either in Madrid, in the company of her friends of the *Generación de los 50*, or in Manhattan.

The French expression '*tranche de vie*' implies the impression of reality derivative of the Realist and Naturalist novel and is linked to the use of the *modo cámara* in narrative. Norman Friedman conceives the *modo cámara* as a kind of external and objective modalisation in which the heterodiegetic narrator[30] transmits what he pretends to see as though he were doing so through a film lens. The characters are shot from without and the narrator, in the third person, makes sure that he keeps his distance.[31] On the other hand, the *nouveau roman*, an experimental trend in French narrative that was prevalent between 1950 and 1960, employs points of view in which a distant objectivity can be practised – that is to say, the narrator does not interfere in the narrative. To chronological disorder is added, in close relationship to cinema, the juxtaposition of sequences.

Spatial coordinates are developed to the maximum, since it is in space that places and objects are defined through abundant descriptions.

In *Irse de casa* it is possible to observe the use of the *modo cámara* through the presence of a heterodiegetic narrator that enriches the story by reproducing, in the form of an interior monologue, the thoughts of the characters and, subsequently, their identity. There exists an insistence upon narrating as though one were looking through a film lens, which the novel's narrative voice enunciates in the moment at which Amparo Miranda decides to go to Spain, motivated by the film script written by her son Jeremy and inspired by the life of his mother, as he explains in the very first pages to Florita, the actress to whom Jeremy offers the text: 'A ella le pediremos la voz en *off* de cuando habla sola, pero la cámara te irá siguiendo a ti ... irá siguiendo tu figura por los suburbios de una ciudad rara' ('We will ask her to use a voice-over when she speaks, but the camera will keep following you ... it will follow your figure through the suburbs of a strange city').[32]

I am not suggesting that *Irse de casa* is a novel that continues in the tradition of the Neo-Realist trend that Martín Gaite experienced in the 1950s. In my view, the writer employs techniques acquired during that period, gradually redefining these in each of her novels in which the gaze centred on everyday life is the cornerstone around which she builds her stories, as is analysed in later chapters of this book. Based on all that concerns and encompasses the look or gaze, she will gradually extract elements that assist in giving testimony of everyday life, mainly from female characters who have witnessed at first hand the socio-political changes in Spain throughout the forty years that the writer dedicated to her narrative output.

The walk or stroll is an important element in this stage of Martín Gaite's life that I would like to underline. In *Esperando el porvenir*, Martín Gaite pays tribute to Ignacio Aldecoa. It is important to bear in mind the reflections that the writer makes concerning him and other writers of the *Generación de los 50*, in particular when she narrates the way in which they obtained material for their stories. This material came from trips through Spain or from walks into the suburbs of Madrid in the 1950s. In *Esperando el porvenir*, Martín Gaite confirms that, at the beginning of the 1950s, the group of young writers that would later become the *Generación de los 50* became increasingly more aware of a reality that 'sistemáticamente silenciaban los periódicos' ('the newspapers systemically silenced')[33] in reference to the rapid development of the suburbs. The exodus from the countryside, which began as early as the 1940s, took on the characteristics of a serious problem in the 1950s with the massive influx to the big cities of farming families in search of work. This is the case of Martín Jurado and Prudencia, the protagonists of Ignacio Aldecoa's short story 'Al otro lado', who leave their town in search of opportunities that they are not going to find in a city in which 'primero son los de la casa, los de la ciudad, y después él y sus vecinos' ('those at home there, from the city, come first, and then him and his neighbours').[34]

In Madrid, the district of Puente de Vallecas was one of the first suburbs in which Martín Gaite helped out in a clinic for the poor and where she came into contact for the first time with 'la descarnada realidad de los suburbios, experiencia reflejada posteriormente en mi cuento "La conciencia tranquila". La mía, de señorita burguesa de provincias, había quedado sacudida para siempre' ('the raw reality of the suburbs, an experience later reflected in my short story "La conciencia tranquila" (*A Clear Conscience*). My conscience as a provincial middle-class young woman was shaken forever'),[35] as she confesses in *Esperando el porvenir*. In the same book, the writer comments:

> La heterogeneidad de los materiales empleados para la construcción de aquellas modestas viviendas hacía de cada una un modelo exclusivo e irrepetible. Aquella manufactura imaginativa, surgida a los dictados de la necesidad, sin otra ley que la de echar mano de lo que buenamente se fuera encontrando (técnica muy parecida a la del 'collage') está descrita en algunos textos de la época.

> The hodgepodge of materials used to build those humble living quarters made each of them an exclusive, irreproducible model. Those fanciful assemblages, dictated by need, devoid of a set method other than that of making good use of what was found lying around (a technique closely resembling collage) are described in a few writings of the times.[36]

Martín Gaite's viewpoint in the above quotation offers an insight into her poetic intentions. Walking or travelling becomes an aesthetic tool with which heterogeneous materials are obtained for the shaping of different narratives. In *Cuadernos de todo*, particularly in 'Cuaderno 8', which contains notes made between 1973 and

1974, Martín Gaite considers that 'hay ciertos viajes que exigen participación porque entras en las casas, en las vidas de las gentes y eso ... te convierte en espectador-participante, te vincula con el tiempo, con la tradición' ('there are certain trips that demand participation because you enter people's homes and lives and that ... turns you into a spectator-participant, it links you with time, with tradition').[37] The writer conceives of herself as a witness seeking to rebuild the memory of her epoch based on her own individual and fragmentary memories. Martín Gaite writes about all that she witnessed and reveals the effects of the milieu through her journeys, trajectories and walks. She makes the city talk, and she makes spaces inside and out talk. It is for this reason that I believe that the journey is the key metaphor and textual strategy that make it possible to denounce what is otherwise silenced. The gaze provides hidden readings in the form of description. Martín Gaite justifies her enunciation through the mediation of the gaze.

Martín Gaite's narrative in the 1950s bases its semantic intentionality on testimony employing character narrators who construct their identity in dismantled societies, with no institution other than the invented tradition of the Franco era vis-à-vis the values of rupture of the new generations.

In the 1940s and 1950s, women writers fought against the social norms that prohibited the intellectual activity of their sex. According to José Jurado Morales in *La trayectoria narrativa de Carmen Martín Gaite*, during the first years of the Franco regime the general attitude of the government was characterised by the belief that it was an economically self-sufficient nation independent of all other nations. This led Spain into total isolation with respect to international life. It was in the small provincial citiesthat the characteristics of an isolated and stagnated society were more noticeable. *Entre visillos* reveals a typical society of post-war Spain. Through the lives of the characters, the oppression and tedium of that provincial city are revealed. The conversations of girls are about boyfriends and marriage. Nevertheless, it becomes clear that some of the young girls begin the struggle against perpetuating traditional norms that have kept women tied to domestic chores.

The Catholic conservative trend became one of the cornerstones of the Franco regime due to its readiness to defend traditional Spanish thought. According to Ramón Buckley, in his study entitled *La doble transición*, this resulted in the identification of 'nation' with 'religion'. Bearing in mind the research by Albert Mechthild in *Vencer no es convencer. Literatura e ideología del fascismo español,* the influence of the Spanish Falangist movement on the organisation of the political regime led to the conception of an authoritarian and centralised dictatorship that sought the construction of a totalitarian state. Subsequently, every Spanish citizen had to adapt to the official ordinances: traditional spirit, conservative ideology and Catholic belief.

Official political propaganda and Catholic activity imposed a rigid moral order and eliminated the freedoms that existed prior to the war. Prominent among the measures adopted were: the teaching of the Catholic religion in all schools; the abolition of divorce; the condemnation of concubinage; and the suppression of civil marriage in favour of Catholic matrimony. In *Usos amorosos de la postguerra española,* Martín Gaite studies the clash between the national discourse and the kind of cinema produced in Hollywood and the United States' way of life. The writer presents her testimony of this period in *Entre visillos,* in which girls are educated to be modest and dependent, while boys should be spontaneous and autonomous. Simone de Beauvoir is correct when she affirms that one is not born a woman; one becomes a woman with time.

Martin Gaite also witnessed and experienced directly the effects of an oppressive and restrictive society, especially for women, in Spain during and after the Civil War. The process through which the Spanish people were obliged to live, from the submission to Franco at the end of the 1930s to the freedom achieved in the latter half of the 1970s, was slow and laborious. With the disappearance of Franco and the beginnings of democracy, the pace of reforms seeking greater liberties increased. It should not be forgotten that it was not until 1978, the year in which the Spanish Constitution was approved, that women were able to open a bank account or travel abroad without their husbands' permission. The socio-cultural construction of gender represented a huge obstacle for women with a poetic vocation: society wanted them to be submissive, home-based, motherly, patient, sweet, dependent and lacking in knowledge. This change in the political, cultural and social life of the country was transcendental because the recovery from the period of the dictatorship and the years of transition were achieved in a situation in which freedom prevails. For this reason, Martín Gaite gradually provides evidence of these political and social changes in her novels. For example, in *Fragmentos de interior*, published in 1976, a microcosm is developed – namely the house at which Luisa arrives – in which a family lives and whose members slowly reveal the context (the macrocosm) – that is life in Madrid.

In *El cuarto de atrás* Martin Gaite reveals and describes the suffocating presence of the Sección Femenina, with its slogans designed to mould and restrict female behaviour: moreover, the novel introduces the reader to *Isabel la Católica* and Carmencita (the daughter of Franco) as models imposed so as to be imitated. In this novel, Martin Gaite reviews the Spanish post-war period by employing two literary discourses: the novel of memories and the fantastic novel. In the text it is possible to read the biography of the writer who lived more than half her life between the dictatorship of Miguel Primo de Rivera and that of Franco, including the parenthesis of the Republican years, plus the twenty-five years of democratic monarchy in the final period of her life. In this novel, the memories of Martin Gaite reflect what she observed and lived and reveal not only how her life was but how she viewed women in that period. She narrates her life and that of contemporary women marked by a rigid education, an ordered life and constrained aspirations in which they found the freedom denied them in the cinema and the romantic novel.

In *Irse de casa*, Martin Gaite tells the story of two women who manage to leave Spain and settle down in New York. However, in their new life they continue to be tied to their memories of the past. Just as in *El cuarto de atrás*, described by Joan Brown as a 'novel-memoir' or 'autobiographical novel',[38] she employs the technique of hybrid composition in which the story of Amparo Miranda is gradually reconstructed fragment by fragment. In her comparative study of *El cuarto de atrás* and *Entre visillos*, Brown considers that both texts are 'one autobiography, twice told'.[39] With *Irse de casa* we would also be talking of an autobiography, told for a third time and in a different manner. Amparo is the obvious subject of the novel's title. '*Irse*' ('to go', 'to leave') refers to the action of getting away from Spain and seeking out a different life, which she finds in New York. It is important to point out that there is no explicit mention of social and political events taking place in Amparo's childhood, but the repressive atmosphere can be glimpsed at through Amparo's mother's refusal to talk about her past, particularly about the true identity of the father. This novel is very representative in the biographical recounting of Martin Gaite. At the age of 54, the writer travels to New York for the first time – an opportunity that would not have been possible in the Franco period due to the rules imposed on women, such as having to ask the husband's permission and complying with social service duties, as was the case when Martin Gaite travelled to the University of Coimbra.

**The 1970s: poetic preamble**
The process endured by Spain, from the imposition of the Franco regime at the end of the 1930s to the full freedom achieved from 1975 onwards, was a slow and arduous one. The internal pressure of forces of varying ideological positions – all pro-Franco in one form or another – as well as the distrust of the regime that prevailed internationally, obliged Franco to implement and apply *Leyes Fundamentales* that would institutionalise the regime and silence all possible attacks. It was in this desire to normalise everyday life that we see the introduction, in 1966, of the new *Ley de Prensa,* which replaced the 1938 law restricting the norms of prior obligatory censorship for newspapers, magazines, books, brochures, radio, cinema, theatre and other forms of entertainment. The new law of 1966 eliminated the obligatory nature of prior censorship in newspapers and books, but not for cinema or theatre. Moreover, it proclaimed the existence of complete freedom, provided that it adhered to 'respeto y a la moral … y a la salvaguardia de la intimidad y del honor personal y familiar' ('respect and decency … and the safeguarding of personal and family privacy as well as honour'),[40] as mentioned by Pedraza Jiménez in *Las épocas de la literatura española.* Nevertheless, the freedom it endorsed was relative in that it did not contemplate the possibility of creating news agencies, these being controlled entirely by the regime itself. The new law further affirmed that the director of the publication was the person responsible for content and it suggested so-called voluntary consultation with the censuring bodies instead of prior obligatory censorship. What was actually offered, therefore, was a diluted and supervised form of freedom of expression. At a later date, reforms seeking greater freedom accelerated with the death of Franco and the beginning of democracy. The March–April period of 1976 was particularly fruitful, with the abolition of the most controversial articles of the *Ley de Prensa de 1966.*

In the prolonged era of the Franco regime we witness the gradual intensification of a justified feeling of hope among the Spanish people. As the 1960s elapsed, a timid and progressive policy of openness on the part of the government became palpable. The *Ley de Prensa*, for one, and the confirmation of Juan Carlos as the future monarch, confirmed this trend. In the 1970s, the assassination of Carrero Blanco and the imminent death of Franco increased the sensation of change. In effect, the majority of Spaniards were confident that a new period in the history of Spain was close at hand –one that would bring with it political and ideological changes and a boom in the social, economic and cultural terrain. Nevertheless, what occured from 20 November 1975 onwards submerged the Spanish people in a state of uncertainty. The political events geared to the consolidation of democracy took place rapidly, while the eternal struggle against the dictatorship receded into the background. With the *raison d'être* of the Opposition gone, the life of its members became meaningless. In other words, politicians, intellectuals, artists and writers were left without the essential referent of their immediate forbears. In the first democratic elections of 1977, citizen participation was so low that the press referred to this extreme apathy using the term '*desencanto*'. This term would later serve to qualify a demoralised and disoriented state of opinion, which Teresa M. Vilarós has analysed in *El mono del desencanto. Una crítica cultural de la transición española (1973–1993)*. In the words of the historian Álvaro Ferray, 'lo que en realidad se quería verbalizar con la expresión "desencanto" o "cultura del desencanto" eran las notables dificultades de adaptación al nuevo escenario político español del posfranquismo experimentadas por un mundo intelectual fraguado, en buena medida, en la oposición crítica a la dictadura' ('what was really meant by the expression "disenchantment" or "disenchantment culture" was the very difficult adaptation process to the new post-Franco Spanish political scenario experienced by an intellectual world set in good part on critical opposition to the dictatorship').[41] During the 1950s and 1960s, Martín Gaite lagged behind writers such as Ignacio Aldecoa, the Goytisolo brothers, Ana María Matute, Alfonso Sastre and Luis Martín-Santos, to mention but a few. Moreover, the writer was seen as the wife of Rafael Sánchez Ferlosio even when she had already won the *Café Gijón* prize for *El balneario* and the *Premio Nadal* for *Entre visillos*. In her article 'Women Writers of Spain: An Historical Perspective' Joan Lipman Brown points out that 'It is only with great difficulty that intellectual status can be granted to women in social systems characterized by the ethic of machismo'.[42] In the 1970s, Martín Gaite and Sánchez Ferlosio separated, divorcing in 1987.

In these years, which go from hope to disenchantment, Martín Gaite published three novels: *Retahílas* (1974), *Fragmentos de interior* (1976) and *El cuarto de atrás* (1978). In this decade, it is possible to say that literature with an exclusively social objective survived with great difficulty. Readers began to tire of the experimentalist artifices of the 1960s and writers were aware that 'la novela estaba en un callejón sin salida, ahogada por sus propios presupuestos teóricos, textuales y técnicos' ('the novel was at a dead end, weighed down by its own theorical, textual and technical presumptions'),[43] as pointed out by Santos Alonso in 'La transición: hacia una nueva novela'. It is not until the 1970s, in keeping with political and literary change, that writers became the central figures of their works. María Elena Bravo refers to the fact that 'el papel del autor sufre una involución, no se representa más que a sí mismo' ('the role of the author goes through a regression, it represents nothing other than itself')[44] and Gonzalo Sobejano, in 'Ante la novela de los años setenta' states that 'en esta nueva novela la imagen del autor se trasluce como la del autor real o como la de un demiurgo: hacedor y señor absoluto de sus figuras' ('in this new novel, the image of the author is seen as that of the authentic author or as that of a demiurge: maker and absolute master of their characters').[45]

In this historic and literary context, the novel sets itself up as a form of self-knowledge for the writer him- or herself. Shape is given to a kind of novel sustained in memory and that presents two narrative possibilities: either it deals with a personal memory, as in *Retahílas,* or it deals with the sum of this personal memory plus the historical memory, as in *El cuarto de atrás.*

After almost ten years devoted to research, Martín Gaite published *Retahílas.* In this novel, an old woman close to death decides to spend her final days in the place where she lived with her ancestors: the country house of Louredo in a village in Galicia. It is there that Eulalia, the old woman's granddaughter, and Germán, Eulalia's nephew, agree to meet, together with Juana, a woman who had been linked with the family since she was little. The novel is made up of a conversation that the aunt and the nephew sustain during a whole night and in which they thread together reflections and memories of other family members and friends. This plot summary reveals the importance of remembering the past, which is the characters' objective and, subsequently, the point of departure of everything that takes place or ceases to take place in the novel. *Retahílas* can be included among that group of novels of the 1970s that find, in personal memory, the basis for their stories and plots, particularly within a subgroup or trend in which the structure of the novels is rooted in dialogue. It is what Gonzalo Sobejano, in 'Ante la novela de los años setenta', has termed '*memoria autobiográfica en forma dialogada*' ('autobiographical memories in the form of dialogue').[46] This mode of writing novels, based on a structure of dialogue, substitutes the kind of novels written in the preceding decade in which the monologue or the auto-dialogue, via the splitting of the 'I', is frequent and makes one think of Juan Goytisolo's *Juan sin tierra*, published in 1975. According to Darío Villanueva, in his article 'La novela', 'desde 1972 comenzó a consolidarse una novela eminentemente comunicativa en la que a través del diálogo de los personajes se planteaban cuestiones de interés a la vez particular y general, se buscaban las "señas de identidad" no desde la soledad del individuo como en el caso de Goytisolo, sino desde la confrontación y el intercambio de dos o más perspectivas' ('as of 1972 an eminently communicative type of novel began to consolidate in which matters of both specific and general interest were brought up through the characters' dialogue. "Identity signs" were sought not from an individual's loneliness, as in Goytisolo's case, but from the comparison and exchange of two or more perspectives').[47] However, it has to be said that, in 1958, Martín Gaite had already written *Entre visillos* with narrators that construct the story from their different perspectives.

Following on from the critical success of *Retahílas*, Martín Gaite published *Fragmentos de interior* in 1976. This novel presents the disintegration of a family from the point of view of a girl who does not belong to this nucleus. The girl is Luisa, who leaves her home town and goes to Madrid with a view to starting anew her amorous relationship with Gonzalo. She begins to serve in a bourgeois family in which ties of affection hardly exist and everyone lives very much in their own worlds. Through the girl, the narrator presents the everyday reality of the family. Agustina is separated from Diego, but she continues to love him. She has had two children by him, and they rarely see or speak to each other: Isabel lives with her father and Jaime with his mother. Diego now lives with Gloria, who works in the cinema and the theatre, and who, at the same time, maintains a love affair with Pablo. At the end of the novel, Luisa decides to leave Madrid when she discovers that Gonzalo is seeing Monique. Agustina commits suicide.

Now I shall proceed to explain the importance of this novel with a view to discerning the importance of the journey as an aesthetic tool with which the narrative is constructed. Luisa arrives in Madrid in search of Gonzalo. In that journey from the small town to the big city we begin to perceive the first outlines or sketches of a new mass urban landscape into which Luisa will venture forth to explore and gradually make her own. By degrees, she will make her own street maps based on her walks about that unknown city. The house at which she arrives becomes a space that she will traverse with her gaze, and with her comings and goings from one room to another she will succeed in sowing memories in each and every corner. The house represents the atmosphere of '*desencanto*' explained earlier, in as much as relations between the members of the family no longer exist. The experience of the journey to Madrid narrated in the present allows us to see the growth of a consciousness. Luisa has ceased to idealise her surroundings, in becoming a more conscious being who observes, analyses and constructs different types of geography.

With the publication, in May 1978, of *El cuarto de atrás*, Martín Gaite continues, to a certain degree, with the narrative modes evident in *Retahílas*. Nevertheless, there is a change: the personal memory of the protagonist coincides with that of the writer, in a desire for autobiographical narrative and because this personal memory cannot be understood without the reconstruction of Spain's most recent past, in an attempt at historical memory.

Martín Gaite joins the list of writers who, in the years of political transition and through their fiction, document the era of the Franco regime. After 20 November 1975, and with the process towards democracy initiated, the recovery of the period of the dictatorship could be carried out from a position of freedom. In 'Ante la novela de la democracia: reflexiones sobre sus raíces', María Elena Bravo expresses the fact that, in that period, there appeared certain works which 'buscan realizar un examen contrastivo del pasado visto a la luz del presente, en todas el narrador (muy cerca del autor) asume una responsabilidad personal' ('look to carry out an examination of the past contrasted with the light of the present, in all of which the narrator (very close to the author) assumes personal responsibility').[48]

In these years, narratives with a marked autobiographical content abound. On certain occasions these narratives refer back to the war years, and at other times to the post-war era, such as *Memoria de un niño de derechas* (1972) by Francisco Umbral and *Memorias de un condenado a muerte* (1978) by José Leiva, to mention just two. The number of writers is considerable and justifies recovering *El cuarto de atrás*, for which Martín Gaite receives the *Premio Nacional de Literatura 1978*. In this novel, the protagonist, C., manages to get to sleep after a lengthy period attempting to do so. Then she is awoken, very soon afterwards, by a telephone call from someone she does not know – a person called Alejandro, who wishes to interview her because she is a writer. In a long conversation between the two, interrupted only by the phone call from a woman, C. talks about Spain's recent history and her memories. She reflects on the passing of time, a dream world and fiction, and she comments on her work and that of other writers. Finally, she wakes up and doubts whether such a conversation really took place or was in fact a dream.

In *El cuarto de atrás*, Martín Gaite employs two literary resources condensed in two aspects: fantasy and metafiction. These two, together with memory in the form of dialogue, represent the most characteristic and innovative features of narrative during the 1970s, according to Sobejano in 'Ante la novela de los setenta': 'parece haber adquirido vigor un nuevo tipo de novela cuyos rasgos determinantes, por paralelismo o en confluencia, vendrían a ser la memoria preferentemente dialogada, la autocrítica de la escritura, y la fantasía.' ('a new type of novel seemed to have acquired strength: its characteristics, through parallelism or intersection, would-be memories expressed preferably through dialogue, self-criticism of the writing and fantasy').[49]

For Manuel Durán it is, likewise, important 'señalar el auge de la literatura fantástica' ('to note the rise of fantastic literature'),[50] as mentioned in his article '*Así que pasen diez años*, la novela española de los setenta'. José Luis Castillo-Puche praises the writers in that she opts for 'esa ruptura con la realidad que permite a la novela explorar mundos fantásticos, oníricos, alucinantes o alucinadores' ('rupture with reality, thus allowing the novel to explore fantastic, dream-like, mind-blowing worlds').[51] Leaving to one side exceptional cases, such as the narrative of Álvaro Cunqueiro or the somewhat distant *Alfanhuí* (1951) by Rafael Sánchez Ferlosio, among others, *El cuarto de atrás* is one of the pioneer novels in this narrative trend, according to assertions made by Sobejano in 'Ante la novela de los setenta'. In *Novela y sociedad en la España de posguerra*, Antonio Vilanova considers *El cuarto de atrás* 'un nuevo concepto de la literatura basado en el culto de la imaginación y de los sueños' ('a new concept of literature based on the cult of the imagination and dreams'),[52] which the writer will develop in later works: *El castillo de las tres murallas*, *El pastel del diablo* and *Caperucita en Manhattan*. In addition, she will construe the concept of interior geography through her use of imagination and dream, as will be discussed in Chapter 3.

In narrative developed in the 1970s, it is possible to observe recurring elements evident not only in the writer's novels but also in her poetic reflections elaborated in *El cuento de nunca acabar* and *Cuadernos de todo*, as well as in her collages. For example, *Retahílas* is structured based on the dialogue between Eulalia and Germán – that is to say, on the weaving of one and the replies (amplifications, digressions or reflections) of the other. It is a literary dialogue, due, among other reasons, to the duration of each intervention. And it is precisely here that the technical innovation of *Retahílas* lies: in the lack of interruption of the interventions of each character. Each weaves what he or she needs to weave so that the other can then take up the thread anew and continue narrating. This is what Martín Gaite will set forth in a technical manner in *El cuento de nunca acabar* under the title 'La interrupción, el proceso':

> Conviene frenar el impulso de interrumpir indiscriminadamente, aun a riesgo de perder, de momento, alguna cosa. Todas las que parecen haberse perdido, reaparecerán a su debido tiempo, si el narrador es bueno; hay que darle un margen de confianza, intentar seguir su ritmo, tener la generosidad de perderse con él … Los coleccionistas de datos estorban el impulso creativo del narrador, el borbotón de una retahíla que solamente puede surgir engarzando los detalles dentro del conjunto de esa manera peculiar.

> Let us resist the urge to interrupt indiscriminately, even at the momentary risk of losing something. Everything that seems to have been passed up will reappear in due time if the narrator is skilful; let us trust them, try to follow their rhythm, have the generosity to get lost along with them … Data collectors hinder the narrator's creative impulse, a continuous sequence that can only advance by stringing along the details within the body of the text in that peculiar manner.[53]

It is important to highlight the fact that *El cuento de nunca acabar* was published in 1983. Nevertheless, Martín Gaite had been writing her *Apuntes sobre la narración, el amor y la mentira* since 1973 and finished them in the autumn of 1982, when she was in Virginia. It is for this reason that I consider it the poetic text in which it is possible to glimpse not only the writer's reflections on narrative, but also the techniques that she employs in creating her work. José Jurado Morales says that 'es una obra fragmentaria e impresionista, hecha de meditaciones, memorias e invenciones' ('it is a fragmentary and impressionist work, made up of meditations, memories and interventions').[54] The structure is divided into four parts entitled 'Siete prólogos', 'A campo través', 'Ruptura de relaciones' and 'Río revuelto'. In the first part, Martín Gaite explains how *El cuento de nunca acabar* began, the fundamental basis for the work being her 'cuadernos de todo' which were published after her death. The second part is made up of eighteen chapters in which she reflects on narrative from different perspectives. In the third part, she outlines the elaboration process behind *El cuento de nunca acabar,* which is interesting to read from the point of view of the possible similarities with collage techniques employed in some of her novels. First, she typed up the notes from 'cuadernos de todo'. Then she cut out the notes and put them in order according to the themes of narrative, love and lies. Later, she pasted the cuttings in a large notebook in which she left a margin on the left-hand side of the page to write in red subtitles such as 'narración avasalladora' ('overwhelming narration'), 'orden y caos' ('order and chaos') and 'geografía narrativa' ('narrative geography'), to mention but a few. The final result were the two notebooks from which she extracted the nineteen chapters grouped under the title 'A campo través'. The final part of *El cuento de nunca acabar* is made up of very short texts dealing with the elements of narrative, love, play and time, among others.

*Retahílas* is structured in fragments of stories in which the memories of Germán and Eulalia (the details) are gradually knitted together to complete the novel (the whole). Each has to undertake a journey back to the family's country house – Eulalia in search of her roots in the place where she spent her childhood and Germán to recall the location of his childhood summer holidays. The journey becomes the factor that sets the narrative in motion. When she meets her nephew, Eulalia tells him:

Ni por las mientes se me estarían pasando semejantes retahílas con el orden que llevan si no estuvieras tú que me las vas guiando, y ese orden es su vida … las historias son su sucesión misma, su encenderse y surgir por un orden irrepetible, el que les va marcando el interlocutor … 'dame hilo toma hilo', me ha hecho mucha gracia eso que le decías tú anoche a Pablo en la borrachera, lo has contado muy bien. Y cada mirada incuba una historia.

No way would I string along sequences in a specific order if you weren't around to lead me along them, and this particular order is its life … stories are their own succession, their own kindling and forming in an unrepeatable order, the order the interlocutor sets for them … 'give me thread take thread', what you were telling Pablo while boozing last night struck me as funny; you've told the story well. And every gaze breeds a story.[55]

It should be pointed out that *Retahílas* is a novel structured around a series of apparently isolated sequences that gradually interlink as they begin to refer back to each other. Each of the narrators takes turns in tugging at the thread of memory and slotting into place pieces of the jigsaw puzzle that is their lives seen from differing points of view, from a place from which they have set forth in order to relate their stories to each other. Narrating a series of fragments is comparable to the pleasure of embroidering in 'La confesión sacramental', which Martín Gaite elaborates in *El cuento de nunca acabar*. In that section, the writer asks herself how she can go about telling a story. Besides using periphery detail and a story within the story, Martín Gaite considers of vital importance the function of the narrator. It is he or she who '*escoge* el color de los hilos [y los] *combina* … a su libre albedrío' ('*chooses* the colour of the thread [and] combines [them] at their discretion').[56] These threads will become fragments or images in the narrative of the 1990s, as I shall analyse in Chapter 2. They are likewise visualised in the collages elaborated by the writer. It is for this reason that I have rendered in italics the actions of *escoger* and *combinar* in that they are analogous activities that will be carried out both in the writing and in the elaboration of collages.

*Retahílas* enquires into the essence of life itself, the remembering of the past that provides the pillars of personal identity. In *La novela femenina contemporánea (1970–1985)*, Biruté Ciplijauskaité articulates a fundamental notion of Martín Gaite's narrative: 'Para saber quién soy debo saber quién he sido y cómo he llegado al estado actual' ('In order to know who I am, I should know who I have been and how I have arrived at this current state').[57] Several critics coincide on this point. For Antonio Vilanova, in 'Carmen Martín Gaite y la teoría de la novela dentro de la novela', 'el tema central en que se inspira es la transmisión de la memoria del pasado, la conservación del legado de nuestros mayores y de las historias de nuestra estirpe familiar' ('the central theme for insipration is the transmission of memories of the past, the conservation of the legacy of our elders and the history of our family bloodline').[58] And if *Retahíla* is the novel of personal and family memory, then Martín Gaite will produce *El cuarto de atrás* (1978), a novel worthy of the *Premio Nacional de Literatura* and, thanks to which Martín Gaite's literary career, will gain recognition inside Spain, as well as fomenting a curiosity outside the country to know her work.

*El cuarto de atrás* is one of the novels most analysed by the critics, and it has been included in the list of writers and works read at universities in the United States. The critics are of the opinion that *El cuarto de atrás* is a novel in which it is possible to glimpse certain biographical features of Carmen Martín Gaite who 'vivió más de la mitad de su vida entre la "dictablanda" de Miguel Primo de Rivera y la dictadura franquista, con el paréntesis cegador de la República y los veinticinco años de monarquía democrática en el último tramo de su vida' ('lived more than half of her life between the "dictablanda" of Miguel Primo de Rivera and the Francoist dictatorship, with the blinding parenthesis of the Republic and the twenty-five years of democratic Monarchy in the last stages of her life'),[59] as pointed out by Inmaculada de la Fuente. In *El cuarto de atrás* there are memories that reflect what has been observed and lived, as in *Entre visillos*, and that describe what Carmen Martín Gaite's life was like during the 1950s, how she viewed her peers, particularly how she viewed women during that period – those provincial women, her contemporaries, marked by a strict upbringing, an ordered life and constrained aspirations, who found in the cinema and the romantic novel the freedom that was denied them; women with other points of view different from hers, to whom she grants a voice in *El balneario*, *Entre visillos*, and *Fragmentos de interior*.

*El cuarto de atrás* was published as soon as democracy in Spain is established. The right to freedom of expression and plurality of opinion allowed Martín Gaite to make a personal assessment of what the presence of Franco meant in her life, and in the life of

Spaniards generally, over a period of four decades. Throughout the novel, the writer establishes chronological milestones referring to the Spanish Civil War and the post-war period. In her historical survey, Martín Gaite mentions rationing cards, the Sección Femenina de Falange, social service, and Carmencita Franco as the prototype of the Spanish women, as well as many other references to historical facts. In *El cuarto de atrás*, her opposition to Franco's dictatorship is evident:

> Así que, desde ese punto de vista, Franco es el primer gobernante que yo he sentido en mi vida como tal, porque desde el principio se notó que era unigénito, indiscutible y omnipresente, que había conseguido infiltrarse en todas las casas, escuelas, cines y cafés … Así que cuando murió, me pasó lo que a mucha gente, que no me lo creía. Hubo quien hizo muchas alharacas y celebraciones, yo simplemente me quedé de piedra, se me vinieron encima los años de su reinado, los sentí como un bloque homogéneo […] sólo podía darme cuenta de eso que le he dicho antes, de que no soy capaz de discernir el paso del tiempo a lo largo de ese periodo, ni diferenciar la guerra de la postguerra, pensé que Franco había paralizado el tiempo.

> So from this standpoint Franco is the first true ruler whom I've felt as such in my life. From the start, it was evident that he was the only begotten child – uncontested and omnipresent – who had managed to sneak into every home, school, cinema and coffee shop … So when he died, I was incredulous, just like many other people were. There were those who celebrated and made a lot of fuss; I was simply stunned, I thought of all the years of his rule, I felt them like a uniform slab […] I could only be aware of what I told you before, that I am incapable of telling the passage of time throughout that period, or differentiating between the war and post-war periods; I believed Franco had paralysed time.[60]

José Jurado Morales acutely observes that the writer 'no elabora un discurso politizado' ('does not develop a politicised discourse'),[61] instead 'prefiere examinar la intrahistoria, recogiendo aspectos varios de la cotidianidad de los años de posguerra' ('she prefers to examine inner stories, picking up on various aspects of post-war everyday life'),[62] such as, for example, the *novedad* of North American cinema, the routine of the spas, the work of dressmakers and, in particular, the life of women. *El cuarto de atrás* is the first novel in which a woman character lives in a flat with her daughter and no mention whatsoever is made of the father; a woman who is able to cope with her loneliness and devote the hours in which she cannot sleep to writing. In *Entre visillos*, Natalia played the role of a novice writer rebuilding in her diary the life of the city. At the age of sixteen and living in a provincial city under the Franco dictatorship, she was unable to aspire to an independent life, much less to living away from her family at a tme when the traditional family structure, defended so vehemently by the Franco regime, was the most valid form of coexistence. Through the notes in Natalia's diary, we can see that she is not prepared to confine herself to provincial routine when she tells her father that 'si tengo que ser una mujer resignada y razonable, prefiero no vivir' ('if I have to be a resigned and reasonable woman, then I prefer not to live').[63] Natalia refuses to accept the submissive attitude of her family and friends, who live under a series of prejudices, and the conservatism of Aunt Concha, whose only wish is to convert her nieces 'en unas estúpidas, que sólo nos educa para tener novio rico, y que seamos lo más retrasadas posible en todo, que no sepamos nada ni nos alegremos con nada' ('into imbeciles; she only educates us to have a rich boyfriend and to be as behind in everything as possible, not knowing anything or getting happiness from anything').[64] If we take into consideration the years in which *Entre visillos* and *El cuarto de atrás* were published, it is possible to appreciate that the difference of twenty years is remarkable not only in Spain's socio-political and cultural arena, but also from the perspective of women and the roles expected of them in society as a whole.

Although, in the 1940s, girls belonging to the bourgeoisie were not allowed to attend university, younger female members of the same families would do so years later. By then, it was not unacceptable to enter marriage with a university degree. Higher studies for women focused on the teaching profession and the arts, while men studied engineering medicine, law or chemistry, according to Oscar Pérez in *Historia de la literatura española contemporánea*. Thus, Tali, the young protagonist of *Entre visillos*, is viewed as a *chica rara* ('a strange girl') by her contemporaries because she wishes to go to Madrid and study natural sciences, a degree subject that was not considered very feminine at the time.

The fear of losing one's femininity was related not only to studying but also to the adoption of lifestyles extracted from North American films shown in the 1950s, as mentioned in the first part of this chapter. Some women of the new generation were prepared to go against the tradition in which they grew up and which the Sección Femenina did its utmost to fulfil, using all the means at its disposal. Drawn to fashion and American cinema, the 'platform shoe' girls recalled by Martín Gaite clung to the most insignificant manifestation of freedom in dress in imposing new styles. A quotation from *Usos amorosos de la postguerra española* reads: 'Las muchachas topolino jamás llevan llave de portal … Los que hemos hablado con las madres sabemos que el negar a sus hijas las llaves del portal es por no renunciar al último vestigio autoritario' ('Platform shoe girls never have the front door key … Those of us who have spoken to their mothers know that by not giving their daughters the keys to the front door they were not giving up that final authoritarian vestige').[65] These girls were unaware of transgression, but life nonetheless made its presence felt even in the narrow confines conceded by their mothers. Some even went to discothèques, smoked, used bad language and began to question virginity before marriage. According to Martín Gaite, in the 1940s, strict control over women began to be a phenomenon of the past.

In spite of the fact that the regime sought to destroy everything that existed prior to 1936, it was unable to erase completely the prototypes of independent women produced by the Republic, such as Victoria Kent or Margarita Nelken. Although their names were forbidden, some of their female companions and comrades in Spain, who moved in circles different from the official ones, succeeded, even through their silence, in creating dissension, which, together with stimulus from abroad, brought about small changes in people's way of thinking.

In her article, 'Writing from Within, with her Own Voice: Carmen Martín Gaite (1925–)' Catherine Davies underlines the fact that *El cuarto de atrás* 'is a novelized social history told, crucially, from a woman's perspective'. The novel narrates the everyday life of women who, like Martín Gaite, grew up in the atmosphere of the 1940s and 1950s. Davies says that, for this reason, the novel is very important in that 'it offers an insider's view of Franco's Spain as only women knew it'.[66] The novel is invaluable for its reconstruction of the everyday life of Spanish women in the post-war period – a life that revolved around sewing, household chores, the bringing up of children and looking after a husband.

Martín Gaite's narrative output in the 1970s, with her novels *Retahílas*, *Fragmentos de interior* and *El cuarto de atrás*, reveals poetic elements already visible in her first period: the journeys of her protagonists in search of a life without family ties; the story of the past in which they grew up and the looking back, which helps visualise in different ways the time and space that once was; and, moreover, the possibility of reconstructing those fragments of stories and converting them into a novel, as in the case of the protagonist in *El cuarto de atrás*. The transition from the Franco regime to democracy is reflected through the lives of the protagonists in these three novels. Eulalia threads and embroiders the text of the family history through her conversation with her nephew; Luisa observes the way in which each of the members of the Madrid family relates to her while, at the same time, observing herself and her own activities. The changes take place without (in the physical surroundings) as well as within (inside the characters themselves). The movements to and fro made by Luisa are similar to those undertaken by C. when the man in black visits her. The difference lies in the fact that the protagonist in *El cuarto de atrás* has already found the space in which she can give free rein to her dreams and memories. She has succeeded in securing her own room, just as Virginia Woolf had demanded. From there, she recounts her life in writing and employs elements of fantastic literature, as well as explaining the way in which she gradually elaborates her novel.

### Consolidation of narrative and visual poetics

I shall present the historical context of the 1990s, focusing on the trips to New York undertaken by Carmen Martín Gaite. These trips were of fundamental importance in the life of the writer, in that they had an impact on her narrative output as well as on a series of collages published in 2005 and entitled *Visión de Nueva York*. The novels and collages of this period are a reflection of Martín Gaite's poetics that she had begun to implement when she was a member of the *Generación del Medio Siglo*.

Due to the success of *El cuarto de atrás*, Carmen Martín Gaite began a series of trips and visits outside Spain, the United States being her main destination. In April 1979, she attended the Primer Congreso de Literatura Española Contemporánea, held at Yale University (Connecticut), at which six papers on her work were presented. The invitation extended to her by Manuel Durán led to the first of many visits. In the autumn of 1980 she was visiting professor at Barnard College and gave a term-long series of seminars on literary theory. During the same period, she also gave a series of lectures at New York University, Columbia, Rutgers, Yale, Chicago and Texas, to mention but a few. In December of that same year, she attended the Annual MLA (Modern Language Association) Congress, as a seminar on her work was programmed for the event. These trips would have an impact on the writer's work in that she would bring her reflections on her poetic narrative to a conclusion in *El cuento de nunca acabar* and would begin a period in which visual images, such as drawing, collage and painting, would commence to form part of a poetics in which she would combine such elements with the act of writing.

It is important to return to *Cuadernos de todo* in order to have a clear perspective of the nature of the process employed by Martín Gaite in creating a poetics that went from the narrative to the visual and from the visual to the narrative. In *Cuaderno 25*, Martín Gaite describes her journey to New York in 1980. In one of the sections, she reflects on the function of her diaries, which was 'ayudar a la memoria a unir las historias múltiples que se suscitan en un día' ('a memory aid to link multiple stories happening in a single day').[67] At that time, the writer's diary was made up of cuttings of images from magazines, photographs, phrases or headings from newspapers or other printed matter, the always implicit desire being that they be 'visualmente divertido' ('visually fun').[68] This diary of collages was published in 2005 and carried the title *Visión de Nueva York*.

Her admiration for New York is expressed by Martín Gaite in a fascination for the fragmentary dimension of the many images that her several visits encompass over time. She is drawn by the instantaneous, the fleeting, the hurried note and the frozen instant, as well as by speed itself which she would like to trap but cannot. Before ever visiting Manhattan, Martín Gaite had already carried in her imagination a city in perpetual construction, consisting of flowing avenues and windows rising up, superimposed one upon the other. This would later contribute to the formation of her poetics. In *Visión de Nueva York*, Martín Gaite writes that Ignacio Álvarez Vara was the person who told her that that city 'se parecía un poco a la Gran Vía de Madrid' ('slightly resembled Madrid's main street, the Gran Vía').[69] It was in 1974, while she was a guest in Álvarez's apartment, that the writer confessed that she saw 'por primera vez la reproducción de un cuadro de Edward Hopper' ('a reproduction of an Edward Hopper painting for the first time').[70] At a later date, the desolate characters of Hopper's paintings would become the source of a wealth of images transformed into narrative, poetry and collage, as will be analysed and discussed in Chapters 2 and 4.

The vision of New York that Martín Gaite gradually created from her first visits in 1979 is so different from that which Álvarez and the cinema of the 1950s had offered her. The writer mentions that: 'yo no sabía lo que era América, ni su tamaño, ni dónde estaba Yale, ni a qué distancia de New York' ('I had no idea what America was: neither its size, nor where Yale was, nor how far from New York').[71] This ignorance would not last long, and Martín Gaite would soon begin to walk the streets of the city and to reconstruct it by blending the lead, glass and wood with the attitude of the people, the light and the differing spaces. As though they were an apparent narrative structure in movement, the novels of the 1990s, and in particular *Irse de casa*, trace exact routes as in plans or maps. The voice that flows collects and accumulates objects, names and anecdotes. Álvarez's descriptions are slowly relegated to memory and what replaces them are streets, floors, buildings, which multiply through associative proximity: noises, trains, streets, subways, radios and shouts. It is worthy of mention that Martín Gaite's approach to New York includes both a land and an aerial perspective. The writer travelled about the city either on foot or by bus, while, on other occasions, her view of the city was taken from the site on which the twin towers of the World Trade Center once stood.

These to-and-from movements about New York gave rise to a series of reflections on a way in which a novel can be constructed, in which the main axis is the walk or stroll. The different urban layouts (as seen in plans, maps and letters) become the models that generate the texts (as can be seen in *Lo raro es vivir* or *Nubosidad variable*), or in which the forward movement of the narrative discourse rests upon an itinerary, such as railway, urban or architectural routes. These itineraries led Martín Gaite to create a *sui generis* terminology in which concepts such as urban, domestic, interior and narrative geography are included. We shall analyse and discuss this in Chapter 3.

Later, in the autumn of 1982, Martín Gaite accepted a post as visiting professor at the University of Virginia, where she taught a course on the *Generación del 98* and another on the contemporary

Spanish short story. In the same year, she took part in the Linguistic Congress held at Wake Forest, and a meeting of the SAMLA (South Atlantic Modern Language Association), the venue for which was the city of Atlanta. In the autumn of 1984, she taught a term-long course on Ignacio Aldecoa at the University of Chicago. In 1983, *El cuarto de atrás* was translated into English for the first time. In the same year, the University of Nebraska published *From Fiction to Metafiction: Essays in Honor of Carmen Martín Gaite*, a book that brings together fifteen essays on her work, written by prestigious Hispanicists. The book also includes five of her collages with the theme of New York. *Cuaderno 28* describes Martín Gaite's stay in the city in the same year in which she wrote her *retahíla neoyorkina* as well as completing the collage that carries the same name. Both will be commented upon and analysed in Chapter 4, on the visual elements in the narrative of Martín Gaite, because it is important to establish the link between writing and the visual dimension in the writer's poetics.

It is important to mention that, in the autumn of 1982, Martín Gaite wrote *Cuaderno 29*, entitled *Cuaderno de América*, in which concepts of her poetics that she would use in her collages and novels of the 1990s appear. *Re-anudar* ('re-tying'), *re-flexionar* ('reflecting') and *re-capitular* ('recapitulating') are actions that link stories from the past with those from the present; they are also a metaphor of 'ir hilvanando cada retal, cada fragmento cotidiano, de ir ordenando cosa por cosa' ('basting every scrap of fabric, each everyday fragment, ordering every element one by one').[72] In the same notebook 29, Martín Gaite emphasises the importance of providing *puntualizaciones de entorno* ('clues to the setting') through the writer-narrator – that is to say, providing the reader with geographical references so as to situate him in the precise time and space of the writing.

In *Cuaderno 29*, the writer continues to set out and describe the principles of her poetics. She points to the *técnica de carta* o *situacionismo* ('letter technique' or 'situationism') in which 'el presente desde el que se narra se enlaza con lo que se narra' ('the present in which the story is narrated links with the narration itself'),[73] but she adds that it is necessary 'llevarlo a sus últimas consecuencias' ('to take it to its ultimate consequences'),[74] which is the collage. This notebook is of vital importance in consolidating the poetics of Martín Gaite, in that the presence of the collage in the narrative is explained as the 'acarreo de papeles de hechos anteriores, recuento de sueños' ('dragging back out of papers of past events, the telling of dreams').[75] In that definition it is possible to perceive another poetic foundation that, later on, will become the *de papeles atados* ('novel of gathered writings').

In 1984, Martín Gaite was invited by the University of Chicago at Illinois to be a visiting professor, imparting a term-long course on the contemporary Spanish short story. During this stay, she gave lectures in Madison and Milwaukee. A year later, she received an invitation from the University of Vassar (Poughkeepsie) to be a visiting professor, analysing her own work and that of Ignacio Aldecoa. During these years of constant trips to the United States, she published the novels *El castillo de las tres murallas* (1981) and *El pastel del diablo* (1985), both of which are considered to belong to the genre of literature for children and young readers, as well as serving as a referent to be borne in mind when it comes to writing *Caperucita en Manhattan* (1990).

In reviewing *Cuaderno 34*, dated 1984, we find a text entitled 'El punto de vista femenino en la literatura', in which Martín Gaite argues in favour of women ceasing to represent the false images imposed by men, especially the writers of the nineteenth century. She makes no specific reference to anyone, but she does feel that the woman 'es presentada como "enigma" que el hombre explora conscientemente como un problema … y al clasificarla como tal, le corta sus alas' ('is presented as an "enigma" that men consciously explore as a problem … and by classifying her thus, they cut her wings').[76] The reflection made in this brief annotation in *Cuaderno 34* would be the basis for the volume entitled *Desde la ventana. Enfoque femenino de la literatura española*, which was published in 1987. In this text, she researches the possible particular mode of writing that women practise compared with men – that is to say, she attempts to ascertain whether it is possible to pinpoint specific aspects of female discourse that are different or absent from male discourse. In the first lecture, 'Mirando a través de la ventana', she reveals the difficulties faced by Spanish women in fulfilling themselves at the secular level, being forever reduced to a domestic life indoors and, in particular, the inconveniences and prejudices faced by female writers. In 'Buscando el modo' she presents the obstacles encountered by certain women who wish to find the time to write, and she uses the life and work of Santa Teresa de Jesús as an example. In this section, Martín Gaite continues her reflections on the importance of the gaze, which she would gradually develop through the female characters of her novels written in the 1990s. In this chapter on poetics, she would explain in greater detail the series of actions that derive from the act of looking, such as the differences between looking into the distance, from a distance, from without, from within, from above and from below. These diverse positions adopted by the writing subject offer fragmented perspectives or points of view that Martín Gaite would gradually assemble to shape the '*novela tipo collage*' or '*novela de papeles atados*' (the inverted commas are mine, emphasising the concepts that form part of the writer's poetics).

In 1985, Martín Gaite was invited to Vassar College (Poughkeepsie) as a visiting professor, to analyse her own work and that of Ignacio Aldecoa. *Cuaderno 35* confirms this visit. It was the seventh occasion on which the writer had travelled to New York. Awaiting her there this time was Juan Carlos Eguillor, whose drawings had inspired her to write *Caperucita en Manhattan*, as we shall see in subsequent chapters. This friendship was crucial in the life of Martín Gaite, as her narrative poetics would slowly merge with the elaboration of drawings, as is analysed in Chapter 4.

In the years in which she travelled extensively, Martín Gaite's literary versatility was enriched by her direct participation in and practice of the genre of literature for children and young readers. She published *El castillo de las tres murallas* (1981) and *El pastel del diablo* (1985). In 1987, she obtained the XV Premio Anagrama de Ensayo for *Usos amorosos de la postguerra española*, in which she provides a historical overview of the initial years of the post-war period and the consequences produced in the amorous habits of the Spanish people. The study takes a close look at certain prominent aspects of life during the Franco regime, such as the Sección Femenina, censorship, education, and Spain's isolation, as commented on in the first section of this chapter. The same year comes to a close with the première of *A palo seco* ('*Monologue in one act*'), which confirms Martín Gaite's resourcefulness regarding the different literary genres. It is important to point out that 'in 1987 she became the first Spanish woman to be elected an honorary fellow of the Modern Language Association, joining an elite group of approximately seventy contemporary world authors (including three fellow Spaniards) who are considered by scholars to be the most significant',[77] as Joan Lipman Brown wrote in 'Carmen Martín Gaite: Reaffirming the Pact between Reader and Writer'.

On 8 November 1991, Martín Gaite arrived in New York once more, as a guest at the Quinto Encuentro de Escritores organised by la Casa de España. During her stay, at the Proshansky Auditorium of the Graduate Center of CUNY (New York City University) she took part in a round-table discussion on female narrative at which Esther Tusquets and Cristina Fernández Cubas, as representatives of different literary generations, were also present. In 1995, she travelled yet again to the United States, to give a series of lectures at the universities of Athens, Charlottesville, New Orleans and Washington. In March 1996, she was invited by the Instituto Cervantes de Nueva York and visited the Universities of Cornell and Delaware during her stay.

The 1990s was a very productive period for Martín Gaite. She published *Caperucita en Manhattan* (1990), *Nubosidad variable* (1992), *La reina de las nieves* (1994), *Lo raro es vivir* (1996) and *Irse de casa* (1998). Moreover, in 1993, *Agua pasada* also appeared and included some of the prologues written for other books by her, as well as a series of articles published in different reviews. Her next essay was *Esperando el porvenir: Homenaje a Ignacio Aldecoa* (1994). This text comprises four chapters and underlines the causes that contributed to shaping the way of thinking of the Spanish people during the post-war period. It also traces the influences of French Existentialism, Italian Neo-Realist cinema, and the North American novel in the writers of her generation, as was seen in the first section of this chapter.

Bearing in mind the incredible length of Carmen Martín Gaite's career, as well as its prolific output, it is important not to overlook the objective of this chapter: to present the socio-political and cultural context to which she belongs, with a view to pinpointing the origins and development of the narrative elements with which the writer constructs her poetics. For her, literature is a journey that, in covering a distance from one place to another, becomes other journeys or is told from differing points of view.

For this reason, I consider the walk or stroll to be the central axis of her narrative. First, they would be through the streets of Madrid in the 1950s, in which, over a period of time, she would register the different parts of the city and then, at a later date, record these parts in writing in her *Cuadernos de todo* so as to leave the reader with a testimony of the different ways of life of post-war Spanish society in general and of women in particular. In that period, a prominent factor is the influence of Italian Neo-Realist cinema, which is transposed to the narrative of the 1990s in *Irse de casa*, which is a novel about a mature woman who travels from New York to Spain and whose story merges with the film script being written by another of the characters.

*Entre visillos* is an ad hoc exponent of the concern on the part of the writers of the *Generación de los 50* to bring to literature what the press preferred to bypass. Their narrative reveals a generational awareness born of experiences lived during the Spanish Civil War and the post-war period and defended through a committed attitude, a willingness to reveal the truth and a desire to achieve greater political, cultural and literary openness. With *Entre visillos*, Martín Gaite ratifies her incorporation into that Neo-Realist trend, a stance that had already been apparent since her participation in the birth of *Revista Española* in 1953. With the publication of *Entre visillos*, it is possible to trace the writer's interest in presenting and developing the points of view of female characters. Such an interest would likewise result in the adoption of a critical attitude towards the expression '*mujeres ventaneras*' ('women gazing through windows'), that is, women who watch life go by from a specific vantage point, which is a theme developed in Chapter 3. In *Entre visillos* the emphasis is placed on the interior spaces to which women have been confined, their only way of escape being the possibility of looking beyond the window, which becomes a metaphor for a greater openness towards other forms of life.

In the 1970s, *El cuarto de atrás* stands out as a novel in which Martín Gaite explores and reviews a specific period of Spanish history – the post-war era – by combining three types of literary discourse: the novel of memories, the fantastic novel and metafiction. The title functions as a symbol of personal development (the protagonist's transition from childhood to maturity) and a historical event (the Spanish Civil War) and its impact on the main character. This room, which Linda Gould Levine has described as being 'a metaphor for freedom, imagination and memory',[78] alludes as much to the physical space itself as it does to the inner and psychological space. In this way, the fundamental task facing the writer is to relate the inner and subjective sphere with the external referent of the historical event. The interlinking of the exterior with the interior is what motivates Martín Gaite to generate a vocabulary associated with the concept of geography. There will be movements to and fro from one type of geography to another: from the domestic geography (represented by the room), a journey will be made to the interior geography (represented by dreams and the imagination), as we shall review and analyse in Chapter 3.

In *El cuarto de atrás*, Martín Gaite includes a dedication to Lewis Carroll, with which she introduces the theme of the fantastic. These are her words: 'Para Lewis Carroll que todavía nos consuela de tanta cordura y nos acoge en su mundo al revés' ('For Lewis Carroll, who still comforts us with so much sanity and welcomes us into his upside-down world'). This phrase serves as a prelude to the presence of two other key figures: Todorov and Kafka. The first is the person who will provide the protagonist with the fantastic elements through a reading of *Introduction to Fantastic Literature*, and the second will appear in the form of an insect, the cockroach, emerging within the novel and, later, in a collage by Martín Gaite that can be seen in *Visión de Nueva York*. However, the novel's contribution does not stop there. The use made of two paintings mentioned at the beginning of the work goes almost unnoticed: *El mundo al revés* and *Conferencia de Lutero con el diablo*. These paintings are inserted into the novel as micro-stories and their function is to create links with the main story so as to, in this way, interlink the visual and narrative dimensions of the work.

Finally, Martín Gaite attained poetic plenitude in the 1990s. First, there was the publication of *El cuento de nunca acabar*, which is a fundamental work in reconstructing the poetic foundations of the writer, as will be analysed in Chapter 2. It is also important to mention the lectures in *Desde la ventana*, the series of articles in *Agua pasada* and *Pido la palabra*, and the notes in *Cuadernos de todo*. In these works it will be possible to appreciate the gradual transformation that is visible in the writer's narrative output and the way in which drawing, painting and collage are progressively incorporated into her writing, particularly that produced in the 1990s. Martín Gaite's narrative reveals the prevalence of a multiplicity of perspectives, the emphasis being not only on inhabited space but on space that is explored, contemplated, foraged, felt, displaced and travelled by women who have succeeded in freeing themselves of the ties imposed upon them in the 1950s.

**2**

# The Poetics of Carmen Martín Gaite

---

*El cuento de nunca acabar* is, in my view, the germinal text in which Martín Gaite creates her own 'nomenclature' with which to explain what she understands by narrative, as well as expounding the elements she uses in its elaboration. In it, the writer introduces certain concepts, such as *preámbulo* ('preface'),[1] *paseos interiores* ('inner wanderings'),[2] *red de cuentos* ('story network'),[3] novels that are *de papeles atados* ('of gathered writings'),[4] *mirar desde fuera* ('looking from outside'),[5] *la geografía narrativa* ('narrative geography'),[6] *las conexiones significativas* ('significant connections'),[7] and *re-anudar* ('re-tying'),[8] all of which she continues to develop in later critical texts such as *Agua pasada* and *Pido la palabra*.

The primary objective of this chapter is to identify the writer's own language and then to show that she creates a poetics that rotates on three axes: the journey, the construction of space and the visual dimension. In this way, it will be possible to demonstrate the way in which Martín Gaite develops her narrative in the 1990s with processes analogous to those carried out in her collages.

It is not possible to analyse the poetics of Martín Gaite without referring to the close ties that exist between *Cuadernos de todo* and *El cuento de nunca acabar*. In her Introduction to *Cuadernos de todo*, María Vittoria Calvi has underlined the relationship between these two texts, and has even gone as far as to consider them *la trastienda* ('the back office')[9] of Martín Gaite's narrative production. The forty *Cuadernos de todo* selected by María Vittoria Calvi provide data from 1961 to 1992. These data have been extremely useful for this research, the objective of which is to show that Martín Gaite creates a poetics that incorporates elements pertaining to disciplines such as drawing, collage and painting that are outside the sphere of literature.

In *Life-Writing in Carmen Martín Gaite's* Cuadernos De Todo *and Her Novels of the 1990s*, María José Blanco establishes a close relationship between *Cuadernos de todo* and *El cuento de nunca acabar*. Blanco shows how some of the ideas about narration that would later solidify were already germinating in *Cuaderno I* (1961). Blanco reorganises the *Cuadernos de todo* and adjusts them in such a way as to show the process of writing of *El cuento de nunca acabar* and the fiction of the 1990s. She also takes times to explain the content of the six *cuadernos americanos* (American notebooks) for the period from 1980 to 1985. These notebooks take their name from the fact that they were written during the various occasions on which Martín Gaite was in the United States as a guest professor. For María José Blanco, the *Cuadernos de todo* are 'a writer's notebooks, for developing ideas on her novels and essays, showing the close link between the author's "diaries" and her work, between life and literature'.[10] Blanco claims that the *cuadernos* are 'therapeutical tools',[11] as it is in writing that the cure is found that allows both the writer and the protagonists of the novels of the 1990s to continue their lives. In 'Presentación de *Los Cuadernos de todo* en Salamanca', María Vittoria Calvi also declares that 'the *Cuadernos de todo* have a very close relationship with *El cuento de nunca acabar*; both works share the rejection of established genres, the search for an aesthetic of the provisional and uncertain'.[12]

Moreover, Pozuelo Yvancos writes that '*Cuadernos* provide a genuine topography to get to know the *place* of Martín Gaite, metonymy of a territory at once vital and literary'.[13] He also establishes the relationship of the *Cuadernos de todo* with 'the gestation processes of the collection of works published between 1962–1994'.[14] He proposes approaching the *Cuadernos de todo* as part of a 'new sibling genre of other genres that I shall call *escrituras del yo* [writings of oneself]'.[15] It is important to point out that Pozuelo Yvancos does not consider them to be memories, autobiography, essays or private diaries. For him, they are 'a subgenre of the *escritura del yo* where various other genres converge and diverge'.[16]

The point of departure for the present chapter is rooted in the reading and analysis of *Cuadernos de todo*. In the notes to 'Cuaderno 14', written in the first three months of 1975, the writer considers the *journey* as the 'tema literario de primera mano' ('first-hand literary topic').[17] Such a concept can be seen a year earlier, in 'Cuaderno 13', when reference is made to the journey as the '*centro*' ('centre')[18] of all narrative, the traveller being obliged to tell the story of his or her arrival at a certain place, or the way in which he or she departed, without forgetting all the possible peripheral stories that emerge once the narrative concerned with the circumstances of the arrival or the reasons for departure has begun. The concept of journey is not only understood as physical movement from one place to another; it also refers to the action of going out for a walk in a city as a way of searching for material that Martín Gaite can use to write a novel. Another instance of journey relates to *paseos interiores* ('inner wanderings'), as developed by Martín Gaite in *El cuento de nunca acabar*. These *paseos interiores* are those roamings about the unconscious via dream and imagination that find their materialisation in writing.

The narrative produced by Carmen Martín Gaite in the 1990s is consolidated in the idea of an ongoing journey through places that gradually give shape to different kinds of geography – the urban, the domestic, the interior and the narrative – each of which will be looked at in depth in Chapter 3. The mere idea of journey implies movement, motion, displacement, trajectory and, consequently, change. For the writer, the journey is the essence of narrative[19] in that the different forms of motion, be they walks in a city, or rambles through the unconscious, via dream or imagination, or movements back and forth within spaces inhabited on a daily basis such as a house, a library, a café or a museum, in one form or another generate a series of actions that gradually divide, producing an aesthetic instrument with which Martín Gaite elaborates her narrative. For this reason, one of the objectives of this chapter is to identify and analyse the series of actions with which Martín Gaite has shaped her poetics. It is important to look at the background to the way in which walks through the city, the unconscious or the narrative text became an aesthetic tool for several writers.

## The journey as poetic search

For Careri, walking is an 'herramienta crítica … una manera obvia de mirar el paisaje como una forma de emergencia de cierto tipo de arte y de arquitectura' ('essential tool … a natural way of

observing the scenery as a source for certain types of art and architecture'.[20] That 'herramienta crítica' has been put into practice by
certain artists who have exercised the activity of aimlessly sauntering about as a form of urban art. In the literary terrain, mention
can be made of Tristan Tzara, André Breton and Guy Debord. With
this perspective in mind, Careri's work centres on three moments
of transition in such a form of art, the point of inflection consisting
of an experience in sauntering. The first transition is from Dadaism
to Surrealism (1921–4), the second from the Lyricist International
to the Situationist International (1956–7), and the third from
Minimalism to *Land Art* (1966–7). With the analysis of these three
periods, Careri pieces together a history of the travelled city that
goes from the *banal city* of Dada to the *entropic city* of Robert
Smithson, via the *unconscious and oneiric city* of the Surrealists and
the *ludic and nomadic city* of the Situationists.

Careri's analysis is of interest because the concept of *recorrido*
('travel', 'route') is linked with three aspects that come together:
the act of passing through (*recorrido* as the action of walking); the
line that passes through space (*recorrido* as an architectonic object)
and the story of the space passed through (*recorrido* as a narrative
structure).[21]

Careri's analysis is interesting, in that viewing sauntering as an
aesthetic practice leads him to the elaboration of a list of words that
he calls *serie de acciones* ('a set of actions') that 'recientemente han
entrado a formar parte de la historia del arte y que podrían
convertirse en un útil instrumento estético con el cual explorar y
transformar los espacios nómadas de la ciudad contemporánea'
('have recently become part of art history and that could turn into
a useful aesthetic tool with which to explore and transform the
nomadic spaces of contemporary cities').[22] Careri presents his *serie
de acciones* in three columns. The first is a list of forty-three verbs –
mostly transitive – such as 'to cross', 'to open', 'to recognise', 'to
descend', 'to ascend', ' to trace', 'to draw', 'to inhabit', 'to visit', 'to
explain', 'to cover' (in distance), 'to observe', 'to find', 'to construct'
and 'to spy'. The second column contains what I call a 'series of
nouns'. This list contains forty-three nouns from which I have
selected those corresponding to the *serie de acciones* mentioned
previously: a territory, a path, a place, a ravine, a mountain, a form,
a point, a circle, a stone, a city, a map, hawthorns, an archipelago,
relations and persons. The third column is another *serie de acciones*

with only eight intransitive verbs which are: 'to walk', 'to find one's way', 'to get lost', 'to wander', 'to immerse oneself', 'to roam', 'to enter' and 'to advance'.

In this chapter I develop the poetics of Carmen Martin Gaite and I consider the *journey* as the cornerstone of her reflections present in her narrative work. In speaking of 'journey' I am referring to all displacement or movement that brings about a transformation in the traveller. Such a journey will contain a series of actions through which the former is carried out, such as: walking, strolling, wandering about, and moving from one place to another or from one thought to another. In these trajectories, the traveller or stroller becomes an observer, or a witness of events. The look or gaze of the person travelling or strolling about the city is of key importance in the writing.

In her own special way, Carmen Martin Gaite puts *flânerie* into practice as an aesthetic exercise through which she will create a series of narrative and visual cartography that will provide testimony of the life of women in different stages of the cultural, social and political life of Spain. The work of the writer encompasses a journey from childhood to maturity and, on a similar level, moves through different moments in the lives of other women. Her constant concern has been to leave behind a testimony of the female condition that would not have been possible without the writer's gaze, and without her particular point of view.

Once again, it is important to point out that the journey is the main axis of Martín Gaite's narrative. Rooted in the journey is the desire for existential change. Travelling is an initiation, a cultural growth, an experience or a search. In the case of Martín Gaite it is a search for words with which she can elaborate her reflections on narration and, in this manner, throw off the impregnable nomenclature of other writers or critics who have also written on the same theme. The writer is *seeking the mode* with which to write her poetics.

In one of the notes from 'Cuaderno 11', dated autumn 1974, Martín Gaite writes that she has been writing *El cuento de nunca acabar*, her fragmented poetic text, for years, because it stems from those notes that she takes while she moves about the city, whether by bus, underground or train. At that time, there is as yet no defined point of view from which to embark upon her reflections on narrative. She takes to the streets in search of a possible answer and says: 'Buscar, hurgar, estoy trabajando por la calle' ('Searching, seeking,

I am working while I walk along the streets').[23] Martín Gaite moves about Madrid following a route through places that are frequented by writers. There are many references to the Ateneo, and to coffee bars and museums. In my view, Martín Gaite is performing *la flânerie* according to the definition provided by Anke Gleber – that is to say, 'a mode of movement that is at the same time a process of reflection and a manner of walking with an attendant presence of mind and close attention to images'.[24]

Martín Gaite uses the *paseo* as an artistic form directly inscribed within a textual space. Madrid is the city that tenders itself as the territory for her artistic experiences. For the writer, 'la ciudad es una geografía de narraciones ... Siguiendo la geografía de la ciudad como hilo conductor, se estructuran nuestras narraciones fragmentarias, desatendidas e internas' ('cities are a geography of stories ... By following the geography of a city as a *leitmotif,* our fragmented, unattended, internal stories are structured'),[25] as she affirms in 'Cuaderno 11'. In this quotation, in speaking about this to-and-fro movement about the city, Martín Gaite mentions certain places such as la Puerta de Alcalá, el Café Gijón or el Ateneo, which will give gradual shape to her own *geografía urbana* ('urban geography') and will be incorporated, at a later date, into her novels, constructing in this way a *geografía narrativa* ('narrative geography').

In her study entitled *Carmen Martín Gaite,* Biruté Ciplijauskaité quotes from the interview that the author agrees to give Miguel Villena, in which she stresses her predilection for *el callejeo* ('wandering').[26] The short journeys on foot or by bus provide raw material with which to write; after all, it is in the street that she can 'capturar el murmullo de la vida cotidiana' ('capture the murmur of everyday life').[27] It is important to underline the fact that the *murmullo* is registered, since it is an indicator that the jaunts that Martín Gaite makes through the streets of the city are absent of danger. It is as though the threads of the different stories that come to her mind are converted into skeins. In her excursions about Madrid, nothing happens; everything is looked at from a distance.

Martín Gaite's meanderings through the streets of Madrid, just like those of the protagonists of her novels, register the *murmullo* of everyday life in that, as her protagonists do, she does so unimpeded. They take to the street so as to get away from domestic life, and they view it from a different perspective – standing back, as it were, and looking at the lives of others. The to-and-fro movement about the city does not imply risk. There are no barriers, either psychological or social, that prevent these protagonists from moving about freely. It is also important to point out that their walks take place during the day or at dusk. Most of them transpire calmly and are wrapped in that *murmullo de lo cotidiano*. The protagonists of the novels of the 1990s travel unhindered, free to move about from one area of the city to another. It is no longer necessary to comply with social security as in the case of the female writer of *El cuarto de atrás*, nor does the daughter have to ask her father's permission to go and study in another city, as in *Entre visillos*.

If, in the work of Martín Gaite, walking is an aesthetic tool with which the writer produces her poetic texts and narrative, then it is possible to identify a series of actions that she employs in a similar manner at different levels. In my view, those levels are the personal, the narrative and the plastic.

At the level of personal experience, I feel that it is important to take up again the idea of the journey as initiation, search or experience. The Indo-European root of the word 'experience' is '*per*', which can be interpreted as 'attempt', 'put to the test' or 'risk'. Many of the secondary meanings of '*per*' refer to movement: to cross a space, to reach an objective and to head outside, as explained by Francesco Careri. In my analysis, I suggest that Martín Gaite converts her experience of walking the streets of Madrid into forays that shape an urban geography. This geography is then transformed into a narrative geography. Unlike the excursions undertaken on foot by the Dadaists or Surrealists, Martín Gaite takes a bus or train in executing hers. I am interested in underlining this fact, in that it is hard to forget that the notes that inspired the *Cuento de nunca acabar* emerged precisely during some of those outings. Martín Gaite took notes while she looked out of the window of the bus at the fleeting images of the city. Here, writing and travelling are simultaneous acts: both actions signal a process, a 'being-in-movement' to attain an objective. In writing while travelling, Martín Gaite traverses the mental space through memory and, at the same time, crosses the textual space by transcribing the visual images provided by the urban geography.

As early as 1948, Madrid became Martín Gaite's residence, as is indicated in Chapter 1 on the historical context of this book. It is thus inevitable that the author begins to tell stories of the past when she goes by el Retiro, heads towards el Ateneo or returns to

Nostromo. For example, in 'Cuaderno 11', corresponding to 1974, the writer jots down that she is travelling in a red bus (a double-decker that is no longer in use) through la Puerta de Alcalá, which evokes the 'estudio de Mampaso [que] estaba ayer en el Gijón' ('Mampaso's studio, located in *El Gijón* yesterday'). She finishes her note by saying: 'Yo conozco su juventud y él la mía. Geografía de Madrid, mi geografía particular, sigo tus huellas' ('I know his days of youth and he mine. Madrid geography, my particular geography, following your footsteps').[28] To walk the streets of Madrid implies, finally, to look at places, which already form part of the particular itinerary of the writer, and to remember friendships. The action of remembering implies telling stories that are deposited in those places, as though we were dealing with a mnemotechnic exercise. The different places pointed out in her itinerary are like the rooms of a house. In travelling about the urban geography and the domestic geography, she reviews the memories that 'se ramifican como los vericuetos de un viaje no programado' ('branch out like the twists and turns of an unplanned trip').[29]

Based on what has been said in previous pages, it can be affirmed that the *leitmotif* of 'the journey' represents the driving force of Martín Gaite's narrative produced in the 1990s. I would also venture to say that it is the thread that unites the four novels. In *Nubosidad variable*, Sofía and Mariana flee, escape and leave home. Mariana takes a decision at the outset of the novel and the reader is gradually informed of the events of the journey via the letters that Mariana writes to Sofía. At the heart of this journey exists a desire for existential change. On the other hand, the story of Sofía consists of her movements back and forth within the domestic geography of her matrimonial home, which she will later abandon, eventually returning to what had formerly been the house of her mother, better known as '*el refu*'. In Sofia's house, the movements back and forth parallel changes taking place within the protagonist. It is important to follow these movements in the domestic geography since it is an indicator of the process of separation of the roles assigned to Sofía as wife and mother. She first abandons the matrimonial bedroom and occupies her daughter Amelia's room instead. It is here that she begins her collage exercises, a very significant act in as much as she discovers the provisional space in which she takes up again the *tandas de deberes* ('rounds of chores'), as she refers to the pleasurable exercise of writing. Amelia's room is her first refuge:

it is the space in which she can begin once again to give free rein to her dreams, which had evaporated due to her time-consuming obligations as mother and spouse. The moments spent in the kitchen represent a pause in which she recapitulates on her life in recent years, during which her 'equilibrio mental estuvo supeditado al logro de recetas de cocina apetitosas y de un comentario aprobatorio' ('mental balance was subordinated to successfully executing tasty recipes and a getting an approving comment').[30] The chapter entitled 'De una habitación a otra' clearly reveals the meditative state in which Sofía finds herself. She continues to entertain a retrospective look on her life, and she does not like what she begins to find out or affirms. One such unexpected encounter is when she discovers that her husband has had a mistress for several years. Knowing and accepting that there is no point in continuing to live with her husband, she makes for the '*refu*', which is an apartment flat where her daughter, Encarna, lives and that she will subsequently abandon to go and live with her friend, Mariana. The fact that Mariana and Sofía find themselves in a kiosk on a beach in the south of Spain affords the possibility of imagining the future of the two friends. It is not known whether both will return to the houses they have been fleeing from, or will seek out another location free of family ties.

*La reina de las nieves* comprises the story of the journeys made by the two protagonists. Leonardo Villalba is a character *in the making*, who undergoes permanent evolution – a process of transformation that is seen in his constant desire to travel. Initially, the narrator plays the lead role in a journey, illustrating, in an irrefutable manner, a wish to get away from himself. He walks the length and breadth of Tangiers, Amsterdam, Verona, Paris, Berlin and Bergamo, like a *flâneur*, roaming the streets in such an erratic manner that he earns himself the nickname of 'the foreigner'. In retrospect, Leonardo sees this period of journeying as a 'huir perpetuamente hacia ciudades que nunca me dijeron: ¡quédate!' ('perpetually escaping to cities that never said "stay!"')[31] Leonardo reveals not only that he is aware that his perennial wanderings entailed escape, but that he had also been conscious that, in that escape, what he sought to leave behind were memories, dates and everything that could tie him in one way or another to a past from which he wished to cut himself off: 'Todos huyen, huimos, de lo mismo, de lo que hemos creído ir dejando enterrado a las espaldas, según nos adentramos por caminos sin dirección' ('Everybody escapes, we escape for the same reasons. We run from what we've thought we buried behind as we aimlessly take the road').[32]

With his release from jail and return to the family home, however, the fleeing comes to an end. Leonardo finally realises that the moment has arrived in which he must come face to face with the ghosts from which had been running, and that the frenetic flight has to come to a close. From that moment, he begins a very different trajectory, in which flight is converted into search. The different rooms of the family house, the notary's office, the streets of Madrid, the house at Almudena, and Monica and the surrounding areas of Quinta Blanca, will become witnesses of his indecisive wanderings, and a reflection of the inner journey that he has embarked upon.

In *Nubosidad variable*, Sofía's movements take her from inside the house to the street outside, to the search for her own space. On the other hand, Leonado's return implies a re-encounter with his past that, initially, he is reluctant to confront. Almost as soon as he arrives, he decides 'condenar la puerta que comunica con los pisos de arriba' ('to condemn the door leading to the upper floors'),[33] and, later, after a brief foray, he returns to the room and closes the sliding doors. In both cases, the desire to set up barriers between himself and the memories that pervade the house becomes evident. Nevertheless, Leonardo gradually makes up his mind to enter his father's office. On one of the four walls hangs a nineteenth-century English engraving behind which is hidden the safe, 'símbolo visible de todas las puertas cerradas de los cuentos' ('visible symbol of all the shut doors in tales'),[34] which contains letters and photographs with which, little by little, Leonardo begins to rebuild the family history. The room, the engraving and the safe are the three elements with which the image of Leonardo, embarking upon a journey towards his inner self, is reinforced.

The protagonist of *Irse de casa* is a woman who, despite the fact that she is no longer overwhelmed by the idea of escaping house and home, decides temporarily to abandon New York, the city where she resides, leaving only a letter for her children. Biruté Ciplijauskaité points out that while the wish to leave home is present in the other novels as a desirable possibility, in this one it is viewed in retrospect. In my opinion, Amparo Miranda has escaped from her home in New York because she has outstanding business to sort out in Spain, in the city where she was born. The idea of leaving home is seen not in retrospect, but in an action that Amparo Miranda embraces on two occasions – one in the past and the second in the present. Unlike Sofía, Amparo does not have to undo marriage ties; instead, she has to solve a personal history.

Until now, I have shown that the journey is the backbone of Martín Gaite's narrative in the 1990s. I would now like to identify and analyse a series of actions that the characters carry out while they are travelling or once they have reached their destinations. In the case of *Nubosidad variable*, Mariana first settles in at the home of a friend but decides to leave that place because it continues to be a prison, preferring to take refuge in a hotel room. It is during these days that she goes back to writing and to projects once abandoned. She alternates this activity with walks in the vicinity of the hotel, where she observes the people whose paths she crosses. In my view, the solitary walks of Mariana in a city that is not hers bestows upon her the characteristics of a *flâneuse*. Through her wanderings, she seeks to attain a state of hypnosis – a disoriented loss of control. They are a *medium* through which she comes into contact with the unconscious part of geographical and mental territory. Mariana confesses that she is lost: 'pero a salvo, por las distintas calles y callejas' ('yet safe, amid streets and alleys').[35] Roaming about blind alleys is a metaphor for the 'cavilación inútil' ('useless ruminations'),[36] in which she finds herself as she 'dudando entre las opciones de *quedarse, irse, seguir huyendo* o *volver a* Madrid' ('wavers between the options of *staying, leaving, keep on escaping* or *returning to* Madrid').[37] These actions are words that travel by 'las calles del cerebro que se mezclan y abrazan describiendo giros caprichosos' ('the mind's roads, which mix and embrace along whimsical twists').[38]

In *La reina de las nieves*, Leonardo decides to take to the street after being freely enclosed for several days with his parents in order to go through certain administrative as well as personal affairs. The walk begins in la Gran Vía as he takes pleasure in everything he sees, stopping from time to time in front of a shop window, and then continuing along 'callejuelas laterals' ('side streets'), 'andando sin prisa ni rumbo' ('meandering leisurely'),[39] like a *flâneur* through the streets of Madrid. In a similar manner, for Mariana in *Nubosidad variable*, walking becomes a 'zigzag entretenido y sedante' ('fun, soothing zigzag'), which opens up to her 'las espirales de [sus] laberintos interiores' ('the spirals of [her] inner mazes').[40] To go out for a walk, then, takes on the meaning of breaking with one's inner self, of crossing a threshold into an outside space, of entering the universe of intimate thoughts, the unconscious, of fantasies. And, just as the walk about the city generates changes within Leonardo, the journey that he makes to la Quinta Blanca at the end of the novel reaffirms two ideas developed up to that moment: the preponderance of sight over the other four senses and the journey as the aesthetic tool with which Martín Gaite constructs her narrative. This is analysed by means of the analogy between 'los repliegues mismos del paisaje' ('the landscape's folds'), which Leonardo contemplates, and which 'no dejan de ser un texto a descifrar, portador de acertijos' ('are still a text to be deciphered, a bringer of riddles').[41] The 'setenta kilómetros ofrecidos al ojo perspicaz que no prejuzga ni descarta nada, sediento de mirar' ('70 kilometres offered to the discerning eye, thirsty of sight, prejudging or excluding nothing')[42] are the material with which the *flâneur* will construct his accounts.

The analogy of walking about the streets of a city, with movements back and forth within the unconscious, reappears in *Lo raro es vivir*. Águeda Soler decides to depart in search of her father, who lives in a new town development. During this search, she gets lost 'por calles, rotondas sin señalizar y descampados a oscuras' ('in unmarked streets and traffic circles and dark vacant lots'),[43] an experience that makes her think that, throughout her whole life to date, she has been accustomed to 'dar vueltas, siempre igual, perdida, sin saber por qué hago lo que hago' ('wandering and getting lost, always the same, clueless as to why I do what I do').[44] For Águeda Soler, it is 'placentero deambular' ('pleasant to wander'), 'caminar perdida entre la gente, a paso perezoso' ('to walk aimlessly among people at a lazy pace')[45] through the city in which a very small stretch of road is capable of evoking memories such as those had by Martín Gaite herself in her walks about Madrid or New York.

Bearing in mind the analysis carried out so far, it may be said that the journey is one of the central axes with which Martín Gaite elaborates her novels of the 1990s. However, the journey *per se* would have little value were we to leave to one side all that which the gaze encapsulates, not to mention the results. If the writer takes to the street in search of specific language with which to explain her narrative strategies, what does she find in the street? What does she observe? How does she go about transforming, in writing, what she registers through her gaze? These are some of the questions that I shall attempt to answer in the following section, which deals with identifying the series of strategies employed by Martín Gaite in elaborating her poetics and, subsequently, her novels.

## Reconstruction of the poetics of Martín Gaite

Martín Gaite wrote four key texts reflecting on her narrative strategies: *El cuento de nunca acabar* (1983), *Agua pasada* (1993), *Pido la palabra* (2002) and *Cuadernos de todo* (2002). In the light of this production, an attempt to reconstruct the writer's poetics would seem appropriate at this stage.

The elaboration process behind *El cuento de nunca acabar* took place between 1973 and 1982. The reason for reconstructing the reflections of a writer on her narrative strategies is the fact that they appear in a fragmented manner throughout the four sections that comprise *El cuento de nunca acabar*, as affirmed by José Jurado Morales in *La trayectoria narrativa de Martín Gaite*.[46] For Jurado Morales, the four sections, entitled 'Siete prólogos', 'A campo través', 'Ruptura de relaciones' and 'Río revuelto' ('Seven Prologues', 'Cross-Country', 'Breaking Up' and 'Raging River'), bear testimony to 'una obra difícil de encasillar genéricamente, a caballo entre el ensayo, el libro de memorias, el aforismo, la narración ficticia' ('writing that is difficult to classify in a genre, somewhere between the essay, the memoir, the aphorism, and fiction').[47] There seems little point in embarking upon a discussion of the classification of *El cuento de nunca acabar*. The important factor for the present study is to present the way in which the aforementioned sections were elaborated – for example, the nineteen chapters grouped under the title of 'A campo través', in that the technique of cutting and pasting fragments of notes in the *Cuadernos de todo* is, in my opinion, used by Martín Gaite to elaborate her novels and collages.

'Ruptura de relaciones' is the section in which Martín Gaite explains the process of elaboration of *El cuento de nunca acabar*. For nine years, the writer took notes in her *Cuadernos de todo*, which revolve around the themes of narrative, love and lies. Later, she typed up these notes, photocopied them, edited them using scissors, finally putting them in order according to themes and pasting those 'tiritas o rectángulos de material mecanografiado' ('strips or rectangles of typed material')[48] in a large notebook. Here, she 'dejaba a la izquierda un margen suficiente para escribir en rojo' ('left enough room at the left margin to write in red ink')[49] different titles, such as, 'narración avasalladora', 'orden y caos', 'geografía narrative' and 'mentira y juego' ('overwhelming story', 'order and chaos', 'narrative geography' and 'lies and games'). By the time she had finished, there were two notebooks called 'Clairefontaine'. The section entitled 'A río revuelto' ('In troubled waters') derives from those notebooks and is an excellent example of the elaboration process explained above, in that it comprises approximately 200 short texts, which, when expanded, provide the structure of the second section – 'A campo través' ('Cross-country') – of *El cuento de nunca acabar* in as much as 'de una nota que tenía ocho líneas en los "Clairefontaine", a veces, habían salido doce folios' ('an eight-line note in the Clairefontaine notebooks would sometimes generate up to twelve folios'),[50] as the writer herself explains.

In the process referred to above, it is possible to glimpse a series of actions that will form part of the poetics of Martín Gaite. For the time being, that series of actions consists of taking notes, typing them up, cutting them out, putting them in order, and pasting them into another notebook in which a space is set aside – a margin in which to write a possible title for those *tiritas* of paper that the writer had pasted to achieve her composition. A similar process is that which takes place in *Cuadernos de todo*, which contain reflections and commentaries on unrelated readings, be they fiction or essay. In this case, reading is combined with the exercise of copying fragments of books by Natalia Ginzburg, Gaston Bachelard, Virginia Woolf, Todorov, Aldecoa or Kafka, to mention but a few. In 'Cuaderno 36', written in 1992, Martín Gaite says: 'Me veo obligada a ver escritas con mi letra en un cuaderno las frases del libro, cosa que sólo se parece al placer preparatorio de los collages. Lo hago verdad, lo hago mío, con sus añadidos y tachaduras' ('I'm forced to see the handwritten phrases of the book, something that is only similar to the preparatory pleasure of collage creation. I make it real, I make it mine, with its additions and erasures').[51]

**Textual collage**

The elaboration process of *El cuento de nunca acabar* is what interests us in this book, as Martín Gaite develops poetics similar to those of the collage. She applies those theoretical principles later, in the elaboration of her collages as well as in that of her narrative of the 1990s, as will be analysed in this chapter and in Chapter 4. According to the definition provided in *Artforms*, the collage is 'a work made by gluing various materials, such as paper scraps, photographs, and cloth, on a flat surface'.[52] Albert Elsen defines it as a 'a *composition* deriving from Cubism and made by pasting together on a flat surface such originally unrelated materials as bits of newspaper, wallpaper, cloth, cigarette packages, and printed photographs'.[53] For her part, Elza Adamowicz defines collage using several approaches:

> As a practice, surrealist collage encompasses a wide range of activities, from encounters with defunct objects at the flea market to the transcription of the multiple voices of the unconscious, the fragmentary images of the dream and all modes of production which stage the clash of disparate elements. As a pragmatic act, collage englobes various complementary or conflictual functions – critical, poetic and political – which cohabit throughout the 1920s and 30s. As a technique, collage is a material mode of cutting and pasting distant elements – or indeed a simulation of that process. ... And as a creative act, it involves the transformation of these messages.[54]

On the one hand, in *El cuento de nunca acabar*, Martín Gaite employs collage as a technique to order *tiritas* of paper, which contain brief reflections written by her and which she pastes into another notebook. Those *tiritas* of paper can be seen in collages composed by the writer, as we shall analyse in Chapter 4 of this book, which deals with the visual elements in the narrative of Martín Gaite. On the other hand, in *Cuadernos de todo*, she has recourse once again to the technique of the collage when she copies texts by other writers and inserts them in her notebooks and novels. In this case, the collage can be identified with the principle of intertextuality as proposed by Henri Béhar: 'Cas limite d'intertextualité, le collage considère l'entier de la littérature comme un discours clos, fini ou finissant, dont les éléments peuvent permuter à l'infini' ('The borderline of intertextuality, the collage considers the whole of literature as a closed, finished or finishing discourse, where the elements can interchange unto infinity').[55] In 'Collage in the Twentieth Century:

An Overview' Katherine Hoffman points out that the concept of collage must be extended so as to include all forms of 'composite art and processes of juxtaposition, plastic, musical and literary'.[56]

In the case of Martín Gaite, intertextuality can be seen when copying fragments of readings from other writers – for example, from *La poética del espacio* by Gaston Bachelard, and inserting them into the 'cuadernos de todo', or placing them within her novels as in the case of *La reina de las nieves*. For Martín Gaite, intertextuality is no more than 'una yuxtaposición de elementos fácil o posible de desmontar ... fértil e inevitable collage' ('a juxtaposition of easily disassembled elements ... a fertile, inevitable collage',[57] as can be read in 'Cuaderno 14'. If 'collage makes poetry with the prosaic fragments of dailiness',[58] as affirmed by Donald Kuspit, the same thing takes place when elaborating a novel. In the work of Martín Gaite, it will be seen that there are clear parallels between the incorporation of elements already existing in the collage and the intertextuality in the literary production. In both cases, it is a question of the transfer of materials from one context to the other. These materials reveal a story in themselves, with which associations are established that resound in the 'new' composition.

If the collage technique consists of cutting and pasting materials from a diversity of sources or, as Elza Adamowicz point out, is a simulation of that process, and if Martín Gaite conceives the novel as *fragmentos de vida* ('life fragments'),[59] as she states in 'Cuaderno 14', I believe that she uses the collage as much in the sense of cutting and pasting as in that of simulating the process. But how and where does she simulate that process? The possible reply can be found in *Fragmentos de interior* (1976), in as much as the title alone is an anticipation of what happens in the novel and the narrative technique employed. The plot deals with the arrival in Madrid of Luisa, a young servant seeking to re-establish amorous ties with Gonzalo. The young girl boards with a well-to-do bourgeois family, where she takes the place of Pura, the old servant. Through Luisa's eyes, the narrator describes the existing relations between the other characters of the novel, who are members of a family. *Fragmentos de interior* alludes to every corner of the house in Madrid where Luisa works. At the same time, it also refers to every nook of the characters' minds. María Vittoria Calvi says:

> I 'frammenti' in questione sono infatti una serie di monologhi interiori dei vari personaggi, che, attraverso la conscienza di uno di essi

– Luisa, la giovane domestica – e la mediazione dell'autore, si ricompongono in una 'struttura' coerente .... Naturalmente, in questo senso il termine *interior* fa riferimento all'interiorità del personaggio.

Ma il titolo del romanzo può anche essere interpretato nella linea semantica di *Entre visillos,* in tal senso, i 'frammenti' sono una serie di immagini succesive di uno spazio preciso: una casa madrileña, vista con gli occhi dei suoi abitori, ma la cui esatta topografia viene definita dallo sguardo esterno di Luisa, che per svolgere il propio lavoro debe, prima di tutto, imparare a mouversi nel nuovo ambiente.

The 'fragments' in question are indeed a series of several characters' inner monologues, which, through the conscience of one of them – Luisa, the young maid – and the author's mediation, recompose in a consistent 'structure' ... Naturally, in this sense the term *interior* refers to the character's inner self.

Yet the title of the novel can also be interpreted in the same semantic line as *Entre visillos,* so the 'fragments are a series of consecutive images of a specific space: a house in Madrid, seen through the eyes of its inhabitants, but whose exact topography is defined by the gaze of the outsider Luisa, who, in order to carry out her work, must, above all, learn to move in the new environment.[60]

We must bear in mind that *Fragmentos de interior* was published in 1976. After a thorough search for reflections on poetics begun by Martín Gaite during those years, I find myself with the notes belonging to 'Cuaderno 14' corresponding to the first three months of 1975. In these notes, the writer summarises one of the artifices that she uses to compose a novel. She begins with a selection of characters of whom we know very little. Then she gradually reveals new aspects of these people as they relate to each other. Finally, Martín Gaite obtains a 'mosaic' shaped with bits and pieces of stories. In my opinion, this notebook is the theoretical foundation for the elaboration of *Fragmentos de interior.* The different bits and pieces of stories are linked through the eyes of Luisa, a character who observes from afar – independently of the fact that the story transpires, for most of the time, inside the house – the inner life of a Madrid family.

We have analysed that the actions of *cutting, pasting and assembling* are pertinent to the elaboration of *El cuento de nunca acabar* and *Cuadernos de todo.* This series of actions will be looked at again when we analyse the author's collages. For the time being, I would like to reiterate the analogy between these actions and that of *tacking.*

In 'Hilos, ataduras y ruinas en la novelística de Carmen Martín Gaite', Kathleen Glenn stresses the importance, for the writer, of the concept of thread in *Retahílas*, on account of the constant use of words such as *tejer, enhebrar, atadura, vínculo, tela* and *tejido* ('to knit', 'to thread', 'tie', 'link', 'cloth' and 'fabric').[61] Through this reiteration, Glenn considers communication as a fundamental theme of the work of Martín Gaite and centres her analysis on an interlocutor's search, which is not always possible to find. With this, she leaves to one side the plastic work of the writer who sticks the *tiritas* of paper in her notebooks to produce *El cuento de nunca acabar* or who brings together the fragments of stories to compose *Nubosidad variable* and *La reina de las nieves,* not to mention the use of thread and remnants in her collages, which we shall look at more closely in Chapter 4.

I previously referred to the fact that *cutting, pasting and assembling* are actions employed by Martín Gaite to put her materials in order and to elaborate *El cuento de nunca acabar* and *Cuadernos de todo.* The analogy of these actions with that of *tacking* is established in *Nubosidad variable* and continues in *Irse de casa.* The letters of Mariana León and Sofía Montalvo's *tanda de deberes* are transformed into a metapoetic text that describes and explains the method that both use to 'write themselves' and the novel the reader is reading. The way in which Sofía works can be compared with the method employed by Martín Gaite, in as much as she dedicates her time to 'pasar en limpio la tanda de deberes' ('make fair copies of the round of chores'),[62] and 'pasar apuntes' ('take notes')[63] from one notebook to another. For her part, Mariana says that she wants to write a novel the main plot of which deals with the escape of a mature woman – this project is clearly the book about her own life – and the composition 'una especie de diario desordenado, sin un antes y un después demasiado precisos' ('a sort of messy diary, with no particularly precise before and after').[64] In the end, the reader has in his or her hands a novel in which the tiny bits and pieces of mirror are synonymous with the fragments of stories or 'retales de material literario' ('scraps of literary material')[65] that Mariana gradually accumulates. The bits and pieces of mirror are *pasted,* the fragments of stories are *ordered* or *assembled* from a 'before' or an 'afterwards' (time references) and the remnants are *tacked.* The analogy established between *tacking* remnants and *assembling* fragments of stories is repeated constantly and thus becomes a *leitmotif.*

In the final chapter, the reader is presented with the dialogue between Sofía and her daughter, Encarna, about literary questions, in which both reach the conclusion that 'todo es coser' ('it's all in the sewing')[66] to obtain, in the end, the textile and textual plot of the novel. In *La novela femenina contemporánea*, Biruté Ciplijauskaité clearly points out that:

> Las novelas se conciben como mosaicos, con grandes blancos o una masa gris que une las piezas del dibujo. Así procede Natalia Ginzburg en su extraordinario *Caro Michele*, así surgen algunas novelas de Béatrix Beck y de Carmen Gómez Ojea. De fragmentos se constituyen *Celia muerde una manzana* de María Luz Melcón y *La trampa* de Ana María Matute, donde la imprecisión notada por Gonzalo Sobejano es buscada, así como lo es la asimetría en las narraciones de Barbara Frischmuth.

> Novels are conceived like mosaics, with great white areas or a grey mass joining the pieces of the design. That's how Natalia Ginzburg goes about it in her extraordinary *Caro Michele* (*Dear Michele*); that's how some novels by Béatrix Beck and Carmen Gómez Ojea emerge. Fragments make up María Luz Melcón's *Celia muerde una manzana* (*Celia Bites an Apple*) and Ana María Matute's *La trampa* (*The Trap*), where the vagueness noted by Gonzalo Sobejano is intentional, just as the asymmetry in Barbara Frischmuth's stories.[67]

Martín Gaite proceeds along similar lines. In *Irse de casa* she goes back to the mosaic composition. The narrator uses the journey of the protagonist, Amparo Miranda, to her native city as a pretext for telling the stories of the other characters belonging to families, such as the Mirandas, the Rocas, the Bores, the Morets and the Sánchez del Olmo. Many stories that had faded from Amparo's memory now reappear, this time transformed. The city, her acquaintances and she herself have all changed. The structure of the novel is rooted in the journey in which Amparo returns to her native city after several years and establishes, during her many walks, an alternation between the description of what she observes as she strolls about and what no longer exists due to the modifications undergone in the city. For example, her mother's sewing workshop has become an antique shop. The place has been remodelled and Amparo is obliged to have recourse to her memories in order to describe what that place was like when she and her mother lived there. On emigrating to the United States, the *cuartito de costura* ('little sewing room')[68] is the only link that both have with the past. The distribution of the space that the narrator describes creates a visual image similar to that of a collage, in that different kinds of elements combine to achieve the following *composition of place*:

> Jeremy miró la máquina de coser, una Singer antigua, el maniquí, el enorme pupitre donde los hilos, retales, tijeras y cuadernos convivían armoniosamente, la lámpara de cristalitos, el retrato grande y feo de la abuela [...] los almohadones sobre los que descansaba ahora la cabeza de María. Y por último la carta recién caída al suelo.

> Jeremy looked at the sewing machine, an old Singer, the mannequin, the huge desk where the thread, fabric scraps, scissors and notebooks harmoniously shared space, the cut crystal lamp, grandmother's large, ugly portrait [...] the pillows on which Maria's head now rested. And lastly, the letter recently fallen to the floor.[69]

That *cuartito de costura* ('little sewing room') is where so-called *desorden y aglomeración* ('clutter') converts into 'ámbito de labores, juegos y adivinanzas' ('a place of work, games and riddle').[70] In this case, the tasks are sewing and writing with which Amparo, as well as her mother, elaborate their creations. The former believes that 'toda creación consiste en lo mismo, en saber coser los elementos dispersos, y entender cómo se relacionan entre sí, da igual que sean historias o pedazos de tela, en el fondo es cuestión de quitar y poner' ('all creations consist of the same thing, knowing how to sew together loose elements and understand how they interrelate, be they stories or pieces of fabric; in the end, it's a matter of removing and adding').[71] Just think of Amparo Miranda's mother, a seamstress by trade, who, with 'un pedacito de cretona floreada' ('a piece of flowery chintz')[72] placed over the torn part of a blue skirt, creates a new line for the autumn–winter collections. In my analysis, I suggest that the action of *patching* one piece of cloth with another is similar to that of superimposing one image on another in a collage. The patch becomes 'un adorno chocante' ('a striking decoration'),[73] by which a different aesthetic is produced. In the same way, the elements of the collage come from other contexts and take on different meanings when, together, they form a 'new' composition.

The action of sewing or tacking to produce an artistic patchwork quilt refers to the study by Miriam Schapiro, and particularly to her neologism, 'Femmage', a 'work by women of history who sewed, pieced, hooked, cut, appliquéd, quilted, tatted, wrote, painted, and combined materials using traditional women's techniques to achieve their art-activities'.[74] Martín Gaite employs the action of tacking as a metaphor for the elaboration of a novel. If the writer conceives the novel as 'fragmentos de vida' ('life fragments'), as previously pointed out, it is necessary to explain the nature of the process of *pasting* or *tacking* such fragments in her novels and, at a later date, in her collages.

In *El cuento de nunca acabar*, Martín Gaite employs the term '*re-anudar*' ('to re-tie', which is a play on '*reanudar*', which means 'to renew', or 'to resume') as 'hilo para tejer lo de antes con lo de ahora' ('the yarn to interweave stuff from before with stuff from now;').[75] That 'before' refers to the stories of the past that are recovered in the present. In her poetics, the writer describes the technique of 'situacionismo' ('situationism') that consists of giving 'puntualizaciones del entorno' ('setting clues') to the present. And in the present, is described the place in which one is situated, this serving as the scenery from where it is possible to link up with stories from the past. Throughout my reading of 'Cuaderno 11', I returned in time to the period in which *El cuento de nunca acabar* was being written, and I noticed that the place from which memories are relived is not necessarily an inner space. The notes dated October 1974 narrate one of the many walks taken by the writer through the streets of Madrid. During one particular walk, Martín Gaite recalls her friendships 'al pasar por las esquinas de las calles [que le] cuentan su historia' ('while walking around the corners of the streets [that] tell their respective stories').[76]

These walks are an example of the writer's use of walking as an aesthetic tool. The meandering walks about the city, in which streets lead to other streets and stories from the past are linked to the present, are a metaphor for the process of reflection in which Martín Gaite finds herself. In the streets she is searching, rummaging and seeking the right point of view to adopt in order to develop the narrative. For the writer, 'la esquina de Narváez con Sainz de Baranda es un estrato sobre el que posteriormente se coloca Sainz de Baranda esquina a Antonio Arias' ('the corner of Narváez and Sainz de Baranda is a layer over which later Sainz de Baranda meets Antonio Arias street').[77] The corner is a stratum, a 'fragment' of a story, which forms part of the whole walk that the writer takes through the urban geography of Madrid. That stratum will become a cutting that the writer will paste in shaping one of the many collages analysed in the previous chapters of this book.

The action of *re-anudar* is analogous with that of *re-capitular*, as suggested by the writer in her 'Cuaderno 29' entitled 'Cuaderno de América', and corresponding to the autumn of 1982, a period in which Martín Gaite is a visiting professor at the University of Virginia. In that notebook, the writer says that 'la mente necesita un mínimo de reposo para recapitular sobre el paso de una situación a otra … momentos de transición' ('the mind requires a minimum amount of rest to recapitulate over the passage from one situation to another … transitional moments').[78] The same idea (using the same words, in fact) is repeated in her article 'El silencio da miedo', first published in the newspaper *El sol* in 1990 and included three years later in *Agua pasada*. In this article, the action *re-capitular* is necessary so as 'no perder el hilo que enhebra los actos sucesivos' ('not to lose the thread that weaves subsequent acts').[79] This repose that the mind needs to go from one thought to another becomes an analogy for taking a rest while walking about a city.

It should be stressed that *re-capitular* consists of 'tomar notas de esos momentos de transición que ocurren entre los diversos quehaceres cotidianos' ('taking notes of transitional moments happening in between various daily tasks').[80] What is Martín Gaite referring to when she speaks of 'quehaceres cotidianos' (daily tasks)? In 'Cuaderno 36', written in 1992, Martín Gaite hints at the fact that the action of *re-capitular* is performed 'mientras se espera el autobús, mientras se hace fila para cobrar en un banco o para que te atiendan en un comercio, ir doblando la ropa' ('while waiting for the bus, while in line to withdraw at the bank or while waiting to be attended at a store, folding clothes').[81] If one resumes (*se re-anuda*) while performing another activity, then has one not found that minimum period of repose that the mind requires to *re-capitular*, as suggested by the writer in her 'Cuaderno de América' and in 'El silencio da miedo'?

Until now, a series of actions has been identified that Martín Gaite employs to elaborate her poetics and her novels. It has been seen that she *takes* notes, *transcribes* them, *cuts* them out, puts them in *order* and *pastes* them in another notebook to produce *El cuento de nunca acabar*. The process of elaboration of certain notebooks included in *Cuadernos de todo* consists of *copying* fragments of other readings that the author *adds* and *crosses out* once she has them in her notebooks. Brief mention was made of the fact that this series of actions resembles the collage technique that Martín Gaite also uses for the composition of her novels. This commentary will be analysed in greater detail in the section entitled 'The visual elements'.

In *El cuento de nunca acabar* – in one of the little less than 200 short texts comprising the section 'Río revuelto' and whose title is 'El desorden artificial' – Martín Gaite says that researching the life of don Melchor de Macanaz (1670–1760) prompts her to reflect on 'el orden de los acontecimientos y su orden de sucesión dentro del relato' ('the order of events and their sequential order in a story'),[82] in that the personal papers of de Macanaz were scattered about, some in Paris, others in Valencia, Madrid and Simancas, which made it very difficult to achieve an overall view of the person. Martín Gaite dedicates seven years to this research, in which she is obliged to *order* the information by consulting Spanish and French archives, reading the works of de Macanaz (most of it unpublished), his letters, the files containing the accusations to which he was subjected by the Inquisition and the minutes of his reports to the King. The writer compares her research work to the artifice employed by certain writers (she does not supply names), who 'inventan (para desordenar adrede su historia) personajes que van aportando a ella informes contradictorios, papeles, cartas. Fingen haberse ido enterando de la historia a saltos, desordenadamente' ('invent (to jumble up their story on purpose) characters who provide her with contradictory data, papers, letters. They pretend to have learned the story in bits and pieces, in disorderly fashion').[83] Martín Gaite calls this type of novel 'de papeles atados' ('of gathered writings'). The term is interesting in that, if it is a question of 'de papeles atados', it requires the action of tying with threads, of *tacking*, so as to be able to repair a 'femmage', employing the technique of collage and incorporating visual elements into her narrative, as we shall see later.

This artifice is the same as the one used by the writer in elaborating her novels. For example, in *La reina de las nieves*, Leonardo and the reader gradually decipher the enigmas hidden behind the names of Sila, Casilda and Silveria. At the beginning of his inquiry, Leonardo believes that they are three distinct people, but as he reads Sila's letters addressed to her father, as well as Casilda's book, he notices 'el acoplamiento progresivo de una mujer con otra, a través de las coincidencias textuales' ('the progressive melding of one woman with the other through textual coincidences'),[84] in as much as they 'aparecen metáforas casi idénticas' ('seem like almost identical metaphors').[85] Furthermore, Silveria is the character of the first draft copy of *El periplo*, Casilda's unpublished novel. Leonardo finds the draft copy in the safe where his father kept his secrets, but that draft is signed by Sila. By reading these different texts (letters–draft–book), Leonardo slowly begins to tie together the different threads of this story. At the end of the chapter, to the Sila–Casilda mirage a third name is added: that of Silveria. In this way, Martín Gaite gradually elaborates a novel 'de papeles atados' ('of gathered writings') in which the fragments of letters and photographs, as well as the notes from Leonardo's notebook, are *tied*, *merged* or *woven*. Note, for example, that the paths fork, the faces blur and the dates superimpose, one upon the other, when Leonardo is trying to complete the jigsaw of stories derived from the female trilogy in which characters create other characters. Thus, *fork*, *blur* and *superimpose* form part of the series of actions with which Carmen Martín Gaite produces an aesthetic instrument geared to the creation of a narrative text in which the inclusion of artistic techniques such as collage is not amiss.

### The gaze

Though some critics have acknowledged the importance of the everyday in Martín Gaite's work, their emphasis has not been on the origin of this gaze upon the everyday, nor on how this gaze opens up the possibility that any object can become aestheticised within the literary text. The key point here is found in what the gaze uncovers, symbolically transforming narrative spaces.

The references used to sustain this investigation, given its interdisciplinary characteristics, combine different forms of studying the act of looking. Using specific examples, it presents a reading of the texts of Carmen Martín Gaite that opens up new interpretations, with the aim of going beyond the purely literary to highlight more interdisciplinary interests.

The review of this approach is important, not only because it highlights how the act of looking distinguishes the poetics of Martín Gaite, but also because, by referring to her gaze and the gaze of others, different acts of looking in a range of disciplines are linked and compared: the studies of the images, and in particular painting.

Despite the approach here traversing different fields of study, they all come together in this investigation and demonstrate the elements that make up the role of the gaze that Martín Gaite uses in her work. To understand this approach to the gaze further, we must first define what we mean by it and what the characteristics of this act are, distinguishing between the acts of 'seeing' and 'looking'. Then we will address the concept of representation, helping to determine the rhetorical strategies that make up a poetics based on the development of a gaze. This will allow us to answer two questions that will act as guides. What is being looked at – or the choice of the objects that are represented – as dealt with in the concepts of Mieke Bal; and how is it looked upon, in turn implying the position of the subject who is looking (from where do they look and how are the objects chosen by the author represented?) These questions are fundamental and are what will guide this analysis of Martín Gaite's work.

In *Travelling Concepts in the Humanities: A Rough Guide*, Mieke Bal traces the journey taken by some of the most representative concepts in the various disciplines of the humanities. In this book, Bal analyses the way in which concepts move between disciplines. For example, an analysis of the gaze, focus and iconicity creates a cartography that shows the journeys and links between these constantly moving concepts. In this book about Martín Gaite, I am interested in developing this idea of following the journey taken by different concepts, because, as Bal writes, 'the best way to think about concepts is with the metaphor of the journey'.[86]

Mieke Bal claims that looking implies an act that needs a visual event, made up of an object (an image, a text, sound or music) and a subject that experiences the visual images as fleeting and subjective.[87] The gaze is framed, bounded and laden with emotion; it is a cognitive, intellectual act that both interprets and classifies. In other words, it means that it is not just what is seen that characterises and defines an object, but also the act of seeing, which involves the sensual, emotional and cognitive as ways of accessing knowledge.

The work of Martín Gaite is constructed in such a way that all of its elements work together to direct the reader to look at those objects, spaces, people and situations that have been passed over in the rush of our lives. That is to say, in the works of Martín Gaite there are no coincidences; everything appears to be arranged so that the reader's look becomes a gaze, revealing to them more than what the eyes see at first sight, and leading to surprise and admiration at what they see. That is, they convert the ordinary into the extraordinary.

Carmen Martín Gaite is a writer interested in the everyday, uncovering the ordinary as an event sufficiently spectacular to be told. The importance of this gaze lies in showing that it is not the context that provides experiences full of wonder, but rather that this wonder is found in the gaze with which we view things. New universes open themselves up to those who know how to look, and anyone can train their gaze to find them.

In the chapter 'Spatial Stories' in *The Practice of Everyday Life*, Michel de Certeau proposes the creation of the everyday through the configuration of the spaces in stories, defined by de Certeau as 'journeys in spaces'.[88] In line with this, both everyday and literary stories are practices in spaces set out by the traveller[89] who directs their view towards a specific point. From directions of how to arrive at a place to a piece that describes the space occupied by its characters, these are frames that organise journeys, either real or intradiegetic. Given that we are interested in finding exactly what route Martin Gaite is proposing for our gaze in her texts, de Certeau's work is highly relevant.

The articles published in *Pido la palabra* (2002) provide a wealth of material with which to reconstruct the poetic principles of Martín Gaite, in that they contain further analysis by the writer of her own production. Such is the case of 'La mirada del escritor' in which Martín Gaite considers sight as the sense prevailing in her work. The person looking can be outside or within, and close to or distant from, the space being looked at. These four options and their possible combinations generate actions that differ among themselves but, at the same time, are grouped together under the heading of 'the gaze'. Such actions are: to look, to contemplate, to peep, to keep watch, to spy or to snoop. Martín Gaite points out that 'el afán selectivo que origina las preferencias se condensa en la visión orientada hacia aquello que el ojo ha elegido a cada instante como tema de curiosidad' ('the selective desire that gives birth to preferences is condensed in the gaze directed towards that which the eye has chosen in each instance as the topic of curiosity').[90] What are those themes that the eye has 'chosen' to look at?

In *Desde la ventana* she brings together four lectures dealing with 'El punto de vista femenino en la literatura española', lectures she delivered in the Foundation Juan March in the autumn of 1986. In these lectures, she looks closely at the (possible) specific way of writing that women display vis-à-vis that of men. In the lecture 'Mirando a través de la ventana' she describes the difficulties that Spanish women have faced throughout history to become independent of a life reduced to the home. More specifically, the author underlines the inconveniences and prejudices that women wishing to become writers have confronted. Thus, in 'Buscando el modo', she briefly describes the life and work of Santa Teresa de Jesús as the story of a woman coming to grips with the written word and the obstacles faced in seeking and being able to find not only her own mode of writing but also her own way of looking.

In 'La mirada del escritor', Martín Gaite establishes two types of gaze, which differ from each other depending on the location of the person observing. The gaze can be from the outside directed inwards, towards the interior of the house; or from the inside of the house directed outwards. In the first case, the interior is the unknown for the passer-by, who imagines, from without, the exciting life within. In my opinion, that passer-by idealises the domestic space. He or she has no reference that helps him or her to possess a 'composition of place'. In the second case, the interior is the known space for the person inhabiting it – usually a woman, who, in the author's collages as well as in her narrative, is looking out from her position in the window. Martín Gaite points out that 'los espacios exteriores y abiertos producían nostalgia a las mujeres que hasta hace pocas décadas salían a la calle menos que los hombres' ('outdoor and open spaces produce a nostalgia in women who until a few decades ago went out onto the street less than men').[91]

Who are those women to whom Martín Gaite refers? For Martín Gaite, the window is the 'punto de referencia para soñar desde dentro el mundo que bulle fuera' ('reference point to dreaming from inside about what is bubbling away outside').[92] Nevertheless, this image, which reinforces the image of 'una mujer recluida en el hogar, condenada a la impasibilidad' ('a woman shut away at home, condemned to impassivity'),[93] does not apply when one thinks, for example, of Sofía's grandmother in *Nubosidad variable*, who takes pleasure watching people go by, engrossed in their own thoughts, in matters in which she is not involved, much less obliged to dream about. The gaze of this woman is remote and could well be that of a *flâneuse* – half visible, half invisible – due to the position from which she gazes. In the gaze of Sofia's grandmother there is that pleasure in 'peeping out at people' from the 'strategic' position that is the window. In this sense, I feel that it is more pertinent to consider the window as a point of reference from which the woman looks at what goes on outside, without being seen, and takes pleasure in that activity. It is not a woman who dreams of the busy world. Dreaming relates to the possibility of imagining stories about the people she watches as they go by the window. She does not dream of being in her place, but that remote gaze is an aesthetic tool that is necessary to elaborate stories that she can later translate into a written form.

We should likewise think of Amparo Miranda in *Irse de casa*, who enjoyed 'espiar sus gestos [los de la gente a su alrededor], intuir lo que ocultaban tras lo que decían, observar cómo se movían, qué terreno fingían ocupar, detectar el punto flaco de sus miedos' ('spying the gestures [of the people around her], sensing what they were hiding behind their speech, observing their movements, what space they pretended to occupy, detecting the weak spots of their fears').[94] In that gaze, it is possible to glimpse the pleasure of 'ver sin ser vista' ('watching unseen'),[95] as stated in the novel. Her vision of the city in which she lived forty years ago has not changed at all. The pleasure of spying continues. Throughout the novel, Amparo Miranda enjoys looking without being recognised. Her gaze provides the possibility of alternating between the description of what Amparo is seeing (that is, the landscapes and people revealed to the reader) and what she had seen previously. Through this contrast, the motives for her journey are gradually unveiled, while the text confirms that what she discovers does not always coincide with what she had hoped to find.

In the following section, I shall analyse the process employed by Martín Gaite in the elaboration of her novels – that is, I will focus on the creative process that is gradually explained in *El cuarto de atrás*, *Nubosidad variable* and *Irse de casa*. I shall establish links with the themes viewed in previous sections: the journey or jaunt from one place to another and the preponderance of looking over the other four senses.

## Exploring Martín Gaite's poetics

Ten years after the publication of *El cuento de nunca acabar,* Martín Gaite published *Agua pasada,* in which she brings together prologues written for works by other writers, articles that had previously been published in magazines and newspapers or which had formed part of a series of lectures such as the one entitled 'Brechas en la costumbre', which was delivered in El Escorial in July 1990 in a symposium on fantastic literature. In that lecture, Martín Gaite sets forth her point of view on narrative by quoting what she had written in *El cuento de nunca acabar.*

> Mientras el narrador no se haya embarcado todavía en el viaje narrativo, mal podrá predecir desde la orilla las vicisitudes del itinerario y tiene que arriesgarse a salir del escondite de lo prefigurado, por miedo que le dé … Da miedo emprender ruta porque cada paso adelante significa internarse en lo desconocido.

> As long as the narrator has not yet embarked on the narrative journey, they are unable to predict from ashore what lies in store and have to risk leaving their hiding place where everything is merely a presage, despite being afraid … It is frightening to start down the road because every step forward means venturing into the unknown.[96]

That *viaje narrativo* is an analogy for the elaboration of a novel that is undertaken via the imagination. In 'Brechas en la costumbre', Martín Gaite considers that to relate progressively the way in which the *viaje narrativo* is executed means gradually becoming aware of its elaboration – that is to say, of its metafiction , as achieved by the writer in *El cuarto de atrás.*[97] The metafictional nature of *El cuarto de atrás* makes it a novel of its time, as confirmed by Emilia Velasco Marcos when she states that it was 'la década de los setenta y hasta mediados de los ochenta el periodo en el que se prodigó con mayor frecuencia este artificio' ('the period in which this artifice was most popular was in the 1970s up to the mid-1980s').[98]

Synthesising theories and studies on metafiction, the concept introduces, basically speaking, two possibilities regarding narrative resources. On the one hand, there is the term 'self-conscious novel', invented by Robert Alter and Patricia Waugh, in which the author consciously underlines everything in his or her narrative that is literary artifice and intertextuality, the objective being to investigate the relationship between fiction and reality. On the other hand, we have the term 'self-referential novel', employed by Robert Spires in *Beyond the Metafictional Mode*, which is one that refers to itself – that is to say, that directs its attention, first and foremost, to the creative process, and only secondly to the world represented by that process. Using Sobejano's terminology, the former may be called 'scriptive' while the latter is referred to as a 'metanovel'.[99]

In *La trayectoria narrativa de Carmen Martín Gaite* José Jurado Morales considers that *El cuarto de atrás* shares characteristics of both possibilities of metafiction, as described above.[100] In his opinion, it is a self-conscious or 'scriptive' novel because it adjusts to the meaning of metafiction developed by Sobejano in which the latter postulates that these types of novels 'ponen de relieve su virtud innovadora, su diferencia epistemológica, su consciencia de una rica intertextualidad literaria' ('highlight their innovative virtue, their epistemological distinction, its conscience of a rich literary intertextuality').[101] Intertextual relations in *El cuarto de atrás* refer specifically to Todorov's *Introduction à la littérature fantastique*, a book without which it would be impossible fully to grasp the whole metaphysical content of *El cuarto de atrás*. The continual explicit references to other authors such as Unamuno, Lewis Carroll, Carmen Laforet, Carmen de Icaza, Machado and Darío, among others, reveals how much literary artifice *El cuarto de atrás* possesses. There exists a self-conscious desire on the part of Martín Gaite to show the way in which she elaborates her novel.

Regarding the view that *El cuarto de atrás* is a self-referential novel or a 'metanovel', it is important to turn to Robert Spires, who establishes that the process of creation is revealed in the novel itself through the attention subtracted from the act of writing, from the act of reading or from an oral discourse between characters. Spires situates *El cuarto de atrás* in the last group, in that, by means of oral discourse, the characters discuss the way in which the novel should be written so that the discourse that they sustain at that moment might be included in it. The novel materialises only if the fictional author, who is generally one of the characters, transforms that oral discourse into writing. This occurs in the conversation sustained by C. with the man in black, and the result of what they talk about that night is precisely the text of *El cuarto de atrás* that the reader is reading. In brief, this is the artifice of the self-referential novel. In her novel, Martín Gaite tells 'la historia de un libro cuyo contenido es la historia de sí mismo' ('the story of a book whose contents is the story of itself'),[102] according to Blas Matamoro in his article entitled 'Carmen Martín Gaite: viaje al cuarto de atrás'.

Published in 1992, *Nubosidad variable* is a novel in the process of being assembled by Mariana León and Sofía Montalvo, using letters and 'ejercicios de redacción' ('exercises in writing'),[103] which each writes respectively. Between both protagonists there ensues a dialogue concerning the narrator, the characters, the space, the time, and the order that the different 'historias despedazadas' ('shattered stories')[104] could possibly take, as well as the way in which these gradually dovetail as the text progresses. The seventeen chapters of the novel are divided into odd chapters and even chapters. The narrator of the former is Sofía, while the narrator of the latter is Mariana. The epilogue is narrated in the third person and describes the meeting of the two old friends in the kiosk, each taking with them the respective sheets and notebooks that form the contents of *Nubosidad variable*.

The initial quotation from the 'Preamble' to *La città e la casa* by Natalia Ginzburg serves as an introduction announcing the fact that *Nubosidad variable* is the result of the exercise of putting together broken mirrors, and fragments of daily occurrences. Stemming from the re-encounter, Sofía and Mariana begin to rebuild their lives and write them. The former begins by writing in the form of a diary, while the latter takes notes on her travels that likewise generate a fragmented form of writing. In the epilogue, Mariana and Sofía meet again and, together, arrange their written memories and reflections in such a manner as to shape a story, entitled *Nubosidad variable*, in 'un procedimiento metaliterario similar al de *El cuarto de atrás*' ('a meta-literary procedure similar to *El cuarto de atrás*'),[105] bearing in mind the analysis of Jurado Morales.

The epistolary exercise established as a 'ritual' between Sofía and Mariana when they were school companions presents a series of 'reglas' ('rules'),[106] to which both have to adhere. These 'reglas', created by Sofía, emphasise the importance of choosing the *place* from which the letter is written, as well as the need to provide references so that the reader–sender can find his or her bearings:

> Ponerse en postura cómoda y elegir un rincón grato, ya sea local cerrado o al aire libre. Luego, dar noticia un poco detallada de ese lugar, igual que se describe previamente el escenario donde va a desarrollarse un texto teatral, es de día, en primer término sofá, por el lateral derecha puerta que da al jardín, lo que sea, para que el

destinatario de la carta se oriente y pueda meterse en situación desde el principio.

Get comfortable and choose a cosy corner, either indoors or outdoors. Then give a somewhat detailed description of the place, just as you would have described the stage where a play will take place, it is daytime, a couch in the foreground, to the right there is a door leading to the garden, whatever, so that the recipient of the letter can orient themselves and put themselves in the situation from the start.[107]

The description of that *lugar* conceived as *rincón* or *escondite* ('corner or hideout') is converted into a poetic principle for Martín Gaite when it is a 'condición previa para jugar con la realidad' ('state prior to playing with reality'),[108] as stated by the writer in 'La mirada del escritor', an article published in *Pido la palabra*. That *rincón* can be situated in a 'local cerrado o al aire libre' ('indoors or outdoors'). In *Nubosidad variable*, Mariana writes the letter to Sofía from 'el espacio más recogido' ('the cosiest place')[109] of her room; in *La reina de las nieves*, Leonardo converts the Puerta de Alcalá into a hiding place where he links the present with the past, based on what he is looking at from that 'lugar estratégico' ('vantage point'),[110] while, in *Irse de casa*, Amparo Miranda goes about the provincial city where she lived for some years and returns to the Plaza del Rincón from where she used to dream of a different life.

So that the reader can 'find his or her bearings', the geographical references are aesthetic tools with which the *preliminares* are built, as reasserted by Mariana:

> Eso es lo más importante de las historias, al margen del final que vayan a tener: registrar sus preliminares, ¿no? Así hiciste tú, al recapitular minuciosamente todos los detalles anteriores a nuestro encuentro, en tu primera tanda de 'deberes'.

> That's the most important thing in stories, irrespective of the ending they'll have: to record its preliminaries, right? That's what you did, when you painstakingly recapitulated all the details prior to our encounter, in your first set of 'tasks'.[111]

An example of the use of *preliminares* or *preámbulos*, as they are also called, is evident in the first chapter of *Caperucita en Manhattan*, entitled 'Datos geográficos de algún interés'. The narrative voice describes New York by using a street map that appears textually at the end of the chapter. The geographical data of the city are the place references with which the preliminaries are created. This novel is a version of the 'clásico *Caperucita Roja* de Charles Perrault, cuyo cuento también era una versión del ya existente en la tradición oral titulado *The Grandmother*' ('Charles Perrault's classic *Little Red Riding Hood*, which was in turn a version of *The Grandmother*, a tale already existing in oral tradition'),[112] according to Jurado Morales's analysis, but, in Martín Gaite's version, the writer has carried out 'una serie de transformaciones con el objeto de adaptarlo a los tiempos actuales y de dar una nueva dimensión al mensaje final' ('a series of transformations aimed at updating it to modern times and to give a new dimension to the final message').[113] The 'transformaciones' to which Jurado Morales refers focus more on the place and the characters. He leaves to one side the journey begun by the protagonist, Sara Allen. A trip from Brooklyn to Manhattan in search of her grandmother can be interpreted as a journey of initiation in which Sara moves physically about the city with which she has already become familiar, thanks to the time spent visually poring over a map of the city that a friend of her grandmother had given her. Mercedes Carbayo Abengózar is of the opinion that we are here dealing with 'un viaje hacia el interior de sí misma' ('a journey toward her inner self'),[114] but I feel that it is more the opposite. It is a journey from within oneself in the direction of the streets, squares and parks that she had already visited in her 'excursión fantástica',[115] via the imagination. The reading of the map 'había dado pie a sus fantasías nocturnas, a sus viajes imaginarios por Manhattan, a sus sueños de libertad' ('had encouraged her nocturnal fantasies, her imaginary trips around Manhattan, her dreams of freedom').[116] Those dreams of freedom cease to be dreams and become reality when Sara Allen decides to take to the streets alone and embark upon a different journey from that she used to make with her mother every week. I am saying that it was a journey from within herself towards the outside because, from the very beginning of the novel, Sara already has 'dos pasiones fundamentales: la de viajar y la de leer' ('two fundamental passions: travelling and reading').[117] In the first part, she travels with the imagination and we know that she is bored with the same trajectory she completes every week with her mother. She knows what she wants. Thus, in the second part, the journey that she undertakes emerges from that desire and from the knowledge that she has already acquired of the city. The journey is a way of externalising everything that goes on within.

On the other hand, the formal structure of *Irse de casa* is a good example of the concept of *preliminares* in that the chapter with which the novel begins is called 'Pórtico con rascacielos' ('Portico with skyscraper'). The 'pórtico' is the antechamber, the narrative space in which Martín Gaite introduces some of her characters whose stories slowly entwine. The skyscrapers of the title serve as a reference in situating the reader in a metropolis the name of which is confirmed as early as the second line of the chapter when the narrative voice provides us with temporal and spatial references: 'Durante la tercera semana de agosto, descargaron sobre Manhattan varias tormentas' ('They dropped several rainstorms over Manhattan during the third week of August').[118] With these references, Martín Gaite constructs the preamble of the fiction as well as the metafiction when she introduces Jeremy Drake as the young writer whose film script deals with the life of his mother, Amparo Miranda, before living in New York. In that *preámbulo* to the novel, Martín Gaite begins 'metiendo en situación poco a poco' ('getting [the reader] into the role little by little')[119] when she provides certain characteristics of her fictional characters and, at the same time, through them or through the narrative voice, gradually explains her way of creating the novel that the reader is actually reading.

In *Irse de casa*, the plot of the metafictional novel begins with the idea that the son of the protagonist has to shoot a film on the life of his mother before her departure for America. The title of the script is *La calle del olvido (Variaciones sobre un tema de J.D.)*. The story is based on memories of his mother, Amparo Miranda, who 'no ha asumido Nueva York y va dejando la vida entre sus calles a medida que sabe cada vez más fijo que aquellas donde pasó su infancia se vuelven un sueño surrealista' ('has not absorbed New York and is dropping bits of her life amid its streets while she is more and more convinced that the streets where she spent her childhood are turning into a surrealist dream').[120] Amparo's journey represents a physical detachment (first from New York to Spain and later the strolls about the provincial city), as well as a journey into the interior geography – that is, into memories. As a result of this journey, which represents the narrative motor, the novel opens out like a fan. The extremely fragmented nature of the story is announced as early as the initial quotation from Clarice Lispector's *Felicidad clandestina*, in which it is said that 'una historia está hecha de muchas historias ('a story is made up of many stories'), each chapter being narrated from the point of view of one or several characters, although the gaze of Amparo Miranda is central. In her presentation of the novel in May 1998, Martín Gaite defined this character as 'una especie de ojo que ve lo que ocurre a su alrededor y lo que le pasa a los demás' ('a sort of eye that sees everything occurring around it and what is happening to others').[121]

The gaze of Amparo Miranda, as well as that of Florita, Jeremy's interlocutor in 'Pórtico con rascacielos', coincides with the critique they make of the script of *La calle del olvido*. Florita considers that 'lo que hay que añadir a ese argumento es gente ... Gente que vaya contando también sus historias, aunque queden a medias ... un choque de historias' ('what we need to add to this topic is people ... People who can also start telling their own stories, even if they stop midway ... a clash of stories').[122] In the 'tercera revisión [que] no consideraba definitiva' ('third revision not considered definitive') Amparo Miranda believes that 'pasan pocas cosas' ('not many things happen').[123] For this reason, she decides to quit Jeremy's script and 'ir de verdad a la calle del Olvido' ('really go to Oblivion Street').[124] The outcome of her decision is her jaunts about the city, 'por callejas en zigzag' ('zigzagging through streets'),[125] as a way of wandering about the unconscious and injecting 'vida al guión de Jeremy' ('life into Jeremy's script').[126] It is thanks to these two characters (Amparo and Florita) that the perspective of both women towards the story of a third is achieved. With this, we witness the annulment of the masculine gaze of Jeremy, which sought to focus continually on the movements of a 'mujer Madura' ('mature woman') in a 'ciudad rara que trata de reconocer sin conseguirlo' ('strange city that she tries, without luck, to recognise').[127] The suggestion of adding people to the film script provides the possibility of having an amalgam of stories of women, who develop at the same time but in different places and whose paths cross in a specific moment of the novel.

Amparo Miranda's walks about the city parallel those taken by other characters. The few encounters occur in the street (Agustín and Marcelo), in the museum (Manuela Roca and Amparo Miranda), in the café (Valeria Roca and Rita Bores) or outside the cathedral entrance (Abel Bores and Amparo) – places that, in one way or another, represent a reproduction to scale of the experience of the modern city. For example, the museum is the place in which 'perdido en la masa, un observador mira sin ser visto, y observa fragmentos de una realidad que entiende sólo parcialmente' ('lost in the masses, an observer watches unseen, observing fragments of a reality they only half understand'),[128] as pointed out by Enric Bou in *Pintura en el aire*. Nevertheless, in the case of Manuela Roca and Amparo Miranda, contact is established through the contemplation of the same painting in the city museum. They are not observers who look without being seen. On the contrary, Manuela Roca becomes aware of the presence of someone else only minutes after she has begun to look at a painting in the Municipal Museum. That presence is a 'mujer extranjera' ('female stranger'),[129] who is also looking at the same painting which 'representaba un enjambre de individuos subidos en las ramas de un árbol frondoso, mientras dos leñadores serraban el tronco del árbol, y ellos tan tranquilos allí arriba, bebiendo y riéndose, alguno con un laud' ('represented a swarm of individuals perched on the branches of a luxuriant tree, and while below two lumberjacks hack at the tree's trunk, the ones on the tree carry on, drinking and laughing, one of them with a lute').[130] As both women contemplate the painting and later comment on the fact that 'ese árbol de la vida lo llevamos por dentro, y nos están cerrando el tronco y no nos damos cuenta' ('we carry that tree of life within, and we don't even notice they're sawing at the trunk'),[131] the museum ceases to be a scaled-down representation of the modern city that the *flâneur* observes with his privileged gaze. Instead, it becomes a place in which contact is established between two women spectators. Amparo contemplates the painting with the gaze of a 'foreigner' or an 'outsider' – that is to say, with a somewhat remote gaze – while Manuela, despite having lived all her life in the city, looks at the same painting to which she had hitherto paid little attention. Through this latter character, Martín Gaite seeks to develop the curiosity for that which is near, yet, looking at it from the outside, at a distance – through a window, so to speak – in order to see what surprising and unexpected elements it might contain.

Ultimately, the role of the gaze that we believe Martín Gaite creates in her work is a way of questioning the reader and their way of looking at life. It is a way of making them see that anything can be aestheticised, just as the wonder in anything can be rediscovered. This is a role of the gaze that goes beyond the pages of a book and looks to show the reader other ways of looking at life, in which the aesthetic experiences are as close to us as we choose and any object, however ordinary it may seem, can lead us to delight and reflect on who we are, what we want and where we are going. These are essential questions that, in the end, are worth trying to answer.

# 3

# The Construction of Space

The 'construction of space', one of the principles evident in the poetics of Carmen Martín Gaite, was first applied in a short story entitled *El cuento de nunca acabar* (1983). For nine years, Martín Gaite had carefully documented her own narrative process and the mechanisms that this process implied. The result was a series of reflections on the concepts of narrator, interlocutor, space and time. It was during that same period that she began to develop ideas for a novel. For her, a novel issued forth from the visualisation of a place – whether it be a city, a house or a room. In looking at or evoking this place, the geographical reference points served as stimuli to write the novel: the neighbourhood in which the events take place, the way in which furniture is arranged, the position of the balconies and the perspective each affords the beholder (in other words, the view of the outside from within, and the view from the outside looking in). In her writings, Martín Gaite employs the language of geography to refer to space. For example, she stresses the importance of location, the need to map out spaces and define boundaries.

For the next ten years, Martín Gaite continued to develop ideas on the importance of space, not only in her work but in the work of other writers as well. 1993 saw the publication of a collection of writings, spanning the 1970s, 1980s and 1990s, entitled *Agua pasada*. In a number of these essays written in the 1990s, Martín Gaite reaffirms the idea that space and time are intertwined in stories occurring in specific spaces such as the room of a house. The creation of individual spaces is necessary in that, at a later date, it is possible to remember where the person was, what he or she could see from there and the changes observed in the occupants of that space, not to mention the transformations in the space itself. In this later period, for Martín Gaite it is no longer merely a question of providing the exact location of where the people live, or a detailed description of the way in which the furniture is arranged, or the direction in which the balconies face. Emphasis is also placed on two key concepts: the look or gaze ('la mirada') and the attitude adopted with respect to the space inhabited and observed.

*Pido la palabra*, published two years after the writer's death, brings together twenty-five lectures, the content of which is notably diverse in that in some of these lectures the author discusses the relationship between literature and cinema, while in others she focuses on the inheritance of the eighteenth century. When exactly these lectures were imparted is unknown, but it is possible to deduce that those dealing with the conception of space date from the 1990s, in as much as, in addition to mentioning her trips to the United States, she analyses and comments on *Nubosidad variable, La reina de las nieves* and *Irse de casa*. In these talks, she reflects on her work and mentions certain influences such as Gaston Bachelard's *La poética del espacio*, a fundamental work in the development of her own narrative, signs of which were already visible in her early short stories and novels. The bachelardian concept of interior space allows us to study the narrative of Martín Gaite as a universe of interior spaces merging with exterior spaces. By 'interior space' Bachelard understands all the poetic images of the abode in which thoughts, memories and dreams reside. In 'El espacio habitable', published in *Agua pasada*, Martín Gaite conceives interior space, as does Bachelard in *La poética del espacio*,[1] as a 'rincón del mundo' (corner of the world),[2] a space lived in, day after day, and which is subject to change. Martín Gaite is interested in the way in which people relate to that space and how they respond to the different situations taking place inside and outside it. The work of Martín Gaite allows the reader to appreciate the way in which that interior space merges with the outside, bearing in mind the precise position adopted by the narrator or protagonist. The author refers to this as the point of view – that is to say, Martín Gaite establishes the position from which that interior space is described.

*Cuadernos de todo*, published in 2002, is a compilation of notes on a wide range of themes of particular interest to Martín Gaite. Some of these notes were converted into essays and published in *Agua pasada* and *Desde la ventana*. Others were transformed into fragments of her novels – for example, *La reina de las nieves* or *Caperucita en Manhattan*. Reading *Cuadernos de todo* provides data not to be found in previous works and which exercised a strong influence on the writer's output. I am referring to the notebooks in which she relates her experiences in New York, a city tht became a reference point for the elaboration of some of her novels (*Caperucita en Manhattan* and *Irse de casa*), poetry ('Todo es un cuento roto en Nueva York') and some collages.

The study of space can be clearly seen in her first novels – namely, in those published between 1958 and 1978. In her analysis of the theory and practice of narrating in Martín Gaite, Mercedes Jiménez González begins her research on the concept of space by asking a fairly straightforward question: where is the story being told? In replying to this question, Jiménez González considers that the places recurring with greater frequency in the first novels can be classified into three main groups: the first refers to urban settings, which she understands as provincial cities, Madrid, or the writer's own house; the second group relates to places of an evocative nature, such as the writer's living room or an old ancestral home; and, finally, the third group includes symbolic locations such as a castle or a seaside resort.[3] However, the critical contribution of Jiménez González to the concept of space fails to offer a convincing argument for why a provincial city, Madrid, and the writer's home should be placed in the same group as though they were spaces sharing the same characteristics. Nevertheless, I draw attention here to the classification in as much as what the critic refers to as 'urban places' – in particular, the city of Madrid – I include as *landmarks* shaping the urban geography that is analysed later in this chapter. For Jiménez González, 'evocative' and 'symbolic' places are converted into part of the trajectory traced in the interior geography, as analysed in the corresponding sections of this chapter.

On the other hand, critics have been keen to stress the prevalence of these interior spaces throughout the first twenty years of Martín Gaite's literary career. Most of them, furthermore, continue referring to the private, domestic, female domain, on the understanding that allusion is also being made to the existence of an exterior space linked with the public, political, male domain. A case in point is José Jurado Morales, who traces the narrative trajectory of Martín Gaite through three of Spain's historical periods: the post-war period, transition and democracy. In his revision of the period of democracy, Jurado Morales justifies the rise of literature written by women in the twentieth century, due, in his opinion, to the personal, social, cultural and political autonomy achieved. He affirms that, in the 1980s particularly, one begins to speak of a 'literatura femenina con diferencias visibles respecto a la escrita por los hombres' ('feminine literature with visible differences in respect to that written by men').[4] However, he does not mention what these 'diferencias visibles' ('visible differences') are, pointing out that female literature 'además de ser escrita por mujeres (recrea mundos que) en la mayoría de los casos se refieren a la esfera de lo femenino' ('as well as being written by women (recreates worlds that) in most cases refer to the feminine sphere').[5] Without describing this 'esfera de lo femenino' ('feminine sphere'), he pursues his analysis, adding that 'los lectores de estas novelas son mujeres quienes se identifican con las historias y los personajes' ('the readers of these novels are women who identified with the stories and characters').[6]

Jurado Morales' analysis establishes the link between Martín Gaite's narrative and the historical context in which events unfold, but he circumscribes literature written by women to the 'esfera de lo femenino' and jumps to the conclusion that the readers are women, too. Does a literature exist that is written by men just for men – that is to say, just for the 'esfera de lo masculino'? It is not the goal of this book to discuss whether these differences exist or whether Martín Gaite actually explores them. What can be salvaged from Jurado Morales' analysis, however, is the historical context and the way in which it reveals the socio-political changes in Spain and the repercussions of these on the narrative of Martín Gaite.

One of the commonplace viewpoints of criticism on Carmen Martín Gaite refers to the writer's narrative obsession with the female condition. The main female characters of the short stories written in the 1950s, as well as the female protagonists of her first novels, find themselves confined to a domestic situation and trapped in the routine role of housewives. In novels written in the 1990s, female protagonists continue to inhabit interior spaces, but they are conscious that they no longer wish to continue living in confinement, and rebel by fleeing the household. The protagonists embark upon a journey in search of their own space. The distances covered physically are an analogy of the transformations taking place within. Little by little, women – and, on occasions, a man – become aware of themselves. In their sorties beyond habitual physical confines they observe everything that surrounds them, but they are likewise captivated by the way in which their bodies now cover space in places already known to them – that is, in locations previously visited when activity was routine.

Martín Gaite constructs a narrative in which the journey as a search for a personal space constitutes a dynamic process in which qualities of movement are established, in that the structure of the journey has an origin and a destiny. The organisation of these, in a text or in the architectural structure of a house, is possible to analyse thanks to the vertical and vectoral composition formulated by Bachelard in *La poética del espacio* and *El aire y los sueños* respectively. Thus, the writer undertakes a detailed description of the places abandoned, or arrived at, or encountered on the 'way to', as seen in 'El viaje como búsqueda' published in *Pido la palabra*.[7] These descriptions, in which the references to time and space are central, instigate the writer to employ a vocabulary consistent with the practice of geography.

Research for this chapter focuses on the link between space and geography established by Carmen Martín Gaite throughout her work. In a close reading of her essays, articles and literary output, it can be seen that the writer employs geographical terminology in constructing four fields. These four fields – domestic geography, urban geography, interior geography and narrative geography – are the object of this present chapter.

The relationship between geography and space established by Martín Gaite opens up new perspectives for the study of her narrative, particularly that produced in the 1970s. Research leads to readings within the discipline of geography and, more specifically, to certain feminist geographers, such as Gillian Rose with her book *Feminism and Geography*. In her article 'Women and Everyday Spaces', she analyses the characteristics of the space normally occupied by women throughout the day, and she researches the styles and moments in which space is conceptualised as male. In addition to studying the ways in which persons move through the different spaces in which they find themselves during the day, she also makes it her task to observe the social roles adopted and experienced by men and women in each of these spaces.

In the work of Martín Gaite, we are presented with a detailed description of the space inhabited by the protagonists of her novels. The writer considers highly significant the expression *cuarto de estar* ('living room' (literally 'being room')) in referring to rooms in which persons change their *estados de ánimo* ('state of mind') depending on the memories they recall as they move about the same room, either physically or visually. From her point of view, *being in a place* is related to the space containing the persons, as well as to the attitude adopted by these persons while there. It also relates to the way in which the same people respond to the different situations experienced inside and outside the space. For this reason, it comes as no surprise to find in her novels women who take on the task of remodelling their houses, whereby the changes taking place within are reflected in the physical space without.

In the case of the narrative writings of Martín Gaite, sight is the one sense that dominates the other four. In some of her novels – for example, *Entre visillos* – Pablo Klein becomes a *flâneur* when he walks the streets and squares of a provincial city. This view from the outside provides only one perspective of the life of that city. The other vision is got from Natalia, who describes, in her diary and through a gaze from within, daily life lived in an enclosure. Using writing as a medium, she documents the nostalgia produced by outside open spaces seen from the inside, from the vantage point of a window. From the outside looking in, and from the inside looking out, both actions reveal fragments of life that, when fused, give progressive shape to a story, which, while dealing with the same incident or the same place, as in the case of *Entre visillos*, is told or described from different points of view. Martín Gaite develops the theme of 'point of view' or what she terms the 'desde donde' (*the from where*) in greater detail in her article 'La mirada del escritor', published in *Pido la palabra*.[8] The point of view also relates to the attitude adopted vis-à-vis the spaces inhabited.

Once the link between space and geography has been established, I shall go on to analyse what the writer has called 'domestic geography', 'urban geography', 'interior geography' and 'narrative geography'. The construction of the first two fields considers space as a geographical concept that contextualises and situates social relations between men and women. It is important to emphasise that social space is not constructed exclusively in terms of gender differences, but also implies aspects such as race and social class, as well as the differences between women themselves, in this way creating multi-spaces. Gillian Rose maintains that recognition of the differences renders two-dimensional social maps inadequate. It is necessary to create structured spaces that encompass as many dimensions as are necessary.

On the other hand, in the development of what she calls 'interior geography', Carmen Martín Gaite refers to the space of the world of dreams, imagination and memory. The writer employs different metaphors to create a universe in which the protagonists throw off the constraints of everyday life. Once again, the writer uses geographical language in creating this particular space, in which free rein is given to the subconscious. But where is that space to be found? How is it constructed? If we are talking about an interior geography, by what means are the excursions into that world traced? Does a link exist with the movements registered in domestic and urban geography? These are the questions that will be explored in this section.

The final part of this chapter focuses on the analysis of narrative geography, the origins of which go back to *El cuento de nunca acabar.* I shall first describe the way in which Martín Gaite develops this central element in her work. The critics acknowledge the great importance that the writer attributes to the concept of place – also referred to as space or setting – in that it is the visualisation of the place in which several of the stories unfold. In narrating a story, Martín Gaite begins by describing the place in which the characters are situated. The story develops out of the description provided by the narrator, references are given and these interweave with stories from the past. It is also probable that these stories from the past transpired in the same place or in different settings. In both cases, those settings become 'hitos de tiempo' ('landmarks in time')[9] – that is to say, in relevant places that, due to their importance, make their mark on the lives of the characters.

The 'hitos de tiempo' serve as an analogy of the signposts traced when drawing a map. They also become a metaphor of the memories that individuals gradually accumulate throughout their lives. In reading a map, those signposts are interpreted from the point of view of the person studying the map, who is probably in a position to add fresh interpretations to those that already exist. The same occurs to persons when they review important scenes in their lives and tell the tales that took place at that time, standing back and being able to link the *how* and the *when* of their personal story with the *when* and the *how* of others. In this way, the places lived in become the reference points with which the narrative geography is constructed. But if we have said that the scenes or settings serve as an analogy of the signposts traced on the map, what is the map in which the narrative geography is traced? How are the movements in and around that geography executed?

To conclude, the objective is to show that the four types of geography are interlinked. But how are those links established? Can it be said that the journeys embarked upon in domestic, interior and urban geography terminate in narrative geography?

## Geography, feminism and concepts of space

In *Feminism and Geography*, Gillian Rose has pointed out that, throughout history, the academic discipline of geography has been dominated by men.[10] It was not until 1982 that a systematic report on geographical studies of women carried out by both men and women appeared.[11] 1984 saw the publication of the study on the relationship between geography and gender,[12] written by nine members of the Women and Geography Study Group set up in 1982 in the United Kingdom. One of the arguments set out in this book refers to the need to study questions of gender within the discipline of geography. The term 'gender' is used to refer to the socially created distinctions between female and male.[13] Feminist geography is 'a geography which explicitly takes into account the socially created gender structure of society'.[14] This field of study includes an immediate reference to the classical text of Simone de Beauvoir, *The Second Sex* (1949), in which the feminist theorist argues that, throughout history, women have been mere objects for men. The concept of 'woman' has been defined from the male perspective and has subsequently negated a woman's right to her own subjectivity. Simone de Beauvoir questioned the socially imposed role of mother, as she considered it yet another of the many obstacles to becoming independent. I believe that the phrase 'One isn't born a woman, one succeeds in becoming one' is closely tied in with feminist geography, given that the task of studying the way in which the distribution of space in society determines the perpetuation of the roles assigned to men and women.

During the 1970s and the early years of the 1980s, feminism of the 'second wave', as presented by Barbara Arneil in *Politics and Feminism*, displays an interest in analysing the contrast between the life of women (centred on the 'private' or 'personal' sphere of the home, the family and domestic duty) and the life of men (centred on the 'public' sphere of paid employment and political involvement). Simone de Beauvoir, Betty Friedan, Sheila Rowbotham, Juliet Mitchell and Kate Millett argue that the differences in the social positions of men and women tend to favour men and result in inequality, as far as power, opportunities and social prestige are concerned. This feminist theorising characteristic of the 'second wave' of feminism analyses the differences between men and women arising from power relations, social position, attitudes and behaviour. It explores the ways in which changes could be brought about in society to free women from the subordination in which they find themselves. Arneil points to the fact that there is no better phrase to encapsulate the way in which these feminists introduce the political dimension into the 'private sphere' than: 'the personal is political'.[15] With this, they reveal that the political exists not only in the 'public sphere', but also in relations between husbands and wives, as well as in the everyday life of women with respect to the clothes they wear, what they eat, how they act, and everything related to the way in which the concept of the 'female' is constructed.

An immediate implication for feminist geography lies in the fact that it is not enough to examine the models of behaviour of men and women, nor the perceptions of space that each may have; it is also necessary to discover the roots of the difference and to document this so as to be able to explain why such differences emerge in the perception of space and in the behaviour to be found therein.

In her article 'Politics and Space/Time', published in *Space, Place and Gender*, and in attempting to find a possible definition of *space*, Doreen Massey comes to the realisation that this concept is used extensively and understood in a multiplicity of ways. In her view, the concerns, as well as the concepts, which, for quite some time, figured in discussions in the field of geography, now hold centre stage in a very broadly based social and political debate. Nevertheless, constant and diversified use explains why the term *space* has taken on a myriad of meanings. Many writers use the terms *space/spatial* and assume that their meanings are clear and irrevocable. In fact, the meanings taken on board by different writers vary enormously. One of the most significant conflicts concerning the definition of space is the depoliticisation of the concept. For some authors, terms such as *centre/periphery/margin* define *space* as actively political. For others, space is the absent sphere of the political.

At first sight, it could be said that, as far as *space* is concerned, there is no immediate evidence of a political dimension in the narrative of Martín Gaite. Yet, after a more detailed analysis, it is possible to affirm that the writer recognises the fact that interior space has been assigned to women throughout history and in different areas of knowledge. These women are anxious to abandon this space, in which they have lived an enclosed existence. In confronting the impossibility of ever being able to escape, they transform the everyday into something extraordinary, in adventures lived through writing. For this reason, the majority of Martín Gaite's protagonists are women who write. The insistence on describing interior space, as well as the to-and-fro movements of the protagonists, is a way of constructing a space that is not void of a political dimension. Rather, politics is practised implicitly through the narrating of everyday activities in that feminism 'remains very much a politics of everyday life. The edge is there: the sense of struggle, the weight of oppression and contradiction', as suggested by Teresa de Lauretis in 'Feminist Studies/Critical Studies: issues, terms and contexts'.[16]

To read the essays of Carmen Martín Gaite with a view to securing a terminology or concrete definitions of space becomes an arduous task that requires the use of the collage technique, with it being necessary to bring together different works published in distinct periods. It is possible to extract a definition of space by reading the diverse articles, essays and novels written by Martín Gaite.

Reference to *El cuento de nunca acabar* is inevitable, for it is in that book that the author develops her poetics on narrative. Throughout the four sections comprising the notes on narrative, love and lies, Martín Gaite establishes as the fundamental principle for the elaboration of a short story the furnishing of references on 'localizaciones de tiempo y espacio' ('time and space localisations').[17] She calls this space 'lugar' and she considers that the initial characteristics to be described of that place are the boundaries and cardinal points. Why are the boundaries and cardinal points so important? In replying to this question, the writer gives priority to these two elements because, in the first place, she establishes the point of view from which that place is described. Secondly, in getting to know the 'terreno' ('lie of the land'),[18] where one is, it is possible to 'mirar alrededor, más lejos' ('look around, further away').[19] It is possible to take the decision to abandon that place. And in using the word 'abandon', I mean leaving that 'terreno' via physical displacements or oneiric journeys, as will be analysed in the section on interior geography.

At a later date, in her article 'El espacio habitable' published in *Agua pasada,* the concept of space conceived as 'rincón del mundo'[20] can be immediately linked with Gaston Bachelard's *La poética del espacio.* The bachelardian concept of house as 'un cuerpo de imágenes' ('a body of images')[21] affords meanings to the two axes of verticality represented by the attic and the cellar. The upper part corresponds to the place inhabited by 'pensamientos claros' ('clear thoughts'),[22] while the lower area represents 'el ser oscuro' ('the dark being').[23] Bachelard applies the psychoanalysis of Jung to illustrate the images of the attic and the cellar as two entities contrasting with each other and, at the same time, complementing each other. Using Jung as a source, Bachelard refers to the lower part of the house as the place where the unconscious resides.

The Bachelardian elements present in the narrative of Martín Gaite are applied in the construction of the space of domestic, as well as interior, geography. The writer uses architectural patterns to construct where the 'verticality' proposed by Bachelard is implemented. In domestic geography, the structure of houses is based on the up–down duality indicated by 'verticality', or on the right-left bipartite structure that points to the direction or sense of movements made within the domestic space. In interior geography, Martín Gaite constructs different metaphors to represent the world of dreams, imagination and memories. She creates the Island of Bergai, the back room, the sewing room, the 'refu' or 'la Plaza del Rincón' as places of refuge that are reached after moving about the different places belonging to the domain of domestic geography.

In 'Tiempo y lugar', published in *Pido la palabra,* the writer elaborates her conception of space. First, she reviews several of her novels the origins of which are rooted in the reference to a place that, generally speaking, represents an interior, or a room in a house. Such is the case in *Entre visillos* (1958), in which the life of a provincial city is observed from a window protected by lace curtains. What can be said of the old family house in which, for six hours, Eulalia and German tell each other a series of stories that form the structure of the novel *Retahílas* (1974)? Four years later, *El cuarto de atrás* was published. The title itself announces a concrete physical place in which the writer lived during certain years of her childhood. In the development of 'Tiempo y lugar', Martín Gaite confesses that 'la obsesión por las habitaciones, por los espacios cerrados' ('the obsession with rooms, with closed spaces')[24] is so prevalent in her work that it has become a metaphor for the unconscious in which 'desorden y la libertad' ('disorder and freedom') reign, as expressed by the protagonist in *El cuarto de atrás*.[25] But if this is the case, how does one explain the creation of the 'Isla de Bergai', 'la Plaza del Rincón' and 'la Puerta de Alcalá' as places in which 'el desorden y la libertad' also exist, as they do in *El cuarto de atrás?*

In pursuing the development of the concept of space presented in 'Tiempo y lugar', Martín Gaite once again affirms that 'la configuración del escenario' ('setting the stage'),[26] also known as 'lugar' ('place'), is 'lo primero que surgía como un acicate para la imaginación' ('the first thing that emerged like a spur to the imagination'),[27] with which she begins to elaborate her novels. It has been said that those 'escenarios' ('stages') are, generally speaking, enclosed spaces. However, she also has recourse to 'espacios abiertos' ('open spaces'),[28] which she conceives as 'paisaje' ('landscape'), be it 'urbano' or 'rural'.[29] Martín Gaite does not go into this concept of 'paisaje' in any depth, which gives the impression that the concepts of 'lugar' ('place'), 'escenario' ('setting') and 'paisaje' ('landscape') are synonymous with 'espacio'. They can all be used in the dichotomy of enclosed–open spaces. For the writer, the difference between enclosed spaces and open ones lies in the fact that in open spaces it is possible to anticipate the geographical location of the house to be erected there.

The 'paisaje rural' is represented in *La reina de las nieves* by the 'faro del Norte' (Northern Lighthouse) built on the cliff's edge and surrounded by seagulls. The 'paisaje rural' contrasts with the 'paisaje urbano', represented by provincial cities such as the one in *Entre visillos*. Madrid is the geographical reference in *Ritmo Lento* and *Fragmentos de interior*. The urban setting for the author's narrative written in the 1990s reveals vestiges of a Madrid belonging to the close of the 1970s, according to a preliminary note by the author in *La reina de las nieves*. In *Lo raro es vivir* it is possible to discern a different kind of Madrid but we also witness the first signs of a New York urban setting that is fully developed in *Irse de casa*.

In the novels published in the 1990s, the interior spaces gradually cease to be claustrophobic and become places suitable for writing. In *Desde la ventana*, Martín Gaite proposes 'habitar un cuarto propio como liberación, no como encierro' ('dwelling in one's own room taken as liberation, not as confinement').[30] Exterior spaces, for their part, begin to predominate to such an extent that if windows were once considered to be the threshold separating and joining domestic geography and urban geography, it will now be seen how certain architectural buildings of the city become the porticos in which the past and the present converge. The past is related to stories emanating from the trajectories covered in the interior geography, and which will gradually produce the textual map signposted in the narrative geography.

**Domestic geography**

In her essay entitled 'Women and Everyday Spaces', Gillian Rose studies such spaces and analyses the movements back and forth produced in them by as they carry out their daily activities. Basing her argument on Ardener, Rose affirms that, through such movements, a 'social map' is elaborated, in which patriarchy creates 'rules' to organise the behaviour of men and women.[31] She argues that everyday spaces have never ceased to be important for feminists. According to the latter, it is through everyday chores that power structures are drawn that limit and confine women. These limits are structured on the basis of the expectations that society has regarding women.

In her analysis of everyday spaces occupied by women, Rose considers the division between public and private space as one of the most oppressive aspects of a patriarchal system. One of the first discussions on the public and the private was developed by Kate Millett, in 1969.[32] Her essay is a revision of 'Of Queens' Gardens', a fundamental manifesto of Victorian society. Its author, John Ruskin, read it in 1864 to an audience of robust women. In the lecture, Ruskin explained that a woman's place was the home. Described in angelic terms, this woman was different from man on account of her passivity, piety and docility. These characteristics were necessary to obtain 'natural perfection' and thus resemble garden flowers. This garden was protected and looked after by the man, who was the head of the household. The task of women, therefore, was to maintain their 'beauty' and to busy themselves in activities that pleased their protectors. Ruskin argued that it was a woman's responsibility to run a household in which tranquillity and love reigned. The house or home thus became a private space, domestic and female. For its part, the male sphere was linked to political life and salaried labour.

Reading Ruskin's manifesto, Millett affirms that the space considered as 'private' was an ideological prison, in that the woman was seen as being totally dependent upon the man and, for this reason, necessarily governed by him. Carole Pateman, for her part, expresses the view that the public–private dichotomy is a topic very much present in the last two centuries of the feminist struggle. Pateman also believes that it is important because it is on the basis of that dichotomy that the politics of space have been created.[33] Gillian Rose concludes her article by affirming that the everyday geography of the kitchen and rooms, as well as the streets, work areas and neighbourhoods, is the geography of space for many women and, thus, becomes a topic of study within feminism. For Gillian Rose, feminism means being conscious of the politics of the everyday, in the same way as one becomes aware of the intersection between space, power and knowledge. In her previously cited article, De Lauretis believes that there exists an epistemological priority 'which feminism has located in the personal, the subjective, the body, the symptomatic, the quotidian, as the very site of material inscription of the ideological'.[34]

Carmen Martín Gaite traces a geography of the everyday by narrating the activities in which her protagonists are occupied. The writer in *El cuento de nunca acabar* is interested in converting into stories all that which, with time, becomes habit in people's lives. Wanting to know *how* and *when* different events take place in our lives, and wanting to link these events with the *when* and the *how* of other people's lives contributes to the development of stories in which the task is to bring together the fragments of an individual's life. This explains why her novels constantly return to the question of how to organise the mosaic of stories that have slowly been put together using all that which enters within the domain of the look or gaze. It is a question of discovering the mode. What is the narrative mode of Martín Gaite? What is the make-up of her narrative poetics? Why is she seen as a writer who describes interior spaces? What are these interior spaces? These are some of the questions to be explored in this section.

Generally speaking, in Martín Gaite's first short stories and novels, the plots deal with the lives of women who live in provincial cities and move to other metropoles to escape tedium, routine, an anodyne existence and narrow-mindedness, and always with their sights set on the future. In her book *Buscando un lugar entre mujeres*, Mercedes Carbayo offers a panoramic view of Martín Gaite's work from the 1940s to the 1990s, from a feminist point of view. In her analysis, Carbayo expresses the opinion that in all her stories fragments of the lives of women are narrated, offering some idea of the situation and society in which they live. Reconstructing these fragments and linking them to those that Martín Gaite develops in her later novels provides us with an image of the social and economic changes in a currently democratic Spain.

In *El mundo de los objetos en la obra de Carmen Martín Gaite*, Emma Martinell Gifre says that critics consider that the writer's narrative is characterised by a predominance of scenes developed in interiors, and in enclosed environments.[35] Martín Gaite makes the following distinction: 'Se dice que la literatura escrita por mujeres, y la mía propia, es de interiores, en general. Aquí hay dos ámbitos, el de los espacios abiertos y el de los espacios cerrados, y se está jugando continuamente con esa dicotomía' ('It is said that literature written by women, including my own, is generally indoors. Here there are two settings – that of open spaces and that of closed spaces – and this dichotomy is continually played upon').[36]

How did Carmen Martín Gaite understand that open–closed dichotomy? Does a literature of interiors exist, and is it specifically confined to women? Did Martín Gaite really see herself as an 'escritora de interiores'? We shall analyse the way in which the protagonists of the novels of the 1990s experienced domestic space. For some, everyday life continues to be a prison. But the realisation of this urges them to take the decision to convert into incentive the space that they view as doom. The protagonists, traditionally immersed in the everyday world, decide to explore this world through writing. They are aware that the places they inhabit can be modified through observation – that is to say, through the point of view that each adopts regarding the respective space that each inhabits.

Domestic geography is elaborated from the to-and-fro movements carried out by the protagonists in the houses or flats they occupy. In each of these movements or itineraries, emphasis is placed on the structure of the house because each room becomes a signpost or 'hito de lugar',[37] as specified by Martín Gaite in *Cuadernos de todo*.

In the introduction to this chapter, it was pointed out that the place conditions the life of those inhabiting it. In this section that argument is corroborated, with the characters experiencing each room in the house in a different way. In reflecting on their lives, the female protagonists inquire into their pasts. This inquiry leads them on a search for their memories, which they have deposited in the different rooms of their domestic world. As we shall see, the protagonists thus move about the rooms, guided by the desire to know where they are. '¿Dónde estoy?' ('Where am I?') is a question that the protagonists in Martín Gaite's prose constantly ask themselves. This interest in wanting to know where they are drives them to explore the lives they lead in their everyday environment. The search is for one's own space but it is also a search into themselves. It comes as no surprise, therefore, that, in the four novels analysed in this chapter, the remodelling of the houses becomes a *leitmotif* indicating the changes in the lives of the protagonists.

The journey through the domestic geography of Martín Gaite's narrative includes different rooms, but a stop is made in the back room, the kitchen and the sewing room because these three places represent the foundation on which the other three types of geography analysed in this chapter are built.

*Nubosidad variable* begins with a chapter entitled 'Problemas de fontanería' ('Plumbing problems'). This simple title refers to the daily duties that it is the responsibility of Sofía Montalvo, one of the protagonists, to carry out. In her role as wife and mother, it is her job to keep the house in order so that her husband does not have to do battle with domestic situations when he returns from work. The life of Sofía Montalvo revolves around household chores. In the first chapter, we find her in the couple's bedroom, where she recalls the refurbishment carried out in the bathroom so as to avoid problems with their neighbours on the seventh floor. Sofía had been obliged to make 'visitas de exploración a la casa de abajo' ('a reconnaissance of the house downstairs'),[38] where she observed that 'las marcas imprevisibles' ('the unforeseen marks')[39] in the neighbours' flat were a metaphor for her 'propia erosión, el deterioro del entusiasmo, de las ilusiones, de (su) fuerza de voluntad y de (sus) capacidades más que discutibles como madre y esposa' ('own erosion, the diminished enthusiasm, loss of dreams, (her) willpower and (her) questionable competence as a mother and a wife').[40] Her married life did not improve after the remodelling of the bathroom, but it was the catalyst that instigated reflections on her own self.

The first chapter provides the preliminaries to the story of Sofía Montalvo. Her life will develop gradually as the novel advances, and through the fusion of different fragments that can be read in the odd-numbered chapters corresponding to the life of Sofía Montalvo. The even-numbered chapters deal with Mariana León, who was a friend of Sofia's at school and who is introduced at the end of the first chapter as a clear example of the application of the poetic principle of Martín Gaite regarding the creation of characters. This was analysed in Chapter 2 of this book.

Continuing with the journey through the domestic geography of *Nubosidad variable,* we follow Sofia's movements through the different rooms of her house. Her daughter Amelia's room is the scene for the following chapters in which Sofía gradually abandons her role of wife and mother and recovers another part of her life that she had given up so as to comply with established norms. The elaboration of collages, as well as writing, represent fragments of that longed-for life. As she moves about physically from room to room, a temporal movement is also taking place, for Sofía has gradually been accumulating different memories in each room. Moving about the matrimonial suite, the bathroom, Amelia's bedroom, the kitchen and Encarna's 'trastero' ('store room') becomes a mnemo-technic exercise in which, through the evocation of her memories, she gradually recovers her own identity. With these movements back and forth, she continually questions herself as she observes the changes that she experiences within her everyday enclosure. All these changes are described painstakingly by Sofía in her letters addressed to her friend, Mariana.

The matrimonial bedroom is a 'landmark' Sofía has no wish to return to, for she no longer has relations of any kind with her husband. She temporarily takes refuge in Amelia's room, where she spends her time 'escribiendo y mirando papeles viejos hasta muy tarde' ('writing and looking at old papers until very late').[41] In this space, and through the process of writing, Sofía frees herself from the ties of everyday life. She attempts to 'piece together' and under-stand past events as though they were 'bits' of narrative, 'incomplete stories' that she has to assemble as best she can so that they can slot into the story line of the letters she is writing to her old friend Mariana. Everything she writes in those letters emerges from her everyday space. Sofía refers directly to this process while in Amelia's room: 'cuánto poso; y sin salir de casa, cada cajón que abro, cada nube que miro pasar por delante de mi ventana, cada palabra que oigo y cada libro que me pongo a leer estalla en mil añicos donde se espejan nuevos fragmentos de vida: historias despedazadas' ('so much sediment; and without leaving home, each drawer I open, each cloud I watch go by from my window, each word I hear and each book I start reading shatters into a thousand shards in which new fragments of life flash mirror-like: shattered stories').[42]

Mariana León, the other protagonist of *Nubosidad variable*, is a fashionable psychiatrist. Unlike Sofía, she has not married and does not have children. She lives in 'una casa antigua en el Madrid viejo' ('a timeworn house on the old side of Madrid'). Mariana's movements about her house share a point of reference in which the public space links up with the private. This she calls 'la boca del lobo' ('the wolf's mouth'). It is a room that 'en realidad son dos habitaciones grandes, separadas entre sí por un arco con cortina de terciopelo, que ahora está descorrida' ('actually are two large rooms, separated by an arch with a velvet curtain that is now drawn open').[43] Here, Mariana receives her patients but she does not dare to analyse herself. Instead, she makes contact with the outside world through them, while closing the doors on her own interior geography. The bipartite structure of the room is an analogy for the separation that Mariana establishes with the events of her past life. She decides to write about what took place years ago as though the events had happened to someone else. She tells the story from a distant perspective in which she becomes the witness–narrator. She is 'sentada contra la pared del fondo, en el espacio más recogido' ('sitting against the back wall, in the cosiest place') and from her table – from the specific place that has become a point of reference within the domestic geography – she can see 'la boca del lobo' ('the wolf's mouth'), a place she only ventures to name in that way 'para sus adentros'[44] ('inwardly, to herself'). To enter that place implies unravelling the threads of unclarified events as though it were a question of undoing the knots that tie her to a past from which she is unable to free herself. Unlike Sofía, Mariana no longer paces about her house, but abandons the domestic space and embarks upon a journey in search of a refuge in which to find her inner self.

Mariana abandons Madrid not because her house is a prison, but because her interior geography has begun to disintegrate. She moves to different places by train or coach. In these places the surroundings mean nothing to her: they are spaces absent of memory. In her house, Sofía, for her part, moves from one room to the next. In each, memories accumulate. Both protagonists, in their movements from one space to another, from one room to the next, trace different geographies the paths of which converge in the *denouement* of the novel.

In her physical and emotional journey, Mariana stays at the home of a friend. This place, which forms part of the geography covered by Mariana, has two levels, each with additional divisions as though we were dealing with Chinese boxes that, in her inner self, too, hold yet more boxes. On the first floor, there are two flats 'de lo más moderno' ('of the most modern sort'):[45] one on the right, and one on the left. The description of the house at Puerto Real is an excellent example of the way in which Martín Gaite structures her interior spaces. Broadly speaking, the writer describes the house in terms of its vertical and horizontal axes, via the ground floor/first floor and right/left division respectively.

The vertical and horizontal dimensions of the house are charged with meanings that refer back to *La poética del espacio*, in which Bachelard defines the house as 'un cuerpo de imágenes que dan al hombre razones o ilusiones de estabilidad' ('a body of images that give causes or illusions of stability to men').[46] To order these images, it is necessary to bear in mind not only the verticality but also the centrality that emanates from the house. The verticality is identified through the north–south poles or via the up–down references represented by the attic and the basement respectively. For Bachelard, the basement is 'el ser oscuro de la casa (…) participa de los poderes subterráneos' ('the house's dark being (…) participates in subterranean powers')[47] and represents the subconscious. The attic, for its part, becomes 'la zona racional de los proyectos intelectualizados' ('the rational area of intellectualised projects')[48] and represents the conscious.

The house at Puerto Real, according to Bachelard's theory and as far as its structure is concerned, is an oneiric abode in as much as the lower level, also known as 'la de los espejos' ('the one with the mirrors'), is a metaphor for the 'cuarto cerrado' ('closed room')[49] that had already appeared in other stories invented by Sofía and Mariana and in which free rein had been given to the unconscious through dreams and the imagination. However, the house does not offer the stability mentioned by Bachelard. Instead, it becomes a 'segunda cárcel' (second jail)[50] for Mariana – the first was

Raimundo's house in Madrid. She therefore decides to go and take refuge in a hotel close to the beach. Once there, she experiences the need to find her bearings, the place being unknown to her and free of memories. She sets about executing a 'composición de lugar' ('place composition')[51] just as Martín Gaite establishes in her 'Tiempo y lugar', published in *Pido la palabra*.

More often than not, the protagonists of her novels are constantly searching, continually journeying, and forever escaping. At first glance, the three states would seem to differ, but they all have a common element: movement. The search, the journey and the escape interweave in the lives of the protagonists who find themselves 'sin arraigo' ('rootless'),[52] They flee from home and embark upon a journey as a way of finding themselves. Take, for example, Mariana in *Nubosidad variable*. She can find neither her voice nor her place: she lacks these two vital elements in her growth as a person.

The first thing that the protagonists do when they get to a new place is to describe it so as to 'procurar orientarse' ('attempt to orient themselves').[53] In this way, that place becomes a point of reference in the different types of geography analysed in this chapter. That 'composición de lugar' is constructed in the following way:

> Aquí, colgado enfrente de mi cama, hay un grabado grande, lo primero con que se topan mis ojos al abrirse. Representa un barco antiguo con las velas desplegadas en el momento de atravesar el pasillo que dejan entre sí dos icebergs (...) Debajo del cuadro, hay una especie de pupitre alargado con espejo y cajones, incómodo como escritorio (...) He pedido una mesa supletoria y la tengo instalada junto a la puerta vidriera que coge toda la pared del fondo.

> Here, hanging in front of my bed, there is a large print, the first thing my eyes see when I wake up. It represents an ancient boat with its sails unfurled, moving through the space left between two icebergs (...) Beneath the painting there is a sort of wide desk with a mirror and drawers, not comfortable for writing at (...) I asked for a table in its place and it stands by the glass door that takes up the entire back wall.[54]

First, a point of reference is established with the word 'aquí' (here), which is where the protagonist positions herself and from where she begins to describe the interior space in which she finds herself. Secondly, the adverbs of place become the signposts of the visual movement that Mariana carries out in the room with which she is still unfamiliar. She thus needs, like the maid in *Fragmentos de interior*, to 'hacerse a la casa' ('get used to the house').[55] In that particular novel, Luisa abandons her town and, for three days, lives in a strange house in which she is obliged to find her way about. She surveys the whole room, her gaze gliding over the surfaces, the telephone, the knobs, the door handles, the tiles and window panes, the purpose being to get to know the contours of that everyday space and consequently become aware of the new situation in which she is immersed. Everything she sees in that house is converted into cardinal points that she will use to find her way on the journey upon which she has embarked alone and in which those cardinal points evoke nothing of her previous life.

Objects are the third and last element used in elaborating the 'composición de lugar'. In this case, the room contains a bed, a large engraving, an additional table, which later on will be covered with papers and books, and the glazed door. In her article 'Dibujo, espacio y ecofeminismo en la C. de *El cuarto de atrás*, de Carmen Martín Gaite', Josefina González states that the third letter of the Spanish alphabet 'es el punto de partida para una secuencia de palabras que denotan objetos que han sido tradicionalmente relacionados con la realidad opresivamente cotidiana y enclaustrada de la mujer' ('is the starting point for a sequence of words that denote objects that have traditionally been related to the oppressively everyday and cloistered reality of women'):[56] the house (*casa*), the bedroom (*cuarto*) and the bed (*cama*). In certain novels by Martín Gaite these three entities are linked with the oppressive life of some of the characters – for example, Águeda Soler, for whom, during the day, the bed becomes a 'potro de tortura' ('torture rack').[57] This, however, is not so with Mariana León, who enjoys lying on the bed and daydreaming.

Josefina González's article provides images of change inside as well as outside C., when she refers to the fact that the sequence *casa-cuarto-cama* 'sugiere un movimiento centrípeto de círculos concéntricos. Un cuarto se encuentra dentro de una casa, una cama se encuentra dentro de un cuarto, un cuerpo se encuentra dentro de una cama y un corazón dentro de un cuerpo' ('suggests centripetal movement in concentric circles. A room is enclosed within a house, a bed is located inside a room, a body can be found inside a bed and a heart inside a body').[58] In the case of *Nubosidad variable*, Mariana is in the room in which there is a bed from which she can see a painting. The movement continues to be centripetal but the painting, like the glazed door, offers the possibility of imagining, of dreaming and of acquiring another perspective on what is seen, which converts the movement, which was centripetal, into centrifugal. The protagonist moves away from the room and from the bed from where she can view the painting. In this way, the limits of the spatial dimensions gradually become superimposed. The painting and the glazed door allow the exterior space to combine with the interior space. They are converted into thresholds where the protagonist can stop and look at the interior, as well as the exterior space as one sole space.

The 'composición de lugar' is a technique employed by Martín Gaite to transform places devoid of meaning into habitable spaces in which memories can gradually be deposited. For this, care is given to the minute description of the space occupied by the protagonist, which is, more often than not, a room. The changes made to large rooms are an analogy of the inner changes taking place inside the person inhabiting these spaces, as well as of the social and economic changes of the city. Take, for example, the modifications undertaken in the old house of Amparo Miranda in *Irse de casa*, which ceased to be the 'Taller Ramona-Modas' ('Ramona-Fashion Workshop')[59] and became instead a bicycle repair shop, a plumber's, a closed business premises and, finally, the antiques shop known as 'Defectos Especiales' ('Special Defects').

The domestic geography that Amparo Miranda had known and held in her memory changed with the reforms undertaken in what was once called 'Taller Ramona-Modas'. Time and space become superimposed in the remodelling carried out. The protagonist arrives at what used to be her old house and, at the same time, observes the modifications, recalling the geography it had had when she lived in what is now 'un espacio amplio, con dos columnas verdes y paredes color ocre' ('a large space, with two green columns and ochre-coloured walls').[60] She adds:

> Resultaba difícil calcular, pero más o menos detrás del respaldo de aquella butaca estuvo el tabique que lindaba con las minúsculas habitaciones de dentro, divididas a su vez por tabiques, ¡cuánto tabique!; aquí en la parte de delante también hubo uno que separaba el probador del taller de las oficialas.

> Volvió la cabeza hacia el fondo. Allí, separado del resto por un biombo de pavos reales, había un rincón a modo de taller con tablero de dibujante y botes de pintura, olía a engrudo; es el sitio donde estuvo un día su dormitorio con el armario de luna.

It was tough to calculate, but more or less behind that armchair's backrest was the partition that acted as a boundary for the tiny inner rooms, themselves divided by partitions (so many partitions!); out front there was also one that separated the officer's workshop changing room.

She turned her head toward the back. There, separated from the rest by a peacock screen, was a corner set up as a workshop with a drafting board and cans of paint, smelling of paste; that's where her bedroom with the moon wardrobe used to be.[61]

The fact that the partitions had been knocked down serves as an analogy of the ties that Amparo Miranda has been gradually undoing. Also worth noting is the centripetal sequence evident in the follwing description: 'detrás del respaldo [...] estuvo el tabique que lindaba con las minúsculas habitaciones de dentro, divididas a su vez por tabiques' ('behind the backrest (...) there used to be a partition that acted as boundary for the tiny inner rooms, themselves divided by partitions').[62] This image is similar to that of the Chinese boxes, which takes us back to the chapter of *Nubosidad variable* entitled 'De una habitación a otra' where Martín Gaite, through the protagonist Sofía, considers that 'los recuerdos están repartidos por habitaciones que el pensamiento visita cuando se le antoja (...) Pensar es ir saltando de una en otra (...) cada habitación lleva cuatro o cinco dentro' ('memories are distributed among all the rooms which the mind visits at will (...) Thinking means jumping from one room to another (...) each room houses one or two').[63] In the structure of the 'Taller Ramona-Modas', that 'minuscule' place was a storehouse of memories of the life of Amparo Miranda. This image evokes *La poética del espacio*, in which the corner of a room is seen as a cupboard full of memories.[64] The remodelling carried out on what was once her old house makes it seem like an 'extraño espacio'.[65] There are very few reference points that allow her to link that house with what took place in her childhood and adolescence. The little sewing room in her flat in New York is superimposed with the 'Taller Ramona-Modas' and becomes the only place that links her to her past. There, she has slowly threaded together the different events that have shaped her life. From the window of that little room she can see the needle that is the Chrysler Building – a needle that, like the one her mother used, 'habían cosido dos destinos, dos trayectorias desparejas [pero] ¿cuándo y por dónde empezó a romperse el tejido?' ('had sown two destinies, two separate trajectories [but] when and where did the fabric begin to break?').[66] The answer to that question requires a journey through the interior geography of Martín Gaite's narrative.

## Interior geography

In the previous section, an analysis was carried out of the importance of the construction of space as place, scene or setting, in which events transpire that will form part of a short story or novel. The trajectories through the different rooms of the house make up the domestic geography. The characters look at and observe everyday spaces and describe them so as to find direction and move about the past of their lives.

In the domestic geography, the characters 'travel' about the interiors of houses and flats whose bipartite structure of up–down and right–left refers back to the Bachelardian theory of constructing an oneiric dwelling. If the houses that make up the domestic geography are located in the city, where are we to find the different worlds pertaining to the interior geography? What is Martín Gaite referring to when she uses the term 'interior'?

In this section, it will be seen that the interior geography is elaborated with the trajectories of the characters through the worlds of dream, fantasy and memory. These three worlds are structured by the unreal, wonder, illusion, literature and memories. The construction of the interior geography allows the characters to free themselves from the domestic geography that is linked with what is tangible, with everyday life, with the real, and with life itself.

In her article 'La mujer en la literatura', which appears in *Pido la palabra*, Martín Gaite expresses the opinion that the woman writer 'ha soñado de niña y adolescente, porque, en general, se ha sentido más oprimida y rodeada de prohibiciones ... ha tenido menos ocasiones de aventura' ('has dreamt as a child and as a teenager because she has generally felt more oppressed and surrounded by restrictions ... she has had less opportunities for adventure').[67] Generally speaking, these dreams are dreams of flight or of escape, in that, having been nourished on solitude, such concepts are unmentionable in nature unless it is through writing. In writing, it is possible to escape in 'los vericuetos secretos y sombríos de la imaginación, por la espiral de los sueños, por dentro' ('the secret and sombre intricacies of the imagination, in the spiral of dreams, inside') as expressed by Carmen, the protagonist of *El cuarto de atrás*.[68]

Martín Gaite's interest in the amalgam of dream and reality dates back to *El balneario* (1954), in which she used a phrase from Unamuno for the epigraph: 'Cuando un hombre, dormido o inerte en la cama, sueña algo, ¿qué es lo que más existe: él, como conciencia que sueña, o su sueño?' ('When a man, asleep or inert in bed, dreams something, what is it that exists most? Him, as a conscience that dreams, or his dream?')[69] The novel is divided into two parts. The first is written in the first person and the protagonist describes her arrival at a seaside resort accompanied by a man who we might suppose is her husband. There are certain elements that make the reader gradually suspect that that first part deals with a dream. The quotation from Unamuno points the way towards the transition between the real and the imaginary. Unlike the first, the second part of *El balneario* is written in the third person and the narrative voice belongs to Matilde, who has woken up from her dream and finds herself in the everyday world offered by the seaside resort she visits during the holidays. It is a place where everyone knows each other and where it is expected that nothing unusual will ever take place. In 'Reflexiones sobre su obra', published in *Pido la palabra*, Martín Gaite considers that dream 'es un vehículo para cuestionar lo que en esa época era tenido por inalterable y para desvelar las decepciones de una vida convencional' ('is a driving force to question what in those times was considered unalterable and to unveil the deception of a conventional life').[70] So Matilde dreams of adventure in the routine world afforded by the seaside resort.

In the development of 'La mujer en la literatura', Martín Gaite considers the role of dreams to be of vital importance. In her opinion, dreams – those of real escape as well as those of literary flight – feed off the assiduous reading of novels narrating stories of women as models to be imitated or rejected. The woman reader, then, is faced with two conditioning factors. The first is the attitude that she adopts to what she is reading – that is to say, the way she receives and incorporates what she reads into her own life. The second is related to the different female models she can choose from as a guide to the way in which she might wish to live – models taken from narratives generally elaborated by men who, as a rule, tend to restrain the dreams and ambitions of women. Even when giving herself up to the pleasure of reading, a woman is frequently given disdainful or caricaturesque features, such as that of a 'chica rara' ('strange girl'). This compels her towards a state in which she can dedicate herself to reading or writing.

The wish for isolation can be so vehement in a woman that it grows in the face of obstacles. The same phenomenon occurs with the desire to escape, or to flee. For Martín Gaite, a pact with the disadvantages can be an experience resulting in literature. 'Convirtiendo en incentivo lo que era condena, la vida cotidiana llega de esa manera a constituir una fuente de inspiración para la mujer extraordinaria que siempre vive a expensas de la ordinaria.' ('Converting what was a punishment into an incentive, daily life thus is able to create a font of inspiration for the extraordinary woman who always lives at the expense of the ordinary.')[71] But that transformation from the ordinary to the extraordinary is possible only through fantasy.

In *La poética de la ensoñación* Bachelard separates dream ('songe') from fantasy ('rêverie') and sees both implying different activities.[72] In the latter, he distinguishes 'daytime fantasy',[73] which takes place 'en la tranquilidad del día, en la paz del reposo' ('in the peace and quiet of the day').[74] This fantasy refers to the 'actividad onírica en la que subsiste un resplandor de conciencia' ('oneiric activity in which the glow of conscience subsists').[75] For Bachelard, 'algunas ensoñaciones poéticas son hipótesis de vidas que amplían la nuestra poniéndonos en confianza dentro del universo' ('some poetic reveries are hypotheses of lives that broaden our own by setting us trustingly within the universe'),[76] which is alien to us: they have a 'carácter constructivo' ('constructive disposition'),[77] which makes them create systems, 'organizar experiencias diversas para intentar comprender el universo' ('organise various experiences to attempt to understand the universe'),[78] discover this universe, and adapt it so that it becomes the world one 'quisiera vivir' ('would like to live in').[79] With fantasy, he says in *El aire y los sueños*, 'el lenguaje escrito crea su propio universo. Un universo de las frases se coloca en orden sobre la página en blanco, en una coherencia de imágenes' ('the written language creates its own universe. A universe of phrases places itself in orderly fashion on the blank page in a coherent set of images').[80] These literary images make us 'cambiar de universo, pero nos albergan siempre un universo imaginario (…) incluso en imágenes literarias aisladas, se sienten actuar esas funciones cósmicas de la literatura. Una imagen literaria a veces basta para transportarnos de un universo a otro' ('change the universe, but they always hold within them an imaginary universe (…) those cosmic functions of literature are felt in action even in isolated literary images. Sometimes a literary image is all it takes to transport us from one universe to another').[81]

Carmen Martín Gaite uses the word 'ensoñación' ('reverie') to refer to the world that is dreamt of while awake. Like Bachelard, the writer draws attention to a difference between dream and fantasy. The two elements stimulate the process of elaboration of a story, but with fantasy one enters the world of the 'como si' ('as if'),[82] as observed by the writer in *El cuento de nunca acabar*. In her article 'Reflexiones en el parque' she argues that narratives, like children's games, share three functions: pleasure, fiction and prediction. From a drawing sketched on the ground in a park or from children playing there, Martín Gaite reflects on the process of narrating, in which the fiction consists of 'echar a navegar la fantasía' ('unleashing fantasy'),[83] becoming immersed in 'el reino del "como si"' '(the realm of "as if"'),[84] so that the drawing can be transformed into a garden, a little house or a shop. The use that Martín Gaite makes of the drawing, be it personally or via the characters of her narrative, is converted into a fundamental part of her fiction in as much as the drawing represents a 'puerto de embarque' (an 'embarkation port'),[85] from which the narrative journey, through the realm of dream and imagination, gets under way. On entering the domain of the 'as if', the trajectory through other surroundings different from those to be found in everyday life begins. The reader is thus drawn away from the obligatory chronology with which, as a rule, stories are narrated.

The creation of 'la isla de Bergai' forms part of the world of fantasy. 'Solamente era necesario mirar a la ventana e invocar el lugar con los ojos cerrados para que se produjera el viaje' ('All that was needed was to look at a window and invoke the place with eyes shut in order for the voyage to take place').[86] The protagonist of *El cuarto de atrás* confirms that the invention of Bergai was due to shortage. Carmen refers back to the years of the war, when she and her sister were no longer given new toys and had to make do with the old ones. In the same way, but in other circumstances, the word 'escasez' ('shortage') related to resolving immediate needs. As a consequence, the word 'placer' ('pleasure') was seen as sharply contrasting with that of 'necesidad' ('need'). At that time, everyone thought of only one thing: 'en comer, en acaparar artículos de primera necesidad' ('of eating, of gathering the bare necessities').[87] So toys were not included in that category, and the pleasure of playing had to be 'amortised' to a certain extent when a new toy was actually purchased. This law of 'amortisation' also extended to the back room, which was the space in which 'reinaban el desorden y la libertad' ('chaos and freedom reigned').[88] Carmen mentions that there exists a 'línea divisoria' ('boundary line'),[89] a frontier indicated by the time–space duality and the personal and social changes in Carmen and the city she lived in. The year 1936 marked an end to Carmen's childhood, at the same time as the back room ceased to be that and became instead a larder that, due to war-time rationing, was used to store 'artículos de primera necesidad' ('basic necessities'),[90] which everyone pooled under one rubric: food. And so those articles replace Carmen's period of childhood play, the larder is superimposed upon the back room and brings to an end a time of life for the protagonist in which she was obliged to invent the island of Bergai as her first refuge, given that the place in which she felt free was converted into yet another everyday space. The creation of that refuge 'se fue perfilando como una tierra marginal (que) tenía la fuerza y la consistencia de los sueños' ('began to take form like a marginal land that had the power and consistency of dreams'),[91] and where everything could be transformed into something else through the imagination. The island of Bergai emerges as the protagonist's reply to an epoch in which the lack of freedom could be found at every level and it was necessary to create new spaces in which it was possible to give free rein to the imagination through play.

In *Desde la ventana*, the writer develops an idea analogous to the drawing, when she refers to the window as 'el punto de enfoque, pero también es el punto de partida' ('the focus point, but also the starting point'),[92] from which domestic spaces are abandoned through fantasy. In considering the window as *a place*, it becomes a signpost within the domestic geography. From there, the eyes scan the house from different points of view, beginning with the interior–exterior duality and then diversifying, depending on the position adopted by the narrator. Thus, the gaze can be from the interior to the exterior ($\rightarrow$); from the exterior to the interior ($\leftarrow$); from the interior to the same interior ($\rightarrow\leftarrow$); or from the interior to other interiors ($\leftrightarrow$). In transferring this image to the interior geography, the journey towards the world of dreams or fantasy is embarked upon through the vision. Mariana says as much when she describes her house to Sofía and confesses that she likes to lie on the bed, looking at the ceiling, because it is her way of preparing herself to dream. By looking upwards ($\uparrow$), the dams of reason are demolished and the imagination overflows.

The gaze from the street towards the interior ($\leftarrow$) becomes a 'motivo de ensoñación' ('reason for reverie')[93] for the passer-by, as stated by Martín Gaite in her article 'La mirada del escritor', which was published in *Pido la palabra*. That interior is unknown to the passer-by, so he or she begins to imagine what life is like inside. In *Entre visillos*, in strolling about the streets and squares of a provincial city, Pablo Klein complements the details he has been afforded by his visits to a particular house with his fantasy, which allows him to make out scenes taking place in those provincial homes: 'mirando las ventanas de los edificios, me imaginaba la vida estancada y caliente que se cocía en los interiores' ('looking at the windows of the buildings, I would imagine the stale, hot life cooking in their interiors').[94] This world faithfully reflects the life of Natalia, who wishes to break away from her enclosed existence, which condemns her to see the same furniture and hear the same conversations day in, day out.

Natalia, like Sorpresa (the protagonist in *El pastel del Diablo*) and Alina (the protagonist in *Las ataduras*), dreams of abandoning the domestic geography, but this dream is only fulfilled when they give themselves up wholeheartedly to the imagination as they gaze out of a window, climb a church tower, stroll along a street or stand on the top of a hill. From these geographical vantage points begins the journey towards the worlds of dream and fantasy in search of a life different from that of the everyday.

Through dream and imagination, the protagonists in Martín Gaite's first novels progressively create a 'brecha en la costumbre' ('rift in customs'), as the writer mentions in an article that carries the same name and that was published in *Agua pasada*, but was delivered in El Escorial in 1990, during a symposium on fantastic literature. That 'brecha en la costumbre' is like the river that Alina contemplates in *Las ataduras* from the top of a rock where she is accompanied by her friend Eloy. From that strategic location, from which what is looked at becomes something else, Alina imagines that the river is 'como una brecha, como una ventana para salir' ('like a breach, like a window to exit from').[95]

That opening made in the wall is an analogy for the interruption of the pulse of the everyday where it is necessary to comply with the many expectations ordained by society. Such is Sofía's case in *Nubosidad variable*, when she recognises that she does not like reality but that she carries out her obligations as 'Dios le ha dado a entender' ('she sees fit').[96] That 'reality' refers to the activities of her everyday life reflected in the accumulation of bills and the like, evidence of implication and a reminder of how she has lived her years. There are 'certificados, recibos, notificaciones de bancos, requerimientos notariales, estados de cuentas, apelaciones, avales, recortes de periódico, radiografías, fes de bautismo, carnets caducados, escrituras de donación, seguros de vida ... libro de familia' ('certificates, receipts, bank notices, notary requirements, bank statements, appeals, endorsements, newspaper cutouts, x-rays, baptism certificates, expired IDs, deeds of gift, life insurance policies ... family book').[97] All these papers link her to her life as a married woman and housewife – roles with which she does not identify and that she knows do not represent her real self. For this reason, as she sits surrounded by papers in one of the rooms of the house, she asks herself: 'Qué hago yo en este sitio? ¿Qué quiere decir "yo"?' ('What am I doing here? What does "me" mean?').[98] This self-questioning makes her more and more aware that she has lived in obsessive confinement and that she needs to recover the Sofía who exists in her memory – a Sofía who liked to have 'vivencias de irrealidad' ('experiences of the unreal')[99] through which she liberated herself from the repugnance she felt for paperwork and a static image of housewife and mother that social conditioning obliged her to adopt with unvarying monotony.

In *Nubosidad variable*, the world of memory is made up of different rooms from the present and the past in which the protagonists move about as they gradually write their respective notebooks. In building a novel as collage, they write fragments of stories that have taken place in a specific place but at different times. Putting these stories in order implies thinking about the 'before' and the 'after' that constantly appears in the novels of Martín Gaite. These signposts in time allows for the superimposing of stories and, subsequently, of scenes. Such is the case of the different stories about encounters narrated in the novel. First, we have the story of Sofía and Mariana at the exhibition; the second story is the encounter and re-encounter of Mariana and Manolo at different times, which we can signpost as *before* and *after* he went to New York; the third story is about the couple on the beach that Mariana sees from the table of the restaurant; the fourth story is that of Mariana and Guillermo; and, finally, there is the re-encounter between Mariana and Sofía at the kiosk.

As stated by Carlos Uxó González in 'La recuperación de la memoria en *La reina de las nieves* de Carmen Martín Gaite', the past can also be evoked: 'a partir de la visión de determinados objetos que un personaje reencuentra y cuya relación con acontecimientos pretéritos pone en funcionamiento su memoria' ('from the sight of specific lost objects a character finds again and whose link with past events and their memory is regained').[100] In *El mundo de los objetos*, Emma Martinell Grife states that 'la incardinación de la referencia a casas, habitaciones, muebles y objetos en la trama novelesca es que en relación con ellos, viéndolos, actuando en relación con ellos, se desencadena el ejercicio de la memoria. Hay un retroceso del tiempo en la conciencia del personaje, que revive historias pasadas, o sea, el pasado de su propia historia' ('the exercise of memory is liberated by incorporating in a novel's plot a reference to dwellings, rooms, furniture and objects; relating to them, seeing them, acting with respect to them. Characters' consciences undergo time regression; they relive past stories, in other words, their own past').[101]

In *Nubosidad variable*, Sofía moves about the domestic geography of the 'refu'. In this house, the area on the right is organised into different rooms: 'la cocina y sus aledaños' ('the kitchen and adjacent spaces'),[102] the bathroom and the 'cuarto de costura' ('sewing room').[103] Here, the threads of several stories are spun and unspun. Sofía's memories are rekindled due to the presence or absence of certain pieces of furniture – for example, 'el camfornio' (the name given to an old armchair).[104] Three stories are developed around this armchair: each refers to a different epoch that Sofía employs to embark upon an interior journey as she moves from one concentric circle to another. The outer circle – the one closest to the present – is linked to the death of Sofía's mother. On that particular night, Sofía falls asleep in 'el camfornio'. This piece of furniture facilitates the link with the following circle, in which certain everyday activities of Sofía's mother are described while she sat in 'el camfornio'. It was there that she 'leía el periódico, hacía labor y resolvía crucigramas' ('would read the paper, do needlework and solve crossword puzzles').[105] The third story, which is situated in the circle that is furthest away from the present, refers to the moment in which the grandmother dies as she is sitting in 'el camfornio' with 'la labor de ganchillo en el regazo' ('the crocheting on her lap').[106]

The story of these three events differs in time, but several elements knit the three together. The first element is the sewing room in which the events take place. It is not the same room but the fact that a sewing room is mentioned allows us to establish a link between the life of the mother and that of the grandmother. Both carried out household activities seated in front of the window. The second element that serves to link the three events referred to is 'el camfornio'. The powerful presence of this object is instrumental in forging the lives of three generations of women: the grandmother, the mother and the daughter. Thus the movement back and forth within 'el refu' reflects a journey through the domestic geography that permits us to appreciate the changes taking place in each generation through everyday activities. To gaze about the domestic enclosure is to gaze into the past from where the journey towards the interior geography begins.

The space covered by a person in the domestic geography produces a parallel movement in the interior geography when this person comes across objects such as photographs, paintings or pieces of furniture. All these objects help the memory to unfold – that is to say, memories are evoked. In *La reina de las nieves*, Casilda Iriarte finds herself in 'el torreón' ('the turret'), which is the place where secrets are kept. She employs a range of words that can be grouped together under the semantic heading of 'geography' to describe what goes on in its interior: 'tenía empapelada el alma de recuerdos, sí, pero me bastaba con orientarme yo sola por esa topografía interior, saber dónde estaba cada cosa, darme un paseo de revisión y ya' ('My soul was wallpapered with memories, yes, all I had to do was to orient myself around that interior topography, to know where each object was, just to saunter about to check things').[107]

The gaze from above is fixed on the world of memory. Take Amparo Miranda, for example. She observes the city from her hotel room. The places she looks at take her back to past events that entwine with her present life. Amparo Miranda recalls her youth spent in Spain forty years earlier and she attempts to incorporate into her 'geografía interior'[108] the urban changes of a city in which she does not recognise anything she sees. The city that she now visits has been superimposed on the ruins of the one ('aquello')[109] where she once lived. In the same novel, in observing the needle of the Chrysler Building from the 'cuartito de costura',[110] Jeremy Drake evokes the epoch in which it was built, since it is a period in which he is interested on account of the expressions of art he wishes to include in his film script. They were the years of art déco in Paris, German expressionism and utopic design. In contemplating the building from the 'cuartito de costura', Jeremy Drake attempts to give a certain unity to the different events that have been sewn together with the needle of the Chrysler Building and with that belonging to Grandmother Ramona, who never returned to the city that her daughter now contemplates from a hotel window. The excursions made by Amparo Miranda about the city contribute, little by little, to the elaboration of the urban geography.

**Urban geography**
In the first section, a review was carried out of the role of domestic geography in Carmen Martín Gaite's narrative written in the 1970s. The house and its different rooms are linked to the interior geography in as much as physical movement produced in the living room, kitchen or sewing room is accompanied by parallel journeys into the past of the protagonists – a past that has driven them from home and into a world of dream or fantasy.

'Urban geography' refers to strolls through the streets of a city by a protagonist who is merely visiting or actually lives there. The characters take to the streets as a way of breaking with the enclosed place or interior space in which they feel imprisoned. The writer of *El cuento de nunca acabar* conceives the city as 'un itinerario de narraciones que se hojaldran' ('an itinerary of stories that form layers like puff pastry').[111] That itinerary is painstakingly constructed with all the fragmented images that the stroller observes during the different trajectories made around the city. These trajectories are covered either on foot or by using some form of transport such as the underground, the bus or the train. Everything observed is converted into raw material from which a short story or novel emerges.

The decadent chalet of *Ritmo lento* was the result of a walk through a neighbourhood in Madrid known as Ciudad Lineal. It was during the 1970s and, at that time, the chalets still preserved their former structure, which dated back to when they were once summer residences for the well-to-do bourgeoisie. In 'Tiempo y Lugar', Martín Gaite tells of the day she went for a walk with her daughter Marta, who was four at the time. They took a tram and strolled about Ciudad Lineal. While her daughter played on a merry-go-round, the writer decided to wander along 'las calles laterales en plan de exploración' ('side streets to do some exploring'),[112] and, all at once, came upon the place that was later transformed into the subject matter of her novel. It was an abandoned chalet and she remembers well 'aquella fachada, aquel jardín, aquel perro surgido intempestivamente y la sensación de tiempo detenido' ('that façade, that garden, the dog that appeared at an untimely moment and the sensation of time stopping'),[113] all of which became a fuse with which to ignite *Ritmo lento*. In 1963, the year in which she published the novel, the expropriation of lands in Ciudad Lineal had already begun, and many houses were demolished, including the chalet that inspired the creation of *Ritmo lento*. Martín Gaite brings her anecdote about a chance stroll to an end by affirming that it is the place that conditions everything that will take place in the book. As far as her own novel is concerned, she says that 'el hecho de que yo viera el chalet poco antes de que lo derribaran condicionó también el contenido de la novela, porque se habla en ella, entre otras muchas cosas, de los barrios amenazados de destrucción' ('the fact that I saw that chalet a little before it being demolished also conditioned the contents of the novel, because in it, among many other things, is the topic of the threat of neighbourhoods being razed').[114]

The settings for novels written after *Ritmo lento* are not the result of strolls taken by the writer through this city or that. Instead, they are enclosed spaces – that is, rooms in which novels are developed, from start to finish. The main story line of *Retahílas* (1974) relates to the theme of memory and the legacy of the dead. The strings to which the title alludes are spun by Germán and his Aunt Eulalia during a six-hour period in an ancient semi-dilapidated ancestral home. The reason for their meeting is the imminent death of Germán's great-grandmother, who is Eulalia's grandmother. While the grandmother is dying, Eulalia and Germán begin a conversation in which memories, events and misunderstandings slowly weave the plot of the novel.

The title *Fragmentos de interior* (1976) offers some indication of what will take place in the novel and of the narrative technique employed in as much as it alludes to each and every corner of the house in Madrid in which the different stories occur. Luisa, a young servant girl arriving in Madrid from a small town, is provided with accommodation in the house of a well-to-do bourgeois family, where she takes over from Pura, the old servant woman. Luisa provides an outsider's view of a space that is well known to its inhabitants but unfamiliar to her. She thus has to learn to move about the new environment and to get to know its cardinal points. It is Pura's task to show her the different rooms in the house and to explain to her where to find the objects she might need. This was analysed in the section on domestic geography.

*El cuarto de atrás* (1978) deals with evoking interiors, as its title suggests. It refers to a concrete physical place that was the writer's play room, but it is also employed as a metaphor for the memory, in that the narrator of the novel describes it as 'un desván del cerebro, una especie de recinto secreto lleno de trastos borrosos, separado de las antesalas más limpias y ordenadas de la mente por una cortina (...) los recuerdos (...) viven agazapados en el cuarto de atrás ('the brain's attic, a sort of secret enclosure full of vague clutter, separated from the cleaner, neater antechambers of the mind by a curtain (...) memories (...) live huddled in the back room').[115] The words *desván* and *recinto* refer to Bachelard's *La poética del espacio*.

New York is the 'paisaje urbano' ('urban landscape') converted in *topoi* in the narrative of Martín Gaite produced after the 1980s. The walks through the city that she visited on more than seven different occasions provided her with visual material that she later transformed into writing. In 'La Libertad como símbolo', the writer looks back on her visits to the city, which helped to sow the seed for her novel *Caperucita en Manhattan*, as well as for her poem 'Todo es un cuento roto en Nueva York' ('Everything is a broken story in New York'), not to mention a later novel entitled *La reina de las nieves*. The 'geografía urbana' ('urban geography')[116] of New York seemed to her 'tan llena de incentivos y contrastes' ('so full of incentives and contrasts'),[117] as though she were seeing a kaleidoscope whose fragmented images were in a constant and rapid process of change.

In her 'Cuaderno de todo' for autumn 1980, Martín Gaite reconstructs New York in two stages: in the first by means of visual images and in the second through her writings. In *Cuadernos de todo*, dated 17 November 1980 a collage appears, entitled 'Retahíla con nieve en Nueva York'. Included in *From Fiction to Metafiction* is a short text written by Martín Gaite carrying the same title as the collage and with a similar date, the difference being that the text was published in the 1980s. Here, however, it is important to point out the nature of the concept of city developed by Martín Gaite, in particular New York, given that it represents a fundamental setting in her narrative of the 1990s.

From her different stays in New York, Carmen Martín Gaite gives shape to a city in which fatigue and freedom fuse and are reflected 'en la actitud de la gente, en la presencia que imponen los objetos, en cómo se relacionan objetos y personas, en la luz y los espacios' ('in the attitude of the people, in the presence objects possess, on how objects and people relate to each other, in light and spaces').[118] From a reading of *Cuadernos de todo* one gets a fragmented vision of New York. Martín Gaite observes the city from different locations. Climbing to the top of the World Trade Center, the writer says that we get a sweeping view of 'todo aquello y de su hermetismo' ('all of it and its hermetism').[119] The view from the World Trade Center takes in more, but does not focus on detail. One looks into the distance from a fixed vantage point, and that produces the sensation of not belonging to the city being observed. The elevation transfigures one into a *flâneuse* and creates a frame of enunciation that constitutes a 'here' and a 'there' once the location of the person observing the city has been taken into account. In this way, the view from the top of the World Trade Center enables the city, in which people live trapped, so to speak, as they move about the streets, to be transformed into a text stretching out under the beholder's gaze, as suggested by Michel de Certeau in *The Practice of Everyday Life*.

In his work, Michel de Certeau conceives the city as a 'text'[120] written by all the to-and-fro movement produced by passers-by on the streets of the metropolis. Yet only the *flâneur* is capable of reading that text, given the distance that he establishes between himself and the world he observes. The routes and trajectories are traced on the map of the city, but these lines only serve to emphasise the absence of the people who have passed that way, as well as the events that have taken place there. For Michel de Certeau, walking implies not having a place and, for this reason, roaming the streets is a metaphor for the search for oneself.

The conception of the city in the narrative of Martín Gaite comes from walking the streets of a city and from the focused observations of the characters. In *La reina de las nieves*, when Leonardo leaves the prison on the outskirts of Madrid, he describes the surroundings from the window of the car in which he is travelling, which explains the fleeting nature of the point of view. The speed of the vehicle is conveyed by listing in quick succession what Leonardo observes: levelled areas, rubbish dumps, and a scrap metal yard. Leonardo is about to enter the city and, here and there, a few buildings begin to appear. There is a pause that allows us to continue moving forward in that centripetal trajectory in which the levelled areas disappear and are replaced by an alternative enumeration of places: blocks of flats, entries to the underground and crossroads with signposting and traffic lights. At this moment of the description, there is, as yet, no sign of people. Entering the city is like passing though the jaws of an animal, devouring the transport system, the emergency services, public safety, noise, and people entering and leaving office blocks in which they will perhaps end up alone. The vision of the city from Leonardo's viewpoint is that of a *flâneur*, of a street stroller amid the crowd observing without being observed. Leonardo looks without being seen and observes fragments of a reality that he only partially understands. The trajectory from the prison to the city facilitates the simultaneous vision of the entire space covered. The continuous sequence of impressions reveals the intense nature of the experience of the space spanned.

During the novel, Leonardo takes a walk or two through the city, as a way of freeing himself from the enclosure to which he has subjected himself. He has come to the family chalet in an attempt to string together the different stories that tie him to a past of which he knows only fragments. In one of his walks he shelters from the rain in La Puerta de Alcalá. From this 'lugar estratégico' ('strategic place'),[121] he contemplates 'los edificios que ahora rodean este islote urbano' ('the buildings that now surround this urban islet').[122] Standing there, in that 'lugar estratégico', he recalls an old engraving that used to be in the grandmother's house – La Quinta Blanca – in which La Puerta de Alcalá 'se ofrece a la vista como un hito solemne y terminal, limítrofe con unos arrabales que no existen siquiera todavía. Cuando Madrid era un poblachón sin luz eléctrica ni alcantarillado' ('can be seen as a solemn, terminal landmark, bordering with outskirts that do not even exist yet. When Madrid was a town without electricity nor a sewage system').[123] La Puerta de Alcalá is a 'lugar estratégico' because Leonardo travels back to other epochs, such as the seventeenth century, which was when the architectural reforms in Madrid were initiated. He also goes back to the years in which he lived with his father, which brings about a momentary change of scenery. Leornardo also calls to mind La Quinta Blanca, a place constantly in his thoughts. A few lines earlier, we said that La Puerta de Alcalá was a 'sitio estratégico', because, from there, Leonardo links past events with the present. In fact, he is able to look in two directions at once, towards both moments in his life, because in that place the frontiers between past and present disappear.

> Hueco abierto de par en par al vacío, la Puerta de Alcalá, armonioso recordatorio de piedra que un día, sin necesidad de apelar a cerrojo alguno, insinuó los linderos entre lo de afuera y lo de dentro, metáfora, acertijo, disparate, puerta que no se hizo para llave y que nunca se cierra; éste es mi refugio momentáneo, abuela, mi isla oculta a los ojos de quienes me hacen señas equívocas, escondite fugaz de las garras del tiempo. Porque ahora – con la pequeña diferencia de que yo me incluía como un bulto minúsculo en el escenario vacío – , la Puerta de Alcalá volvía a ser la del grabado que mi padre me enseñaba de niño: por aquí se sale de una ciudad transitada por carruajes.

> A wide-open cavity like a vacuum, the Puerta de Alcalá, harmonious stone reminder that one day, without needing a lock, it hinted at the fringes between what's outside and what lies inward, a metaphor, a riddle, utter nonsense, a gate never made for a key and that is never shut; this is my momentary refuge, grandmother, my island hidden from the eyes of those who make ambiguous signals at me, a fleeting hiding place from the claws of time. Because now – with the small difference that I'd include myself as a minuscule lump on an empty stage, the Puerta de Alcalá was once again the print my father showed me as a child: this the exit way from a city where carriages circulate.[124]

In analysing this fragment by way of associations, it is possible to appreciate a list of nouns corresponding to La Puerta de Alcaláthat are to be found on repeated occasions throughout Martín Gaite's narrative. In the domestic geography, the window was the point of reference from which the woman prepared to dream of the world that she discerned and imagined, being in her inner redoubt. La Puerta de Alcalá shares the characteristic of 'hueco' ('cavity') with the window, but differs from the latter in as much as it is open to the 'vacío' ('vacuum'), which means that the gaze does not come to a halt when confronted with walls as one looks towards the interior of a house through a window. In addition, La Puerta de Alcalá is converted into 'refugio' ('refuge') while the window is 'el punto de enfoque (y) también el punto de partida' ('the focus point (and) also the point of departure'),[125] according to Martín Gaite in *Desde la ventana*. From there, one looks at oneself and, from there, oneiric journeys are begun. Both the window and La Puerta de Alcalá point to frontiers, but if the window is 'símbolo de lo fronterizo, limítrofe entre el espacio cerrado y el abierto, entre lo familiar y lo inexplorado' ('a symbol of a frontier, a borderland between indoors and outdoors, between the familiar and the unexplored'), according to Iñaki Torre Fica in 'La mujer ventanera en la poesía de Carmen Martín Gaite'.[126] What are 'los linderos entre lo de afuera y lo de dentro' ('the borderlands between outdoor and indoors') to which La Puerta de Alcalá points? What is being referred to when the word 'fuera' ('outdoors') is used? What does 'dentro' ('indoors') mean?

In the domestic geography, 'lo cerrado' ('that which is closed') was linked to the interior of the houses and rooms, while 'lo abierto' ('that which is open') had to do with the street. The window was the strategic place from which women imprisoned in the home peered out on and dreamt of the outside world and from which they were free to look without being seen. In the urban geography, La Puerta de Alcalá is a 'hito de tiempo' because the setting foments and brings alive events from the past and the present of Leonardo's life. Feeling protected there, the narrative geography operates in the background, as the thread of all that has been gradually changing in the life of Leonardo: the city's architecture, his relations with people who have died, as in the case of his father. As he contemplates the buildings that surround his 'islote urbano' ('urban islet']', all these fragmented and muddled narratives appear, emerging one by one as they are called forth by the geographical references of the place in which Leonardo has taken refuge.

Leonardo's walk through the streets of Madrid is gradually converted 'en un zigzag entretenido y sedante' ('into a fun, soothing zigzag'), which distances him more and more from 'las vías concurridas y abriendo las espirales de [su] laberinto interior' ('the crowded streets and the spirals of (his) inner labyrinth').[127] His walk implies digression and the discovery of self. His urban meanderings transform the city into an analogy of the human psyche, which is explored with a view to recovering the amnesias of his past life. Take, for example, the use of 'echar a andar por la Gran Vía' ('take a walk along the Gran Vía'),[128] to take pleasure in the walks, to go down 'callejuelas laterales' ('side streets'),[129] 'continuaba andando sin prisa ni rumbo, dejándome rozar por otros transeúntes perezosos de la media tarde' ('carried on walking unhurriedly and aimlessly, allowing other lazy mid-afternoon strollers to brush against me').[130] As he walks, he gradually gives shape to the setting appropriate to engage in a telephone conversation with a person who will provide him with details of his past.

Amparo Miranda, the protagonist in *Irse de casa*, becomes the *flâneuse* due to her solitary strolls through the streets of a city in which she ceased to live forty years earlier. From the moment she arrives, she adopts an observer's stance and acknowledges the fact that her vision now is the same as it was then: to see without being seen.[131] In the previous novels, some of the characters also looked from their windows without being seen. But that look already contained a certain pleasure, as can be seen in *Nubosidad variable*. Sofía Montalvo's mother liked to 'atisbar a la gente pasando por la calle, con sus penas, con sus paquetes, con su frío y sus prisas, y yo a salvo de asuntos que no iban a salpicarme ni a meterme en líos, como cuando vas al teatro, sentada a la camilla, cosiendo junto al mirador' ('peek at people walking on the street, with their worries, their packages, their chill and their hurry, while I am safe from matters that were not going to splatter me nor get me into trouble, like when going to see a play, sitting at a brazier table, sewing by the bay window').[132]

Valeria Roca, a character in *Lo raro es vivir*, also becomes a *flâneuse* when, in one of her walks around the city's Ensanche, the name of which is not mentioned in the entire novel, she stops to have breakfast in a café, from where she sits, on a chair by the window, she begins to look out on 'la avenida ancha con bloques de quince pisos por la que pululaban muchos coches y se veía circular a peatones que parecían saber adónde iban' ('a broad avenue with 15-floor buildings; there was heavy traffic and there were pedestrians who looked as if they knew where they were going').[133] The to-and-fro movement of pedestrians, who are strangers for her but who might happen to know her family and feel 'de aquí de toda la vida' ('they've lived here all their lives'),[134] leads her to reflect on the changes in the city and, finally, on the social and economic transformations taking place in recent years. It is a period in which buildings are being pulled down and avenues widened, and a time to modernise the old and erect new neighbourhoods, new spaces representing a new iconography in which the two strata of the city – the 'casco' and the 'Ensanche' – are superimposed, one upon the other. Some of the commercial premises of the Ensanche have large, brightly lit and modern fronts, yet are decorated with 'un toque de antigüedad' ('a touch of antiquity'),[135] while the few businesses in the 'casco viejo' ('old downtown area') have been revamped, preserving their old façades while the interiors exhibit the most modern of refurbishments. Such is the case of the shop known as 'Defectos Especiales', which was built on what used to be the 'Taller Ramona-Modas'. The description of the spaces reveals several stories, one being that of Amparo Miranda and Rita Bores who are likewise superimposed. Is this superimposition also presented with the different types of geography analysed in this chapter? Is the domestic geography linked to the interior geography and/or the urban geography? How does this link operate?

A possible reply can be found in another section of the previously analysed fragment. Valeria Roca is 'mirando a través del cristal una calle anónima, que daba pie a situarla en cualquier sitio, puedo pensar que he hecho un viaje a otra ciudad, se dijo, una ciudad donde nadie me espera ni me conoce' ('looking through the glass at a nondescript street that could easily be located anywhere, I can even believe that I've travelled to another city, she told herself, a city where no one is expecting me or even knows me').[136] This fragment is converted into the point of contact of several types of geography in that it presents elements that Martín Gaite implements in her narrative geography. These elements are the gaze, the window, the journey and the imagination. The word 'pensar' ('to think') is used as a synonym for *inventing a story*. In this story, Valeria, the *flâneuse*, strolls about an unknown city in which she passes the time of day hiding behind a cloak of anonymity, as in the story of Amparo Miranda. In this way, the story of the urban geography in which we see Amparo walking about the streets of 'una ciudad rara' ('a strange city')[137] is superimposed on the dream of Valeria Roca, which is developed in the interior geography in that she is imagining a similar story to that of Amparo Miranda.

*Irse de casa* is a novel in which domestic geography disappears almost completely in order to move on to an urban geography, in which the settings are the streets of Manhattan and the provincial cities of Spain. Amparo Miranda, the protagonist, could well be the woman in Edward Hopper's painting *Hotel Room.* Nevertheless, as the plot develops, Amparo Miranda does not remain in her room reading a newspaper, but goes out for a walk in the city in which she has to make an effort to remember that she is not in Manhattan, but in the city where she spent her childhood.

The structure of *Irse de casa* differs from previous novels in that each chapter has its own title. It begins with a preamble called 'Pórtico con rascacielos' ('Portico with Skyscraper') followed by 28 numbered chapters that terminate in 'Apertura a otros pórticos' ('Opening to Other Porticoes'). In *Carmen Martín Gaite (1925–2000)* Biruté Ciplijauskaité considers that 'el énfasis en la casa se recalca' ('the emphasis on the house is stressed'),[138] due to the use of these titles instead of the usual prologue and epilogue. And she goes on to underline the quality of 'casa abierta' ('open house'). However, the word 'rascacielos' ('skyscraper') refers to an image of the city that does not necessarily become the 'casa abierta' ('open house') suggested by Ciplijauskaité.

During this analysis, it has been pointed out that Martín Gaite places great importance on the decription of *place* and, by doing so, she slowly creates the framework of or the preamble to the stories it is her intention to tell. In the case of *Irse de casa,* 'Pórtico con rascacielos' provides a time and place reference that situates the reader in Manhattan, whose 'bóveda ficticia se rasgaba en charcos de claridad intempestiva' ('fake vault tore itself in puddles of untimely clarity')[139] at certain times of the day and, at others, would unleash torrential rain. These climatological changes refer to the weather forecasts of *Nubosidad variable,* in which mention is also made of possible 'Nubosidad variable con algún chubasco en todo el Suroeste' ('variable cloudiness with a few showers throughout the south west').[140]

As Jeremy Drake, the character in *Irse de casa,* wanders about Manhattan and observes its changeable 'bóveda' ('vault'), he reflects on the need to be attentive to the surprises that light can produce, in that 'son instantes así los que sirven para tener una visión diferente de la realidad y conseguir otro enfoque' ('those are the moments that are most useful to get a vision other than reality and find another viewpoint').[141] The different walks he takes through the city, like the gaze executed from afar, gradually convert him into a *flâneur*.

Like the other characters of Martín Gaite's fiction, Jeremy devotes his time to writing. But, in his case, we are no longer dealing with a diary or letters, or notebooks like those written by Leonardo. Jeremy is writing a film script and the plot is about 'dos desarraigos idénticos, de alguien que no ha asumido Nueva York y va dejando la vida entre sus calles a medida que sabe cada vez más fijo que aquellas donde pasó su infancia se le vuelven un sueño surrealista' ('two identical uprootings of someone who has not come to terms with New York and is leaving behind scraps of their life amid its streets while they become more and more certain that the streets where they spent their childhood are turning into a surreal dream').[142] For this, it is necessary for the protagonist to wander 'por los suburbios de una ciudad rara (...) exteriores en plan mutante, estética cubista' ('through the suburbs of a strange city (...) exteriors as a mutant, cubist aesthetic').[143] During the novel, there is constant reference to exterior space, and in particular to the streets, the *set* for which 'tan pronto era interior como exterior' ('was as much interior as exterior').[144] Interior spaces, such as rooms, are transformed into streets and these, in their turn, seem like prisons. In employing this approach, the limits of the interior–exterior duality are obliterated, thus opening the way to a different conception of space. In the words of Martín Gaite in *Irse de casa*, an 'estética mutante' ('mutant aesthetic')[145] is created.

In this 'estética mutante' ('mutant aesthetic'), the Plaza del Rincón becomes 'una especie de sala de espera o promontorio ignorado desde el cual lanzar el anzuelo hacia aguas más alborotadas e incursiones de mayor riesgo' ('a sort of waiting room or ignored promontory from which to cast the bait into the most troubled waters and riskiest forays').[146] For Amparo Miranda, the space that forms part of the urban geography is converted into a refuge, into a clandestine place, as 'allí en el repliegue más arrinconado de la ciudad, al abrigo de miradas indiscretas, cerraba los ojos para entregarse a sus fantasías de futuro, igual que estaba haciendo ahora para recuperarlas' ('there in the furthest folds of the city, safe from indiscreet eyes, she would shut her eyes to abandon herself to fantasies of the future, just as she was now doing to retrieve them').[147]

The transformation of the Plaza del Rincón into a hiding place in which free rein is given to fantasy links in with the interior geography, in which the protagonists embark upon a journey to a universe of dream and imagination, leaving behind those highways and byways of a domestic geography in which the everyday becomes a bond in a world holding no attraction whatsoever. In the domestic geography, it was revealed how spaces are lived as enclosures, but there are certain houses that are also converted into refuge. Such is the case of Lagasca's flat in *Nubosidad variable,* better known as 'el refu'.[148] At the end of the novel, Sofía takes shelter there after deciding to break the ties with her life as a married woman. The denouement of *Nubosidad variable* presents us with two women who have given up their domestic geography in order to embark upon a journey in which writing becomes *the* refuge. The stories told throughout the novel become key moments in the narrative geography.

**Narrative geography**
In the previous sections, we identified and viewed the different types of geography developed by Martín Gaite. In the domestic geography, the concept of space was analysed from the point of view of the interior–exterior duality. This revealed how the house represented either imprisonment or liberation. In the second section, space referred to the world of dreams, fantasy and memory, strategies employed to prevent having to move about the domestic geography. In the third section, space alluded to the concept of a city that is explored by the passer-by whose observations gradually constitute the female point of view in the urban geography.

In my opinion, the narrative geography is the place in which all three types of geography converge. Before putting forward my arguments for this, I feel it necessary to speak of the origins of the 'geografía narrativa'. For this, a change of scenery is necessary, we must go back to the years in which *El cuento de nunca acabar* was being written, a period that partly coincides with Martín Gaite's several visits to New York. It is in the autumn of 1982 that the writer finally completes a work begun nine years earlier. During her prolonged stay in Virginia, Martín Gaite concludes her reflections on narrative, love and lies.

In Chapter 2, I indicated the way in which the writer creates her stories from scenes set in everyday spaces, be they interior or exterior. In looking at a simple street corner, scenes from the past proliferate, superimposing themselves on other scenes – this time from the present. In *El cuento de nunca acabar*, Martín Gaite tells the story of a walk with her mother through the streets of Madrid. They both stop in front of the house in which her mother lived when she was young. Looking at this previously inhabited space, the mother begins to tell a story from her youth, which took place inside that old house. In this manner, the past is brought forward to the present in which Martín Gaite and her mother are looking at the house from the outside.

The gaze from the outside refers to the urban geography. As she walks, the *flâneuse* encounters places visited on a previous occasion, which she gradually incorporates into her interior geography, thus impregnating them with memories. A story is rooted in the everyday as it tells how the people whom a person knows gradually change direction, how these people are forced to relate to each other, speak about each other, dealing with each other in this or that way. To put together a story based on these changes taking place in the everyday lives of people allows one to link the past with the present. In the terminology of Martín Gaite, time is signposted with the adverbs 'antes' ('before') and 'después' ('after'),[149] which 'hay que saber marcar en la historia' ('authors need to know how to mark in stories').[150] But that 'saber marcar' ('how to mark') does not mean establishing limits. What is important is to narrate the changes that have taken place in the persons as well as the places.

In her article 'La libertad como símbolo', which appears in *Pido la palabra*, Martín Gaite provides us with a resumé of her different trips to New York referred to in the interior geography and the urban geography. For the writer, each visit became a journey of recognition of places previously visited. The combination of the story of what took place in her first walks in New York City with the tales arising from her later jaunts shapes the techniques of the 'geografía narrativa'. But, at what moment are the trajectories indicated? Who embarks upon journeys in that geography?

In Chapter 2, I pointed out that Martín Gaite establishes an analogy between going for a walk in a park that a person knows and copying old notes into new notebooks. Both actions have to do with a process, with a *doing by degrees*, with a *being in movement*. The notebook in which notes are being taken with which to write a story or a novel is the physical space in which actions are generated with which the narrative geography is constructed. In other words, the narrative geography is that trip through writing and reading. In order to demonstrate my hypothesis, it is indispensable to review the notion of literature as hiding place put forward by Martín Gaite in *Retahílas* (1974). Eulalia, the protagonist, recalls her first encounters with books:

> Leer (…) se convirtió progresivamente en tarea secreta y solitaria (…) Leer era acceder a un terreno en el que se ingresaba con esfuerzo, emoción y destreza, terreno amenazado y siempre a conquistar, a reinventar y defender (…) la puerta de ingreso a este recinto, además de secreta debía ser empujada preferentemente de noche.

> Reading (…) turned out to be a progressively secret, solitary task (…) Reading was gaining access to territory whose entryway was traversed with effort, emotion and skill; the area was under threat and always required conquest, redefinition and defence (…) the entry gate to this enclosure, besides being secret, needed a push, especially at night.[151]

From that early period, there are already signs of the use of geographical vocabulary when defining the act of reading as 'terreno' to be conquered and defended. Access to that space included within certain limits is secret. It is also a journey made alone. In a similar manner, in *Nubosidad variable*, Sofía and Mariana build a 'territorio'[152] with words. The term 'territorio' ('territory') appears again later, as being synonymous with 'patria' ('homeland'). Mariana describes it in the following way:

> Mi patria escabrosa y recóndita, siempre esperando por mí. Riachuelos por cuya corriente huyen los peces rojos del pretérito imperfecto, montañitas dentadas de gerundios, cuestas arriba flanqueadas por signos de admiración y puntos suspensivos, angostos desfiladeros donde se hila la oración compuesta, árboles frondosos de adjetivos o desnudos de ellos, praderas atisbadas en sueños y a las que sólo se llega por el puente inestable del condicional.

> My rugged, recondite homeland, forever waiting for me. Streams in whose current red fish of the simple past place themselves to escape, ragged little gerund mountains, uphill and flanked by exclamation marks and ellipses, narrow ravines where compound sentences file through, trees full of adjectives or devoid of them, prairies glimpsed

in dreams and to which one arrives at only by crossing the unstable bridge of the conditional.[153]

In the previous quotation, geographical vocabulary is employed to describe the configuration of the 'patria' of writing, which is 'escabrosa' and 'recóndita'. There are streams, mountains, sharp inclines, narrow ravines, leafy trees and meadows. It is as though the description were of a countryside whose scenery was idealised and where no one lived because there are no houses. The only inhabitant of that 'patria' is the person describing it and who lives there as a refuge.

During the entire novel, Sofía remains in her house. Only at the end does she escape her domestic geography and head for the 'refu' – a concrete physical space that functions as a metaphor for writing. It is by no means gratuitous that Martín Gaite should insert a quotation from Pessoa in the conversation held between Sofía and Raimundo, a friend of her children whose story also forms parts of one of the fragments of the novel's collage. Raimundo suggests to Sofía 'que construyera en sueños las calles de (su) nuevo país, y las casas, ladrillo por ladrillo. Se había dado cuenta de que estaba triste, perdida. Y poco a poco lo (dejó) de estar, creó para (ella) una pequeña patria de palabras, un albergue provisional' ('that she lay the streets of (her) new country, and build the houses brick by brick, in her dreams. He realised she was sad, lost. And a bit at a time she ceased to be; he built her a small homeland made of words, a temporary shelter').[154]

Metaphorically speaking, the 'refu' ends up becoming the actual writing, as I mentioned earlier. That physical space belonging to the domestic geography – also called 'el cuarto derecha' ('the room on the right')[155] – is transformed into the text that Sofía and Mariana are writing. Mariana confesses that she does not have 'más refugio que el de la escritura' ('a refuge other than writing').[156] She pronounces this phrase when she finds herself in the house at Puerto Real, which ends up becoming a cell, and, for this reason, she decides to escape.

In another fragment of *Nubosidad variable*, Martín Gaite gradually indicates the vantage points from which the different stories progressively shaping the narrative geography are constructed. Sofía is writing to Mariana, and she tells her that 'ha tocado el turno a la historia de Guillermo' ('it's time to tell Guillermo's story'):[157]

En este momento, en este 'ahora' acampado entre dos polos de 'siempre', me siento instalada en un territorio estratégico para montar el catalejo y otear muy allá, sin olvidar el punto de mira que he tomado ni, por supuesto, que vale rectificarlo. Y aunque el lugar te parezca metafórico, existe; y el suelo que estoy pisando es de fiar. Créeme, por favor. Además hoy no tenemos alrededor comparsas que nos interrumpan. ¿Quieres entrar conmigo, Mariana, en el recinto del cuento?

Como necesito imaginar, aunque sea aproximadamente, tus puntos cardinales, mientras aparejo los bártulos para la pesca de esta historia esquiva.

This very moment, in this 'now' set between two 'always' poles, I feel myself installed in a strategic territory to mount the spyglass and scan far over there, without ever forgetting the focus point I've chosen nor, of course, that I can adjust it. Even if the place seems metaphoric, it exists; and the ground I'm standing on is trustworthy. Please believe me. Besides, today there are no extras around to interrupt us. Mariana, do you want to venture inside the story's enclosure with me?

I need to imagine, even if approximately, your cardinal points, while I ready the gear to fish out this elusive story.[158]

In the above passage it is possible to identify a wide range of vocabulary grouped under what Carmen Martín Gaite calls 'geografía narrativa': the 'ahora' ('now') serving as a time reference or 'hito de tiempo' in which past and present are the axes indicative of movement, while the 'allá' ('there') is the story still to be told and before which a distant gaze characteristic of the *flâneuse* is sustained. It is the strategic territory as well as the technique to be employed in narrating the story of Guillermo, which, according to Sofía, is the collage, the spyglass – the tool or material with which to elaborate the collage – like the love letters written between Sofía and Guillermo and the bits and pieces of a diary that she began when her mother died, as well as notes written only days earlier. Looking through the sight of a gun ('punto de mira') becomes a graphic equivalent for what Martín Gaite terms the 'point of view', while the interior space of the story corresponds to the preamble in Guillermo's tale. In the case of the love story between Sofía and Guillermo, she decides to tell 'los preliminares',[159] and nothing more – in other words, she establishes the frontiers of what she wishes to narrate.

The construction of 'la patria de la escritura' shares elements similar to those analysed in previous sections. In the interior geography, rivers were breaches through which the protagonists escaped towards the universe of dreams represented by meadows in the narrative geography, while bridges became thresholds uniting the world of dreams with the world of reality. In this way, it can be seen that the different types of geography constructed by Martín Gaite progressively interlink, and the frontiers between the three geographies – domestic, interior and urban – gradually disappear.

In the *Cuadernos de todo*, particularly in 'Cuaderno 35', written in the University of Vassar in 1985, we read a complete and meticulous description of the place in which the writer lived as visiting professor for a semester. The history of the town of Poughkeepsie and of the founder of Vassar College merges with the description of the apartment flat that she occupies. Combined with these stories, there is also the detailed description in 'Cuaderno 35' summoning up other stories. Among these, Martín Gaite tells of a dream in which that notebook is gradually transformed into the garden of Vassar:

> Se entraba al cuaderno por la solapa trasera (...) pero luego ya se salía a la luz (...) total, que entrar en el cuaderno de todo era propiamente salir, y a donde se salía era al parque de Vassar, cada línea un caminito que ya conocía o que iba explorando y todos los personajes en que iba pensando o que veía de verdad andaban al mismo tiempo por allí juntos e ingrávidos (...) todo confundido, todo permitido (...) O sea que el jardín de Vassar es el texto mismo y también el escenario de sus transformaciones.

> Entry to the notebook was through the back flap (...) but then you would go out into the light (...) after all, entering the notebook of everything really meant exiting, and the place I exited to was the Vassar park. Each line was a path I was familiar with or that I was exploring and all the characters I was thinking about or that I was actually seeing were walking along together, weightless (...) everything mixed up, everything allowed (...) In other words, the Vassar park is the text itself as well as the stage for its transformations.[160]

In the domestic geography reference was made to Bachelard, who sees the house as a refuge. The principle involved in constructing an oneiric abode the vertical axis of which is charged with different meanings, and where the lower and upper areas are related to memory and fantasy respectively, is also employed in the narrative *terrain*. Mariana says that what she writes is at times converted into 'un túnel excavado (...) una galería subterránea de palabras' ('an excavated tunnel (...) an underground gallery of words');[161] on other occasions, what is written rises to the surface, 'las palabras abren brecha hacia (el) incierto refugio' ('the words open a breech to an uncertain refuge'),[162] where Sofía is to be found. Through writing, a liberation slowly takes place in that, via the medium of words, it is possible to 'atravesar fosos (…) escalar muros (y) saltar de rama en rama por los árboles' ('cross moats (…) scales walls (and) jump from branch to branch in the trees').[163] In this way, the text that Mariana and Sofía gradually produce progressively unites what is within with what is without. The frontiers are slowly dissolved and a space is created in which the different types of geography evident in the narrative of Martín Gaite converge.

In this chapter I have detected two differences regarding the concept of space that Martin Gaite exposes in *El cuento de nunca acabar*, *Agua pasada*, *Pido la palabra*, and *Cuadernos de todo* and that she gradually and simultaneously employs in the narrative itself. In the first place, the writer defines space as the place, the scenario in which a story emerges or in which the events of a short story or novel occur. This statement constitutes the basis of her poetic narrative. The other characteristic concerning space points directly towards the everyday space inhabited by women, be they of the author's generation or that of the protagonists in her novels. I have linked this notion of space with the theories on feminist geography, with one of the themes studied in this discipline being the everyday geography of the household and kitchen, not to mention the streets, places of work and neighbourhoods, among others. The main idea is to create an awareness of the politics of the everyday. In my opinion, Martin Gaite is an excellent observer of the everyday life of women in Spain in different historical periods.

On the one hand, the creation of these spaces emerges from the personal experience of the writer – that is to say, Martin Gaite describes places in which she has lived, such as, for example, the room in *Cuarto de atrás* in which she and her sister played during their childhood. On the other hand, spaces are imagined or dreamt, like the Isla de Bergai. Martin Gaite substantiates that the gaze is essential for the formation of both spaces: those that are real and those that are imaginary. The place, the 'aquí', as Martín Gaite specifies in her articles from *Pido la palabra,* is the point of departure for the narrative. Once the character is situated in that 'aquí', she begins to describe that place and, for this, she must choose a 'desde donde' ('from where') in which to begin to carry out that

activity. That 'desde donde', in other words, is 'the point of view' –
the narrator´s 'punto de mira' – that orients the narrative
perspective.

Throughout the writings in which Martín Gaite reflects on the
way in which she creates her own narrative, she acknowledges the
*gaze* as a vital part of the text's machinery and, consequently, puts
forward a series of characteristics of that *gaze*. The first of these is
the fact that we are dealing with a *female gaze* for two simple reasons:
she is a woman writer and the characters of her novels, generally
speaking, are also women. The house and home are the everyday
space inhabited by these women. The movements they make about
this sphere are what results in the emergence of the domestic geography. In this section, I showed that the most common spaces are
the kitchen, the sewing room, the parents' bedroom and the back
room. All these places have been designated to women without
asking them if they were appropriate for them. Take, for example,
the political ideology of the Sección Femenina, which introduced
the figure of the mother and the submissive wife as female prototypes whose duty it was to fulfil all domestic chores. The protagonists
in the narrative of the 1990s break with this stereotype. For example,
in *Nubosidad variable*, Sofia decides to abandon the matrimonial
bedroom because she realises that the relationship with her has no
meaning whatsoever. From that moment on, she dedicates herself
to the activities that she enjoys, such as reading and the creation of
collages. Later, she leaves home and retires to the 'Refu' – the flat
in which she spent the first years of marriage. The most important
factor in this movement about the domestic geography lies in the
fact that the protagonists gradually become aware of the lives they
are leading and of the need for change and the struggle required in
shaping a life of their own. These women free themselves from
family and social ties. The movement from one room to another
represents a kind of personal growth in as much as, by scanning
with their eyes each of the objects occupying the rooms, they begin
to remember past events, and they set out to re-encounter personal
memories.

Another feature of the *gaze* in the poetics of Martín Gaite is the
dichotomy of looking from without or from within. The former
requires a distance, be it temporal or spatial, and consists of being
witness to events, as in the case of Pablo Klein in *Entre visillos*, Luisa
in *Fragmentos de interior* and Amparo Miranda in *Irse de casa*. The

gaze from within, for its part, implies looking from what is familiar (the interiors of houses inhabited by women) towards what is unknown (the exterior). The window thus becomes a relevant and obligatory factor in the work of Martín Gaite. The window is a symbol of the frontier between open and closed spaces, between what is familiar and the unknown, between routine life and adventure. Furthermore, the window conditions a particular kind of gaze – looking without being seen – and it becomes a halfway hiding place. From this place, women give free rein to the imagination and this is a transgression of the rhythm of everyday life in that it is now possible to transform the ordinary into the extraordinary, or dream of other worlds that they have not yet explored. In *Desde la ventana*, Martín Gaite traces the history of the female focus in Spanish literature and, for this, she introduces each of the women writers discussed within a broad spectrum encompassing the rights or lack of rights of women and the expectations of society regarding their behaviour. Martín Gaite points to the fact that, living a caged life, women were obliged to seek ways out that were not so obvious. Literature was one such possibility of escape.

*Displacement* and the *gaze* become fundamental elements in the poetics of Martín Gaite, as can be confirmed in the section on urban geography. There, I show that this type of geography is constructed from walks to and fro through the streets of the city. I have looked at novels that I situate at crucial moments in the life of the writer: before and after New York. The eyes, attentive to what is going on in the street, emphasise the precept of finding inspiration in life. I have mentioned that the writer was in the habit of strolling the streets of Madrid and, later, those of New York. The street signifies continuous movement, changes, transitions, the unexpected, disorder and improvisation. As the writer walks, her eyes scan a street corner and awaken memories in her. In *El cuento de nunca acabar* she says: 'una esquina cualquiera de una calle se pone a dispararme, al mirarla, escenas superpuestas y aglomeradas de mi paso por allí en otras ocasiones' ('any corner of a street catapults me, by looking at it, into superimposed and amassed scenes of previous times I have passed that way').[164] That place viewed from a different perspective – in this case due to the distance recorded in time – evokes past memories, which fuse with present events, the objective being to combine the 'before' with the 'after' and thus be able to weave a complete story.

*Retahílas, Ritmo lento, Fragmentos de interior* and *El cuarto de atrás* belong to the stage prior to New York. The spaces described include a provincial city or a house or flat in Madrid. The political and social issues that were being experienced in Spain under the Franco regime have had strong repercussions in the work of the writer, as I have indicated in Chapter 1. The narrative of the 1990s refers directly to New York, and this is explained by the journeys made by the writer as early as 1979. First, I have presented the vision of New York that the writer has and that is recovered in *Cuadernos de todo*. In these notebooks, we can find a description of her movements to and fro about the city of Manhattan, the place or the 'aquí' from which *Caperucita en Manhattan,* as well as the poem 'Todo es un cuento roto en Nueva York' emerge, not to mention the series of collages that will be discussed in the next chapter. In addition to the aforementioned, I then reviewed the movements of the characters present in the narrative of the 1990s and, with this, I explored the application of the series of actions linked to such movement back and forth, such as strolling, exploring, stopping and taking a pause.

In the case of interior geography, I have indicated that it refers to the world of dreams, fantasy and memory. In this geography, the characters free themselves from the ties imposed upon them by the domestic one. Finally, there is a close link between both spheres because the dreams of the protagonists, who look out of the window, involve fleeing and escaping. The dreams will feed off the imagination, reading, writing and the collage. It is for this reason that the protagonists dedicate their time to one or several of these activities, at the same time as they slowly recall their past lives. The aspect of fantasy relates to daydreams and to the creation of imaginary places that are converted into refuges – or hiding places, as in the case of the island of Bergai. Reading and writing are also a shelter for women uprooted culturally, as I explained and analysed in the section on narrative geography.

Ultimately, movement takes place through reading and writing. Reading is considered to be an activity that has to be conquered and defended or an enclosure that one visits at night. These concepts imply that reading is considered something prohibited, which explains why it has to be visited late at night, or as a space difficult to maintain. This peculiarity makes one think of the struggle that women have had to confront in order to have a space of their own (as suggested by Virginia Woolf) in which they would have access to reading and writing with no restrictions whatsoever. This view confirms the fact that Martín Gaite had her mind centred on exposing the obstacles existing throughout the history of women to holding a prominent place and at the same level as that enjoyed by male writers. Martín Gaite analyses this situation in *Desde la ventana* and, moreover, she herself lived a personal situation in which her work was not recognised until the publication of *El cuarto de atrás*. Furthermore, this recognition did not even occur in her own country but in the United States. One of the possible factors in that situation, as expressed by Joan Lipman Brown in 'Carmen Martín Gaite: Reaffirming the Pact between Reader and Writer', is 'the marginalization of women writers in most Spanish literary histories'.[165] According to Martín Gaite, narrative geography and interior geography are the spaces in which women have been able to free themselves. In both spheres, imagination, fantasy, dreams and memories prevail. Nevertheless, these two environments are juxtaposed or interlinked with the domestic and urban geography that contextualise and situate social relations between men and women. Martín Gaite testifies to the way in which those geographical differences are implied, and in particular to the female condition of Spanish women from the 1950s to the 1990s.

The process of looking, of moving to and fro between these four types of geography, plays an indispensable role in the poetics of the writer. The most challenging task is to know how to weave the threads of the domestic, urban, interior and narrative when shaping the history of the everyday.

# 4

# Visual Elements in the Narrative of Martín Gaite

The journey is the central axis of the writer's narrative in the 1990s. Each journey takes place within the sphere of domestic, urban, interior or narrative geography. As each transpires, the gaze plays a fundamental role in as much as everything seen is converted in material with which Martín Gaite assembles her stories, poems, novels, essays, drawings and collages.

The writer's drawings and collages have received scant attention from critics. We do have the excellent article by Kathleen Glenn entitled 'Collage, Textile and Palimpsest: Carmen Martín Gaite's *Nubosidad variable*', in which she analyses in detail the collage that adorns the cover of the novel and that she considers 'a visualization of the novel's content and structure'.[1] Years prior to the publication of this novel, Martín Gaite had elaborated other collages. Five of these appeared in *From Fiction to Metafiction*. With the publication of *Cuadernos de todo*, visual materials elaborated by the writer increase so as to include not only collage but drawing, too. Anyone who has read *Caperucita en Manhattan* will have realised that the drawings in the novel are the author's own work. In the 1990s, Martín Gaite wrote lectures in which she commented on the work of Spanish painters such as Dalí, Murillo, Maura, Montaner and Tuset. In the same period, she took part in a conference at the Museo Thyssen Bornemisza with her commentary on Edward Hopper's *Hotel Room*.

I shall deal with the drawings, collages and articles on the afore-mentioned artists, given that in all of them there exists the idea that the visual dimension is material for the literary dimension, and that the literary interlinks with the visual. I am interested in showing the process by which Martín Gaite uses the visual image and converts it into text. In my view, there exists a series of actions similar to those identified and underlined in Chapter 2. I shall also analyse the inverse process – that is to say, to begin with a text that is later represented visually. With this, my intention is to show the intrinsic relationship between the visual and the literary via collage and painting in Martín Gaite's narrative work produced in the 1990s.

## Drawing as a source of narrative

The link between drawing and the elaboration of narrative writing in the work of Martín Gaite dates back to the period in which the writer lived in New York. It was the summer of 1985 and she was staying at the home of her friend, 'un conocido ilustrador de literatura infantil' ('a well-known illustrator of children's books'), as he is referred to in 'La libertad como símbolo', published in *Pido la palabra*. In that article, Martín Gaite states that the shaping of her novel *Caperucita en Manhattan* stemmed from the drawings on which Juan Carlos Eguillor was working, which formed part of a folder entitled 'Castillos de Manhattan'.[2] These drawings were 'unidos algunos de ellos por un conato de trama argumental, aunque todavía endeble, a modo de comic' (linked by a semblance of topic, though still weak, a little bit like a comic book).[3] In them, one could see 'una niña con capa roja, una especie de Caperucita moderna, que iba volando por encima de los rascacielos o se metía por el interior de las alcantarillas' ('a little girl wearing a red hood, a modern Little Red Riding Hood of sorts, who was soaring above the skyscrapers or going down through a manhole').[4] According to Eguillor, this little girl lived in Brooklyn and the cake for the grandmother had to be taken to the north of Manhattan. These were the only clear details for Eguillor, which is why he asked Martín Gaite's help in 'configurar la leyenda de cada viñeta' ('configuring the captions of each strip').[5]

*Caperucita en Manhattan*, published by Siruela in 1990, does not include the drawings that inspired it, but rather those elaborated by Martín Gaite herself. In total, there is one drawing in each of the 13 chapters that make up the novel. The first is a map of Manhattan that appears at the end of the chapter and that does not correspond entirely to the description given by the narrator:

Manhattan es una isla entre ríos. Las calles que quedan a la derecha de Central Park y corren en sentido horizontal terminan en un río que se llama el East River, por estar al este, y las de la izquierda en otro: el río Hudson. Se abrazan uno con otro por abajo y por arriba. El East River tiene varios puentes, a cual más complicado y misterioso, que unen la isla por esa parte con otros barrios de la ciudad, uno de los cuales se llama Brooklyn, como también el famoso puente que conduce a él. El puente de Brooklyn es el último, el que queda más al sur, tiene mucho tráfico y está adornado con hilos de luces formando festón que desde lejos parecen farolillos de verbena ... Vigilando Manhattan por la parte de abajo ... donde se mezclan los dos ríos, hay una islita con una estatua enorme de metal verdoso que lleva una antorcha en su brazo levantado.

Manhattan is an island between rivers. Streets to the right of Central Park running horizontally end at a river called the East River, because it lies to the east, and the left-hand streets run to the other river: the Hudson. They embrace each other from beneath and above. The East River has several bridges, complicated and mysterious all of them, which join the island on that side with other neighbourhoods, one of which being Brooklyn, like the famous bridge leading to that neighbourhood. The Brooklyn Bridge is the last one, the southernmost, it has a lot of traffic and it is decorated with strings of light that form festoons; from afar they seem like little lanterns lighting up Spanish street festivals ... Gazing at Manhattan from the lower part ... where the two rivers meet, there is an islet with an enormous greenish metal statue holding up a torch high above its head.[6]

This description, and the whole first chapter, in fact, serve as *preámbulos* – an element of Martín Gaite's poetics – providing necessary geographical references with which Sara Allen, the protagonist, can find her bearings in an urban geography that she dreams about and that she will explore in later chapters. From the previous quotation, two semantic fields emerge when associating certain words. The first has relates to location: 'right', 'left', 'up', 'down', 'east' and 'south'. The second is linked with urban geography: 'Manhattan', 'island', 'statue', 'rivers', 'bridges', 'districts', 'streets' and 'traffic'. This map was a present for Sara Allen, who learned to read at the age of two with the help of a *puzzle*. I use italics for the word *puzzle* because Sara manipulates cubes that 'llevaban en cada cara una letra mayúscula diferente, con el dibujo en colores de una flor, fruta o animal cuyo nombre empezara por aquella letra' ('had a different upper-case letter on each face, plus a colour image of a flower, fruit or animal whose name began with that letter').[7] She places them in rows, turns them over and combines the letters in a manner analogous to the way in which the different materials used to make a collage or the fragments of stories employed to write a novel are manipulated.

Sara Allen's method of apprenticeship consisted of combining the letters of the alphabet with 'perfiles divertidos y peculiares' ('fun and unusual profiles') of certain objects.[8] For example, 'la E parecía un peine, la S una serpiente, la O un huevo, la X una cruz ladeada, la H una escalera para enanos' ('E looked like a comb, S a snake, O an egg, X a lop-sided cross, H a ladder for dwarves'),[9] among others. This method of apprenticeship, in which the letter is *combined* (the italics are mine) with an image, is the first indication of the relationship between the visual and the written. In my view, this step is similar to the preparatory stage of a collage in which a selection is made of possible materials, be they texts or images.

The letter–image combination will later become the drawing–story concept. For the time being, the hypothesis consists of showing that there is no difference 'entre dibujar y escribir' ('between drawing and writing'),[10] as suggested by the writer through Sara, who devotes her time to 'pintar unos garabatos que imitaban las letras y otros que imitaban muebles, cacharros de cocina, nubes o tejados' ('painting squiggles which stood for letters and others simulating furniture, kitchen utensils, clouds or roofs').[11] Based on these drawings, it can be implied that Sara's gaze is directed towards the interior when she draws furniture and 'cacharros de cocina' ('kitchen utensils'),[12] and towards the exterior when she depicts clouds and roof tops.

The drawings inserted into *Caperucita en Manhattan* are justified in that they fulfil a need to illustrate. Each chapter contains a drawing, the story of which can be found in the text. By observing the thirteen drawings it is possible to see recurring elements in the work of Martín Gaite. For example, the drawing that accompanies the second chapter shows Sara Allen leaning on a windowsill and looking out; a speech balloon that would normally be seen in comics hangs from one side of the window. The balloon contains the word 'Miranfú', which was 'invented' by Sara by mixing consonants and vowels when she began to write. This word appears in the final drawing of the book, which shows Sara Allen throwing herself

down a drain leading to 'Freedom'.[13] The meaning of 'Miranfú',
according to what is written in *Caperucita en Manhattan*, is that 'va a
pasar algo diferente' ('something different is going to happen') or
'me voy a llevar una sorpresa' ('I'm going to be surprised').[14] The
surprise, the speech balloon, the window and the female figure in
the window are reiterative elements in the work of Martín Gaite.
They appear in her novels, in her essays, in her drawings and also in
her collages. They are her textual and visual references.

Juan Senís Fernández and Marta Sanjuán carry out a comparative analysis of *Caperucita en Manhattan* and *Visión de Nueva York*
through their representation of the city. They believe that both
texts 'make up the summum of Martín Gaite's poetics about New
York, through the important role that the city plays in both, and of
her graphic and visual activity'.[15] For the authors, *Visión de Nueva
York* is linked with the *Cuadernos de todo* as both are 'private types of
work',[16] given that they were not written for immediate publication.
Senís and Sanjuán coincide with Debra Ochoa and Gladis Granata
de Egües in not analysing these texts as though they were diaries.

The use of drawing in the narrative of Carmen Martín Gaite
occurs prior to the publication of *Caperucita en Manhattan*. In one of
her lectures, entitled 'Tiempo y Lugar', which, moreover, appears
in *Pido la palabra*, the writer answered the question that many critics
of her work had been continually asking: '¿Cómo se le ocurre a
usted una novela?' ('How do you get ideas for your novels?')[17] A
novel, the writer from Salamanca says, emerges as soon as the
setting has been cast. She adds that the geographical location is also
very important and that, in her case in particular, that place is
usually an 'espacio acotado, un interior' ('delimited space, an interior').[18] To illustrate these previous affirmations, Martín Gaite
offers as an example her novel, which, in her opinion, has been
'una de las más analizadas y despiezadas por la crítica literaria'
('one of the most broken down and analysed by literary critics'):[19]
*El cuarto de atrás*. In this novel, according to the writer's analysis,
there are three geographically located back rooms. The first is
where the narrator, C., is sleeping; the second no longer exists, but
the narrator knows it and evokes it as the games room in her house
in Salamanca; and the third is the room that the narrator has never
entered but that the memory of her mother bequeathed to her.
This legacy was made in a conversation the topic of which was old
houses. The narrator asks her mother to draw her a plan of the

house in Cáceres so that, in this way, she can imagine what it is like. The narrator goes on with her story and says that 'a medida que el dibujo de cada habitación daba pie para errores de encaje, se encandiló y se fue a buscar papel cuadriculado para ver de solventarlos, hasta que, al final, estábamos las dos tan interesadas que nos olvidamos de poner la mesa para comer, y yo le dije que los cuentos bonitos siempre hacen perder la noción del tiempo...' ('as the drawing of each room gave cause for mistakes in the layout, she grew animated and went in search of graph paper to try to correct them, until, in the end, we were both so absorbed that we forgot to set the table for a meal, and I said that beautiful stories always make one lose track of time').[20]

In her article 'Tiempo y Lugar', which we mentioned earlier, Carmen Martín Gaite points out that she finds it 'curioso que tanto en el cuarto de atrás legado por (su) madre como en la evocación de (su) casa de Salamanca medie un dibujo' ('curious that so much in the back room left by (her) mother as an evocation of (her) house in Salamanca draws a picture').[21] Nevertheless, it is not at all 'curioso' given that, as a result of the explanation of that drawing there emerges 'un cuento fresco e irregular, tejido de verdades y mentiras, como todos los cuentos' ('a fresh and irregular story, sown of truth and lies, like all stories'), as expressed by the protagonist in *El cuarto de atrás*.[22] In this novel, the narrator is stretched out on the floor of her current back room and, from there, she begins to draw the room in which her childhood took place.

> Pinto, pinto, ¿qué pinto?, ¿con qué color y con qué letrita? Con la C. de mi nombre, tres cosas con la C, primero una casa, luego un cuarto y luego una cama. La casa tiene un balcón antiguo sobre la plaza pequeña, se pintan los barrotes gruesos y paralelos y detrás de las puertas que dan al interior, abiertas porque era primavera, y de la placita (aunque no la pinte, la veo, siempre la vuelvo a ver) venía el ruido del agua cayendo por tres caños al pilón de una fuente que había en medio, el único ruido que entraba al cuarto de noche. Ya estamos en el cuarto: se empieza por el ángulo del techo y, arrancando de ahí para abajo, la raya vertical donde se juntan las paredes. Bueno, ya, al suelo no hace falta llegar porque lo tapa la cama, que está apoyada contra la esquina, una cama turca; de día se ponían almohadones y servía para tirarse en los ratos de aburrimiento, es fácil de pintar: un simple rectángulo sin cabecera, las dos líneas un poco curvas de la almohada, la vertical del embozo y el resto del espacio cuajado de tildes de eñe, imitando el dibujo de la colcha.

Paint, paint, what should I paint? Which colour should I use and with which letter? With the C of my first name, three things that begin with C, first a house, then a room and then a bed. The house has an old-style balcony overlooking a small square, the wooden bars are painted thick and parallel and behind the doors leading indoors, open because it was spring, and from the square (even if I don't include it in the painting, I see it, I always see it again) there came the sound of falling water spewing from three spouts of a fountain set in the middle, the only sound that came into the room at night. We are now in that room: let's start from the angle of the ceiling, and, moving down from there, the vertical line where the walls meet. All right, that's enough, it's not necessary to reach the floor because the bed is there, set against the corner, an Ottoman; by day it had big pillows and you could lie there when you were feeling bored, it is easy to paint: a simple rectangle with no headboard, the lines for the pillow a bit curved, the vertical line of the fringe and the rest of the blank space filled with squiggles, imitating the design of the coverlet.[23]

In the above quotation, two elements appear that are of key importance in the narrative of Martín Gaite: colours and letters, or, to put it another way, drawing and writing, as implemented in *Caperucita en Manhattan.* Once the letter to be employed in the painting is selected, then a decision is taken on what to represent. In this case, the option taken is a house (*casa*), a room (*cuarto*) and a bed (*cama*). The order of the three elements allows for the creation of a three-dimensional space in that what one paints first is the house with 'un balcón' ('a balcony'), indicating the frontier between the outside and the inside. From the balcony, it is possible to see the 'plaza pequeña' ('small square') and, from the square, perhaps, it is likewise possible to glimpse the inside of the house, provided that the doors are open, as they would be in spring. In the centre of the square there is a fountain, and the water it receives produces a certain noise that one can hear from the room.

Here we have an excellent example of the way in which the transition from the outside towards the inside takes place. In the room, on the other hand, one traces 'el ángulo del techo' ('the angle of the ceiling') and then a 'raya vertical' ('vertical line') where the walls meet. It is impossible to see where that 'raya vertical' ('vertical line') finishes because a bed is visible 'que está apoyada contra la esquina' ('that is placed in a corner'). The narrator, we must not forget, is stretched out on the floor, looking at the ceiling, for she has begun to draw one of the angles. It is important to follow the direction of her gaze, which first rests on the ceiling and then begins to lower until it meets the ottoman located in one of the corners of the room. The drawing of the bed is executed with a rectangle, two curved lines, a vertical line, and 'el resto del espacio cuajado de tildes de eñe' ('the rest of the space is set like the line above the Spanish ñ') that mirror the drawing on the bedspread.

In the same way in which, from the explanation of a drawing, it is possible to extract a story, the elaboration of maps in *Nubosidad variable* generates stories that arise from an explanation of the distribution of space. For example, Mariana describes to Sofía the place from where she is writing her a letter.

> Bien. Dos referencias para que te sitúes, una de tiempo y otra de luz. Hace un rato han dado las once y media en el reloj de pared que estuvo siempre en la calle de Serrano, al fondo del pasillo. Segunda referencia: te estoy escribiendo a la luz de la lámpara que también conoces. Es aquella de mesa que tenía mi abuelo en su despacho, ¿te acuerdas?, una con pantalla de cristal verde billar por fuera y blanco por dentro, con soporte dorado. Te incluyo un plano en papel cuadriculado y marco con una R. y una L. en rojo los lugares que ocupan esos dos viejos conocidos tuyos dentro de la habitación donde ahora paso la mayor parte de mi vida … En realidad son dos habitaciones grandes, como verás, separadas entre sí por un arco con cortina de terciopelo, que ahora está descorrida. En total cincuenta y ocho pasos de largo (los cuento cuando me paseo de un extremo a otro), y cuatro huecos a la calle. Los tres marcados con una b. son balcones, y el último de allá, con m., un mirador hermoso.

Two references to get your bearings, one based on time and the other on light. A little while ago the clock that has always been in Serrano Street, at the end of the hall, struck eleven thirty. Second reference: I'm writing you by the light of a lamp you are also familiar with. It's that table my grandfather had in his office, remember? It has a bottle-green glass screen on the outside and is white on the inside, with a golden frame. I'm including a diagram on graph paper in which I marked with a red R and L the places where these two old acquaintances of yours are located in the room where I now spend most of my life… Actually, they are two large rooms, as you can see, separated by an arch with a velvet curtain that is now drawn open. They total fifty-eight steps in length (I count them when I walk from one end to the other), and have four openings to the street. The three marked with a b are balconies, and the last one further away, with an m, is a beautiful bay window.[24]

To situate the reader by using references to the place from where
one is writing is a fundamental element in the poetics of Martín
Gaite. In one of her notes published in *El cuento de nunca acabar* and
carrying the title 'Geografía narrativa', the writer says that memories are rooted in settlement, in situational milieux – that is to say,
'el lugar es su estructura, y desde él se recoge presente también'
('place is its structure, and from there the present is also brought
together').[25] In another article belonging to the commentaries,
readings and notes that she made on narration, love and lies and
entitled *El cuento de nunca acabar*, the writer states that a sense of
direction is the most important thing for a human being, as 'al
describir el lugar, se desplega su poder de convocatoria' ('in
describing the place, their power to summon up unfolds'),[26] and
new stories subsequently arise. She adds that this sense of direction
is similar to the references to *decor* in a play. In the case of the quote
from *Nubosidad variable*, we find ourselves with two references: a
wall clock and a lamp. Both references are objects that appear on
the map via the first letter of their respective names. This process is
similar to that which the narrator of *El cuarto de atrás* employs when
she paints three elements that begin with the C. of her name, or
what Sara Allen does when she links a letter with the 'profile' of an
object, a flower or an animal.

When Mariana explains that she is drawing a room that 'en realidad son dos habitaciones grandes' ('is really two large rooms'), is
actually creating a three-dimensional space when she positions
herself in a specific place from which she describes what her gaze is
observing. In this case, Mariana is to be found 'sentada contra la
pared del fondo' ('seated against the back wall') and from the table
that is in the corner she can see the 'arco con cortina de terciopelo'
('arch with the velvet curtain') that separates the two rooms, the
total length of which is 'cincuenta y ocho pasos de largo' ('fifty-eight
steps').

The term 'drawing-story' appears in *Irse de casa*,[27] when Caroline
describes one of her drawings in the following way:

> Es un castillo para refugiarse. El río que tiene alrededor es el de las
> cosas que no se entienden, por eso lo he pintado de color marrón.
> Algunas veces crece, porque ha llovido mucho y sube el agua removida
> con barro y bichos grandes que se meten por las ventanas. Entonces
> hay que desplegar la bandera y subirse a la torre.

> It's a castle to seek refuge in. The river around it is made of things that are incomprehensible, that's why I painted it brown. It sometimes rises because it's rained a lot and the water is mixed with mud and big critters that enter from the windows. That's the time to unfurl the flag and climb up the tower.[28]

In this case, the creation the story stems from the drawing. A similar process takes place with Leonardo, the protagonist in *La reina de las nieves*, who draws Gerda and Kay – Hans Christian Andersen's character – in different ways. At times, he would place them 'separados pero mirándose y sonriéndose por la ventana; otras, sentados juntos en sus taburetes de madera, con un fondo de muchos tiestos llenos de flores' ('apart but looking at each other and smiling through the window; others, sitting together in their wooden stools, with a background of many flowerpots').[29] Leonardo says that the model for his drawings were 'las ilustraciones del libro donde venía contada aquella historia' ('the illustrations in the book where that story was told'),[30] but that 'aquella copia inicial se ramificó en múltiples variantes añadidas por (su) imaginación ('that initial copy branched out in multiple variants fueled by (his) imagination').[31] This is a similar process to that which occurred to Martín Gaite on seeing the drawings of her friend Juan Carlos Eguillor – drawings that were the basis and point of departure for Martín Gaite in writing *Caperucita en Manhattan.*

The drawing is an essential tool employed by Martín Gaite in developing her narrative. In *Lo raro es vivir*, Agueda is writing a doctoral book the title of which is 'Un aventurero del siglo XVIII y su criado'. Luis Vidal y Villalba is the name of the adventurer who, together with his servant, Juan de Edad, is suspected of having taken part in a conspiracy to secure the independence of Chile and Paraguay. The function of this research into the archives is to provide an example of a particular process in the poetics of Martín Gaite: to awaken the reader's or listener's interest by inserting a 'pista engañosa' ('red herring'). In a conversation with her husband Tomás, Agueda tells him about the development of the investigation in which she finds herself immersed. One of the relevant details is the fact that Don Luis Vidal y Villalba was prisoner in the *Cárcel Real* of a town called Las Rozas. In this place, on 13 June 1785, Don Luis handed over his belongings to the jailor. Among these items there was the 'retrato de mujer en miniatura en ovalo con el cerco de madera, dentro de una cajita también de madera' ('miniature oval portrait of a woman, with a wooden frame, inside a little wooden box').[32] Agueda says that once she had finished telling her husband 'las peripecias de aquella historia' ('the misadventures in that story'),[33] she began taking notes on what she had told him. The explanation of what was essentially historical research was transformed into a story with the potential to be a novel. There were so many enigmas to solve that it prompted one to write about them 'en forma de novela' ('in the form of a novel').[34] The enigmas or 'puntos oscuros' ('dark points')[35] are jotted down on 'papeles y fichas' ('paper and index cards')[36] and returned to later with a view to piecing together the whole story. Nevertheless, it is necessary to consult these notes not only so as to be able to tell the story but also to make a drawing in order to explain how all the events occurred. Thus, Agueda draws 'el mapa de América y el contorno de España arriba a la derecha' ('the map of America and the outline of Spain on the upper right'),[37] and affirms: 'la historia no puede entenderse sin la geografía' ('the story cannot be understood without its geography').[38]

In *Lo raro es vivir*, in addition to the drawing of maps, plans are also traced in order to get to a specific destination. Drawing maps reveals the importance of being able to conceptualise spatial relations. The most common situation in which the elaboration of maps is required is when it is necessary successfully to transmit geographical knowledge to another person, as pointed out by Yi-Fu Tuan in the chapter 'Spatial Ability, Knowledge, and Place'.[39] But is it only geographical knowledge that is transmitted? Yi-Fu Tuan focuses his study on the concept of space and place from a general and humanistic perspective in which the 'human being' is represented by the man who goes out and explores an unknown space with the objective of converting it into a place he can settle down in.

In my view, maps and plans, in addition to providing another person with geographical references, presuppose a narrative idea in that they are conceived with a particular itinerary in mind. A map is the 'memorandum de la sucesión de etapas, el trazado de un recorrido' ('memorandum of a succession of stages, the drawing of a route') as stated by Italo Calvino in 'The Traveller in the Map'.[40] In the case of Martín Gaite, the explanation of plans and maps is equivalent to writing a kind of script so as not to get lost when telling a story that has an excessive number of ramifications.[41] Each landmark is a pause, a stop, so as to order the story. Returning to our analysis of *Lo raro es vivir*, Agueda's father draws a plan so that she can visit him in his new house, located in a new urban development near Las Rozas.

> Sus dedos siempre ágiles y aquellas líneas raras que iba trazando sin prisa para ayudarme a encontrar cierto camino (se debía haber dado cuenta de que andaba sin brújula), tal vez puente o quien sabe si túnel, daba igual, todos los jeroglíficos sacan de lo estancado y estimulan la aventura solo con ponerse a entenderlos.

> His ever-nimble fingers and those strange lines he was unhurriedly drawing to help himself find a certain path (he must have realised he was without a compass), perhaps a bridge or maybe a tunnel, it didn't matter, all hieroglyphs get him out of a rut and rouse him to adventure just by attempting to understand them.[42]

The tracing of 'líneas raras' ('strange lines') becomes a map, or a 'hieroglyph', which has to be interpreted by the person looking at it. In *El cuento de nunca acabar*, Carmen Martín Gaite tells about the period in which she and her daughter would go to the park where they would meet other children who, at the beginning, were reluctant to invite strangers to take part in their games. The tactic employed by the writer was to draw or trace 'líneas raras' ('strange lines') that gradually awakened the interest of the children who then began to 'descifrar' ('decipher') them. The plot of one or various stories gradually took shape by observing the lines and the interchange of different ways of seeing and interpreting the same drawing.

The elaboration of maps and plans as visual elements that foment the creation of stories is an analogy of the processes evident in the poetics of Martín Gaite. Agueda's father draws a plan the route of which is 'opción nº 1',[43] but is crossed out because it is the main road leading to Las Rozas. That option receives the name of 'pista engañosa' ('red herring'),[44] because to go that way guarantees getting lost. That 'pista engañosa' of the map is also an element that appears 'en todos los juegos infantiles, en los cuentos de hadas, en las adivinanzas' ('in all children's games, in fairy tales, in riddles'),[45] which are likewise a *leitmotif* in the narrative of Martín Gaite. Let us recall the conversation between Agueda and Ambroise Dupont, a lecturer at the Sorbonne who had gone to Spain to research the situation of the Spanish clergy at the end of the eighteenth century. In that conservation, Agueda confesses her interest in fairy tales

and their ability to convince more than any other kind of story by
providing the possibility for characters to be transformed. Later on,
Agueda adds that the 'pista engañosa' also appears 'en las novelas
policiacas, y en la investigación judicial' ('in detective novels, and
in police investigations'),[46] which refers us to the doctoral book she
is currently working on and which is inserted as a story that, at
times, is superimposed upon the other stories of *Lo raro es vivir*.
Agueda says that 'hay varias partidas simultáneas que se juegan en
el mismo tablero (y que) nunca estamos atendiendo una sola'
('there are several simultaneous matches played in the same board
(and that) we are never just playing one').[47] This leads us to think
of the bits of mirror mentioned in *Nubosidad variable* or in the
collage technique, which consists of gradually pasting together the
fragments of different stories whose point of union ends up being
what Agueda considers 'un nudo, un cruce de vías, parada en Las
Rozas' ('a knot, a junction, a stop in Las Rozas')[48] – in other words,
a recapitulation in which several stories come together and are
superimposed one upon the other.

In this section I have pointed to the importance of drawing as a
narrative source – that is to say, as a visual element from which one
or various stories emerge to shape a short story or novel. *Caperucita
en Manhattan* is the only novel in which it is possible to find drawings made by the writer herself. I have said that to assess the quality
of the drawings does not form part of this study. I am interested in
the idea that a novel or short story is built upon the tracing of 'líneas
raras', which represent people near a window, or plans and maps
providing geographical references to get to a particular place or to
describe the place in which the narrator can be located.

In the novels of the 1990s, Martín Gaite creates characters who,
in one way or another, are linked to the drawing. In the description
of these drawings, which are not seen but read, it is possible to find
elements and actions which will turn up again in the elaboration of
the collage. For example, in *La reina de las nieves*, Leonardo draws
'paisajes irreales' ('unreal landscapes') the composition of which is
the following:

El mar invade los bosques, trepa por los edificios, anega a los habitantes estables de la zona, los desahucia. Animales antiguos con cola
de sirena o colmillos de morsa se asoman por rendijas y balcones,
barcos de guerra andan varados por las azoteas junto a tiestos de boj,
y los pasillos de los rascacielos se vuelven navegables, estallan y

vomitan cascadas de agua y barro … Algunos de los esbozos mejores los coloreo con acuarela. Y todos llevan arriba, abajo o en el centro, en forma de serpentina, bandera, nube u oleaje, fragmentos del texto de Casilda Iriarte, copiados con letra pequeña y cuidadosa entre el caos reinante.

The sea invades forests, climbs up buildings, floods the area's fixed denizens, evicting them. Ancient animals with siren tails or walrus tusks peer in through cracks and balconies, warships are left stranded in rooftops beside boxwood pots, and the corridors of skyscrapers become navigable, they blow up and vomit cascades of water and mud … I watercolour some of the best sketches. And all of them, either on top, below or in the middle, serpentine, or in the shape of a flag, a cloud or waves, fragments of Casilda Iriarte's text, copied in small, careful handwriting amid the reigning chaos.[49]

This drawing describes the method used by Martín Gaite in elaborating her collages. Notice the selection and positioning of the elements. The city invaded by the sea is that 'paisaje irreal' the destruction of which is being contemplated. The sea ceases to be inanimate and takes on life as it 'climbs up' the buildings, the ancient animals are seen reflected in the window panes, and the warships navigate up and down the corridors of the skyscrapers. It is important to highlight the use of watercolours and the insertion of fragments of a text cut-out in the form a streamer or cloud in as much as these resources are the same as those used by the writer in her collages, as well as in her novels, as we shall discuss in the following section.

I have analysed the importance of drawing as a narrative source in Martín Gaite. In *Caperucita en Manhattan*, Sara learns to read with a game of cubes, the faces of which carry letters corresponding to coloured drawings of flowers, fruits and animals. Sara manipulates the cubes, turns them this way and that, and *combines* the letters to form 'new' words such as 'Miranfú', which means 'surprise', and which she uses in those moments in which she wishes to escape the everyday. This novel is the only one that contains drawings elaborated by the writer. However, I have shown that drawings described by the characters in other novels such as *El cuarto de atrás*, *Nubosidad variable*, *La reina de las nieves*, *Lo raro es vivir* and *Irse de casa* are necessary preambles to telling the stories. The description of the drawings is full of geographical references that help to situate, in time and space, the person reading. The letter–image combination becomes the drawing–story concept. It is no longer a question of linking a letter with its image, but of telling a story based on lines traced on paper. The maps and the plans are a kind of script that helps the reader to stay on track when telling a story with many different ramifications. Note, here, the analogy between drawing a map and writing a script, with which I reintroduce the concept of the journey analysed in Chapter 2. The drawings of maps and plans serve as a guide for travellers. There are signposts, suggestions of places to visit and information on the unknown *space* that travellers have set out to explore. On their trips, they point out their routes as they go, and slowly convert unknown spaces into familiar places holding particular memories or arousing special emotions. In this way, travellers gradually create 'hitos de lugar' ('landmarks') that they represent with signals on their maps so that, at a later date, they can provide geographical references for others or tell the tale created from the itinerary traced on their map.

## Painting: from contemplation to writing

Write and contemplate, paint and perceive. Exercises in looking that are construed as aesthetic acts, where what is intelligible and what is perceivable come together in the same experience. In Martín Gaite's writing, literature is nourished and supported by painting. When looking at a painting, a story emerges. In *El punto de vista literario y visual: Hopper y Martín Gaite*, I analysed the way in which Martín Gaite establishes dialogues between painting and literature. To do this, I studied two articles published in the 1990s, in which Martín Gaite reflects on the representation of women by Dalí, Murillo, Tuset and Hopper. In that article, I showed that the approach by the writer to the paintings was that of a spectator. However, I would now add that Martín Gaite repeats and tries out her poetic proposal of writing a novel or a story starting from visual references in two essays that she wrote about these painters.

The essay called *Los incentivos de la ventana* is to be read in the context of the exhibition *El espacio privado. Cinco siglos en veinte palabras*. The aim of the exhibition was to reflect on the way in which Spanish culture uses space and fills it with images, as pointed out by Emma Martinell in the preface to the third edition of *Desde la ventana*. Carmen Martín Gaite took part in the exhibition with an essay about the function of the window, starting from its representation in pictures by the following artists: Salvador Dalí, *Figura en una finestre*; Murillo, *Dos mujeres en la ventana*; Maura Montaner, *Sin Tarea*; and Salvador Tuset, *Horas de Labor*.

The window has been a constant theme not just in Martín Gaite's literature, but also in her essays, collected in *Desde la ventana*. In that book, the writer traces the history of the feminine gaze that, for centuries, was confined to interior spaces. The window 'era un elemento tan ineludible como peligroso de transgresión' ('was as inescapable as it was dangerous as an element of transgression').[50] Luis Vives, Antonio de Guevara and Father Luis de León, among other 'tantos conspicuos varones … daban por supuesto que una mujer no podía asomarse a la ventana más que movida por un aliciente pecaminoso, para atender a los requerimientos de algún enamorado' ('conspicuous men … assumed that a woman could not lean out of a window except with a sinful purpose, to attend to the requirements of a love').[51] Further on, she continues the defence of the woman 'ventanera' – this was the adjective frequently used in classical Spanish literature, applied to frivolous women looking to enjoy themselves, who leaned out of the window in order to be seen[52] – saying that there was no idea of the woman who leaned out of the window because her soul was thirsting to leave the indoors within which it had been confined for so long. That is the soul that leads several protagonists of Martín Gaite's work, when faced with a window, to use their imagination to travel. The window, therefore, 'es el punto de enfoque, pero también el punto de partida' ('is a focus point, but also a point of departure'),[53] as it is from there that other worlds are created, that free the woman from the 'enjaulamiento que durante siglos se ha supuesto como algo inherente a un papel voluntariamente aceptado por la mujer' ('imprisonment that for centuries has been seen as something inherent in the role willingly accepted by women').[54]

Continuing her reflection of the function of the window, Martín Gaite says that interiors are the domain of the woman adjusting to the role socially imposed upon her. Therefore, it is not strange that 'toda la pintura y la literatura de interiores nos (tenga) acostumbrado al protagonismo de la mujer como alma del espacio domestic' ('all the paintings and literature about interior spaces have accustomed us to the leading role of the woman as the heart of the domestic space').[55] And, in this way, the writer accesses the interior space represented in the four paintings previously mentioned. According to the writer from Salamanca, the first thing to stand out is that, in the four paintings, 'las figuras enmarcadas por la ventana o sentadas cerca de ella son figuras femeninas' ('the figures framed by the window or sat near to it are feminine').[56] She considers that 'el recuadro liberador de una ventana, para que la mujer pueda alzar de vez en cuando los ojos a ella y descansar de sus tareas, o soñar con el mundo que se ve a lo lejos, es una referencia constante tanto en pintura como en literatura' ('the liberating presence of the window, to which the woman can occasionally raise her eyes and rest from her chores or dream of a world seen from afar, is a constant reference in painting as well as in literature').[57]

The Thyssen Bornemisza Museum was the stage on which Martín Gaite could present *El punto de vista*, a lecture in which she analysed *Hotel Room* by Edward Hopper. Her first contact with the work by the American painter was in 1980, when the Spanish author visited a retrospective that celebrated the fiftieth anniversary of the Whitney Museum in New York. That exhibition led her to making a notebook of collages as a homage to the artist who had showed her how to look not just at the interiors in American life, but also at the exteriors, where 'soledad aureolaba las gasolineras contempladas al pasar, las casas con jardín donde la dueña está a la puerta, inmóvil, con un perro, los palos de telégrafo, los edificios color salmón, los supermercados, las tiendas de segunda mano' ('loneliness emanated from the petrol stations seen in passing; the houses with gardens with the owner standing at the door, not moving, with a dog; the telephone poles, the salmon-coloured buildings, the supermarkets, the second-hand shops').[58] Some images like this, as well as some critical texts collected in the notebook of collages, were useful material for the author from the *Generación de los 50* to access the work and life of Hopper.

One element in the poetic narrative of Martín Gaite is the establishment of 'el antes y el después de las cosas que van a referirse o sobre las que se enfoca circunstancialmente nuestra atención' ('the before and the after of the things that are referred to or those that accidentally catch our attention').[59] For this, the writer considers it important to 'definir el carácter de Edward Hopper y situar el ambiente y la época en que se desenvolvió su trabajo' ('define the character of Edward Hopper and situate the role of the environment and the era in which he carried out his work'),[60] before beginning an analysis of *Hotel Room*. For Martín Gaite, the work of Hopper can be compared with that of some American authors of the same period, 'caracterizados por la mirada testimonial de quien pretende esconderse o pasar inadvertido para mirar lo que va a describir' ('characterised by the symbolic gaze of someone trying to hide or remain unnoticed in order to see what they are going to describe'),[61] given that the painter from New York does exactly the same: 'fisgar apasionadamente, unas veces desde dentro y otras desde fuera' ('passionately spying, sometimes from inside and others from out').[62] Thus the window is one of the most important elements in his paintings. Martín Gaite considers that the main theme of Hopper's work is 'la mujer en un interior con fondo de ventana' ('the woman indoors with a window in the background')[63] – also a favourite theme of Vermeer, another one of the artists linked to Martín Gaite's writing.

In his article *Amistades de ida y vuelta a través del texto*, Juan Senís Fernández reflects that reading the work of Carmen Martín Gaite provides 'un caudal de sugerencias, citas, influencias y deudas que conduce a otros textos' ('a flow of suggestions, quotes, influences and doubts that lead to other texts').[64] Some of these literary reso-nances are related to Primo Levi or Natalia Ginzburg, for example. Other links are established between Martín Gaite, Vermeer and Hopper. According to Senís Fernández, all three base their work 'en la poética del espacio que se extiende y se trasciende desde un rincón mínimo e íntimo, desde una simple habitación poblada por figuras que están muy lejos de la heroicidad convencional. Es, en definitiva, una estética de la aparente insignificancia' ('on the poetics of the space that extends from and transcends the smallest and most intimate corner, from a simple room full of figures very far from conventional heroism. It is, ultimately, an aesthetic of the seemingly insignificant').[65] This is exemplified, for Senís Fernández, in *Retahílas* and *El cuarto de atrás*, where 'el espacio en que se sitúa a los personajes es reducido e interior, pero la palabra y la memoria lo llenan de emoción y recuerdos ' ('the space in which the charac-ters find themselves is reduced and indoors, but words and memories fill it with emotions and reminiscences').[66] Likewise, Vermeer and Hopper reflect 'los matices psicológicos en un gesto mínimo y certero, de un lado, y las gamas de luces, sombras y colores, de otro, para ubicar a sus personajes en clara ligazón con el ambiente' ('the psychological nuances of a minimal and distinct gesture on one side, and the array of light, shade and colour on the other, in order to give their characters a clear link with their environment').[67] Further on, Senís Fernández says that, on the one hand, we can imagine Mariana in *Nubosidad vairable* as one of the women in Hopper's hotels, sat next to the window, trying to fill their loneliness and uneasiness with the light of some southern beach. On the other hand, in *El cuarto de atrás* there is a Vermeerian atmosphere in the black and white squares of the floor and the semi drawn red curtain in the corridor. Juan Senís Fernández concludes with a comparison between Hopper and Vermeer: the first is a master of painting the disconnect between man and his surroundings, while the latter concentrates on the complicity between his characters and the space that they occupy.

*Hotel Room* impressed Martín Gaite so much that it led her to invent a story about 'la mujer recién llegada a la habitación de un hotel desconocido' ('the woman recently arrived in a room in an unknown hotel'),[68] and it was also the starting point for her poem *Todo es un cuento roto en Nueva York* in which 'una mujer inconcreta, buscada acaso por la policía y que va convirtiéndose en otra a lo largo del poema, acaba refugiándose en un cuadro del Museo Whitney, se sienta en la cama de una pensión anónima y ya no espera nada' ('an unspecified woman, who is perhaps wanted by the police and changing into someone else over the length of the poem, ends up hiding in a picture at the Whitney Museum, sitting on a bed in an anonymous bed and breakfast and no longer waiting for anything').[69] For Carmen Martín Gaite, a painting is already a novel in itself, as she writes in reference to *Hotel Room*. She adds that not only in this painting, but in all of Hopper's work, 'los seres sugieren escenas anteriores y posteriores a ese momento en el que reposan, esperan, leen, piensan o están en tensión' ('the people suggest previous and upcoming scenes to this moment where they rest, wait, read, think or tense up').[70] According to Martín Gaite, 'ese proceso de establecer un antes y un después de una escena determinada es lo que caracteriza el desarrollo de la novella' ('that process of establishing a before and an after of a particular scene is what characterises the development of a novel').[71]

Carmen Martín Gaite believes that 'nadie sea capaz de mirarlo (el cuadro) sin imaginar casi inmediatamente el antes y el después de esa mujer sentada en la cama de un cuarto que no es el suyo, anónimo, sin recuerdos, descarnado de cualquier adorno que pueda dar pie a la fantasía' ('no one is able to look at (the painting) without almost immediately imaging a before and an after of that woman sat on the bed in a room that is not her own, anonymous, without memories, striped of any adornment that could give rise to fantasy').[72] The contemplation of the painting leads us to pose various questions about the women. Those questions are the starting point for the elaboration of many of the stories that can change depending on the position of the person observing, as well as the person narrating. Martín Gaite views that painting from outside and says that in *Hotel Room* 'pesa tanto lo que se ve como lo que no se ve, todo eso que no se cuenta, pero que se ofrece como enigma a descifrar' ('what you do not see is as important as what you do, all that is not told, but is offered like an enigma to decode').[73] For her, the paper that the woman has in her hands is this enigma that allows for the creation of stories about its possible content. Martín Gaite comments that, after having viewed the painting on several occasions, she thought that the woman was holding a letter. However, after having carried out some investigations, she found out through some notes written by Josephine Nivison, Hopper's wife, that the yellow paper is a train timetable. Faced with this information, Martín Gaite says: 'He mirado bien. He aprendido a mirar como Hopper me enseñó.' ('I have viewed it correctly. I have learnt to view like Hopper taught me.')[74] For Carmen Martín Gaite, the women in *Hotel Room* is 'un ser humano acosado por sí mismo, por sus equivocaciones y tropiezos, cuyo deseo es escapar cuanto antes de donde está. ¿Escapar por qué y hacia dónde? ¿De qué pasado?' ('a human being pursued by herself, by her mistakes and blunders, whose desire is to escape from where she is as soon as possible. Why escape and where to? From what past?')[75] asks the writer. In these questions, Martín Gaite concludes, lies 'el germen de las muchas novelas posibles que sugiere la contemplación de este admirable cuadro' ('the seed of many possible novels that the contemplation of this admirable painting suggests').[76]

In these two essays – *Los incentivos de la ventana* and *El punto de vista* – the link between painting and literature is established. This link can also be seen in Martín Gaite's fiction. The novels of the 1990s can be read as a journey through the history of art, stopping, it is worth mentioning, in specific periods such as the Italian Trecento, German Romanticism and Surrealism. Martín Gaite establishes a relation between literature and painting by introducing, literally, some paintings over the course of her literary narratives. The introduction of a painting – described or interpreted by the voice or gaze of the narrator or of a character – changes the meaning of the story that is narrated and thereby, more generally, of the whole literary work. In other words, the literal presence of a painting in the narration produces a twist that impacts on the meaning of the painting that is spoken about as well as the text in which it appears. For Enric Bou, this wealth in the production of the meaning of the literary text is due to the use of a characteristic rhetorical image in descriptions: an *ekphrasis* that indicates 'la reproducción mediante palabras de un modelo o referencia visual' ('the reproduction in words of a visual model or reference').[77] In the novels of Martín Gaite, this practice can usually be found in references or allusions that the narrator or characters make regarding a pictorial work. In this way, the object is incorporated into the narration through a process of description that frequently only tries to present a textual version. In Martín Gaite's narration the use of *ekphrasis* proposes a change in the direction of meaning, which is explained through a series of transformations carried out through the voice and gaze of the narrator. This gaze of the narrator has added weight to the meaning of the painting by its introduction in the verbal context.

In *Lo raro es vivir*, a textual space in which Martín Gaite's two aesthetic interests overwhelmingly converge is created – on one side literature, and on the other painting. Águeda Luengo, the protagonist and narrator, unravels several stories about life and death. This theme is repeated throughout the novel in the various intertwined stories. One of these refers to Águeda's evocation of Rosaria Tena, the glasses-wearing teacher, with whom she passes through the history of art, focusing on the painters of the Italian Trecento: Giotto, Ambrogio, Lorenzetti, Orcagna and Leonardo da Vinci. On their journey, the pictures are explored by themes rather than following a chronological sequence, as in the Italian Trecento 'todo se superpone, es un periodo de mucho fermento, de historias que fluyen sin cesar y sin cesar mezclan sus aguas' ('everything overlaps, it is a period of great ferment, of stories that flow without stopping, and never cease to mix their waters'),[78] according to Rosario Tena. She also adds that, in the pictures they see, the themes of *The Divine Comedy* frequently appear – for example: 'ascensión y caída, levitación y abismo, miedo y coraje, y siempre la amenaza de la muerte rondando como un cortejo invisible a la vida' ('ascension and fall, levitation and the abyss, fear and courage, and always the threat of death circling like the invisible crust of life'),[79] or, in other moments, 'las tropas de la vida acosan el castillo de la muerte' ('the troops of life harry the castle of death').[80]

Reading Carmen Martín Gaite's work provides a flow of suggestions, references, influences and doubts that lead to other texts. Some of those literary resonances are related to writers such as Primo Levi or Natalia Ginzburg, for example. Other established links emerge with painters like Hopper and Vermeer, who form part of the imaginary museum of Martín Gaite. The concept of the imaginary museum is the evocation of paintings through *ekphrasis*.

The imaginary museum of Martín Gaite can be seen through her novels, as she draws upon specific paintings that 'illustrate' narrative sections. In *Nubosidad variable*, the main scenario, which consists of leaving home as a way of breaking family and social ties, is reinforced with Remedios Varo's painting 'Rompiendo el circulo vicioso'. In the painting, a woman, with huge eyes that stare as though she were in a trance, gathers all her strength to break that rope that binds her body. Her hair is standing on end, as she has been electrified by the force of what she has done, and, upon breaking the 'vicious circle', a dense green wood appears in her chest, the deep home of her subconscious, now made accessible. In *Nubosidad variable*, *ekphrasis* appears in the following way:

> Abrí la puerta con todo sigilo y me deslicé de puntillas escalera abajo … Y cuando salí, con mi maleta en la mano, no me atrevía a mirar para atrás … Era aún casi de noche, y oyendo resonar mis pasos en la calle desierta, camino de la estación, me acordé de un cuadro de Remedios Varo que se titula 'Rompiendo el círculo vicioso' y representa a una mujer que lleva dentro del pecho un bosque rodeado de alambradas. Nada me consuela tanto en este momento, Sofía, como pensar que puedas conocer ese cuadro.

> I very carefully opened the door and slipped on tiptoes down the stairs … And when I left, with my bag in my hand, I did not dare look back … It was still almost night-time, and hearing my footsteps echo in the deserted street on the way to the station, I remembered the painting by Remedios Varo called *Rompiendo el circulo vicioso*, that showed a woman with a forest in her chest surrounded by barbed wire. Nothing consoles me more right now, Sofia, than the thought that you might see this painting.[81]

The use of *ekphrasis* in literary texts is usually found in references and allusions that the narrator or characters make regarding a pictorial work, as in the case of the section quoted above. In this way, the object it incorporated into the narrative through a process of description that generally only tries to show a textual version. This type of *ekphrasis* becomes an invitation to the viewer to compare the pictorial object with its textual description. However, in the section above the use of *ekphrasis* proposes a change in the direction of meaning, explained through some transformations that take place in the narrator and person she is talking with. Both have decided to break the 'vicious circle' that they are living in.

In *La reina de las nieves*, Martín Gaite alludes to Caspar Friedich's *Wanderer above a Sea of Fog* in a similar way as Dalí's *La persistencia de la memoria* in *Nubosidad variable*. In this case, Casilda Iriarte, a fictitious character, writes *Ensayos sobre el vertigo*, the cover of which is Friedrich's painting. Unlike *Nubosidad variable*, there is not a chapter with the same name as the painting, but the person with his back to us in the picture becomes a character in the novel, and is also seen in Leonardo's drawings.

*La reina de las nieves* also has Romantic elements. Vertigo, according to Casilda Iriarte, is the confusion of the Romantic hero, infected by nature's excesses, but at the same time able to take in these phenomena.[82] Night, the sea, a storm or love are all inexplicable phenomena, inexpressible for the Romantic hero. Casilda says that pleasure lies in the transient, the ethereal, in enjoying the moment that the waves break, or even the moment that day gives way to night or vice versa, but as if everything were seen in a picture, because neither the sea, the night, the storm, nor love can fit into a space, no matter how big we imagine it, because they are phenomena that cannot be confined.

Leonardo and Casilda share literary affinities, as well as having the same opinions about the German painter Friedrich's work. They both believe that he 'sí supo recoger en sus pinturas esas ansias de infinito que inculca la naturaleza desatada en las figuras como temerosas que contemplan la escena y la padecen, de espaldas a nosotros casi siempre' ('knew how to arrange in his pictures those fears of the infinite that untamed nature instils into the timorous figures, both contemplating and suffering the scene, almost always with their back to us').[83] And as Friedrich captures the figures with their back turned, contemplating an infinite landscape, so Carmen

Martín Gaite constructs a space in which her characters are positioned with their backs to the spectator, while also sharing other characteristics in tone, colour and composition.

In *La reina de la nieves* and *Lo raro es vivir* the references to colour, the positioning of characters in space, and the detailed description of places, among other aspects, produce an effect of plasticity in the literary tale. *Lo raro es vivir* is a novel where the themes of life and death are intertwined not just in the story of the two Aguedas – mother and daughter – but also in that of all of the characters that gradually appear as though drawn slowly onto a canvas. Mother Agueda is a famous painter whose student is Rosario Tena, in turn the substitute teacher of history of art of Agueda, the daughter. One of the 'accessory' characters, the teacher at the Sorbonne, says to Agueda (daughter) 'nos pasamos la vida decidiendo, por mucho que nos agobie decidir, ésa es nuestra condena, la sed de infinitud chocando contra los barrotes de la jaula' ('we spend our life deciding, as much as deciding weighs us down. This is our sentence, the thirst for eternity, knocking against the bars of our cage').[84] In this novel, there are some moments in which the characters try to explain – either to themselves or to others – the aesthetic experience that defines the contemplation of different paintings. Rosario Tena projects some frescos from the Campo Santo in Pisa attributed to Orcagna and 'se limitaba a hacer breves comentarios, a medida que iba ampliando detalles significativos e insignificantes, como si explorase uno por uno los rincones de una habitación. Todo con mucha lentitud, para que se nos quedara grabado en la retina, que en eso consistía – dijo – el placer de la contemplación' ('confined herself to brief comments, while expanding on significant and insignificant details, as though she were exploring the corners of a room one by one. All very slowly, so that is would remain etched on our retina. It is of this, she said, that the pleasure of contemplation is made').[85] Take note here of the analogy between the visual journey through the painting that is undertaken and that of exploring the corners of a room. The interior geography is equated with the imaginary museum of the characters and of the writer herself.

In Martín Gaite's writing, a painting cannot be seen, understood or appreciated in the same way before and after its appearance in the textual context. The visual object – whether it be a painting or a collage – adds new meanings to and intensifies the plastic dimension of the literary work. The gaze of the writer pauses for an instant on those fleeting images where fragments of her life interweave with or superimpose themselves upon her reflections about her own process of writing. It is a writing full of visual references, because, according to the main character in *Lo raro es vivir*, 'para contar un cuento se necesita un dibujo' ('in order to tell a story, you need a picture').[86] The gaze of Martín Gaite pass through an urban geography and gives testimony of this journey in her *Visión de Nueva York* collages.

## The artistic strategies of collage

In Chapter 2 I have shown that Martín Gaite used collage techniques in the elaboration of *El cuento de nunca acabar*, her first book of reflections on writing. The technique of collage, understood, explained and used by the writer, consists of a series of actions, needing a notebook, a typewriter to write up notes to another type of paper, scissors for cutting up the notes that have been typed up, a reorganisation and classification of these written materials, and another notebook with which to stick and order all of the previously mixed-up ideas. The series of actions can be reduced to simply compiling material, cutting, organising and sticking. However, Martín Gaite builds a series of actions through which she develops her narrative techniques, which are also reflected in the making of her collages.

I believe that this journey is the backbone of Martín Gaite's poetics. As the writer says, a story is born in the moment that the narrator begins to tell about the arrival or exit of the characters, who are usually women. Julia in *Entre visillos* leaves for Madrid; Sofia Montalvo and Mariana León escape their respective family home and work commitments; Amparo Miranda quits Spain to move to New York, but after several years decides to return to the land of her birth. A similar situation happens with Pablo Klein – a character in *Entre visillos* – who travels to a provincial city where he spent his childhood, in order to relive the past that he spent with his father. Not to mention Leonardo in *La reina de las nieves*, whose confusion starts upon leaving jail. His stay at his father's house serves as a form of preparation for the journey into his past that he will have to take, as represented by the Quinta Blanca.

In Martín Gaite's poetics, travelling is closely linked with the idea of the journey, roving, rambling, strolling and exploring. All of these actions are a constant in her narratives, and are carried out in different ways. For example, you stroll around a town, down dead ends, around the cityscape; your rove around a room with your eyes, down side streets, around gardens and fences, around objects; you explore the city, pot plants or an object; a journey is not just physical, but can also take place by looking from one wall to the other.

All of these series of actions relate to movement, which is something that Martín Gaite translates to other areas of her poetics. For example, the action of strolling around an urban landscape is converted into the feat of wondering, meditating, reflecting, thinking. And remember, in *Nubosidad viable*, Sofia says that 'Pensar es ir saltando de una habitación a otra [por] habitaciones que se dislocan, bifurcan e intercambian volúmenes y adornos cuando surgen en los sueños' ('To think is to jump from one room to another [through] rooms that shift, split, swap sizes and decorations when they appear in dreams').[87] From my point of view, this quote is a metaphor for the relevance of memory in Martín Gaite's work. Her characters are generally sunken in their thoughts as they try to order the events of the past. Rooms are the space *par excellence* in which to deposit their memories. This is where the importance and imperious need to describe the place where the characters are writing a letter or their diary comes from. There is a focus on the description of objects so that these can serve as reference points, or 'hitos de lugar' as Martín Gaite called them. So far, I have demonstrated how a series of different actions are brought together in Martín Gaite's narrative production. The key point now is to show how these actions are used in the elaboration of collages. From my point of view, movement in collage is achieved through the use of the overlapping, juxtaposition or interlinking of images or cut-outs of various materials. In this way, we can see layers of faces, texts, dates and advertisements in the collages. References to time and place are juxtaposed.

Carmen Martín Gaite accumulated collages after her first visit to New York in 1980. Some of these collages left the private space of her 'notebooks about everything' and were published in 2005, entitled *Visión de Nueva York*. In this book, the collages are presented in chronological order. They deal with the period from September

1980 until January 1981. That point in time takes us back to a series of events in the writer's life. One of these is the process of writing *El cuento de nunca acabar*, a key text in her poetics that she finished in New York.

According to a letter written by Martín Gaite to her friend Ignacio Álvarez and published in the first pages of the book, *Visión de Nueva York* came about as a homage to Edward Hopper. In 1980, the writer started her notebook of collages with one called *Vision of New York*. Elide Pitarello carries out an analysis of this collage. To do this, she reproduces with words the visual references, in which the use of the photography of Hopper, as well as his paintings *Approaching the City* (1946) and *Early Sunday Morning* (1930), stands out. The homage to Hopper is also seen in the hominine collage made by Martín Gaite on 28 September 1980 and published in *Visión de Nueva York*. The collage, over two pages, is made up of different materials: cut-outs from newspapers, cut-outs from reproductions of the painter's work – again, *Early Sunday Morning*, but cut into two segments. In between the two pieces of the image, the writer placed a reproduction of another painting, *Automat* (1927); we can also see hand-written annotations by the writer – a constant presence in her collages. This fragment of text shows us a section belonging to a diary, as it says in the first person, 'Hago este collage el 28 de septiembre de 1980' ('I am making this collage on 28 September 1980').[88]

Writing – on the one side – and the making of collages – on the other – deploy a hidden or explicit dialogue with other texts, discourses and fragments, which they interweave and assimilate. The technique of collage allows us to bring together a number of pre-existing sections from other texts and integrate them into an artefact, with the aim of producing a new text that shows the differences and similarities as representation of its meaning. After visiting the Whitney Museum, Martín Gaite sees the world as though it were another painting. This is why she says that, in New York, images are quicker than words. However, the adoption of pictorial themes or the references to different painters (Vermeer, Remedios Varo or Hopper, to give some examples) is not just simple intertextuality, but also has a more complex meaning. There is a first, elemental level of *ekphrasis*, the literary description of a work of art, but at a second level there is the contribution of diverse intertexts that complicate the perception of the lecture that she writes about *Hotel*

*Room* (1931), and carries out an *ekphrasis* at several levels: she recomposes the diverse sections that are evoked, and combines them with her experience as a visitor to the museum as well as with multiple literary references and her own voice represented in first person, as seen in some of the fragments in some collages. With all of this she creates a picture, collage or new text. The reader is left with the recomposition and interpretation.

In *Collages and Narrative in Carmen Martín Gaite*, I identify and classify the textual and visual materials used by the writer in her collages. The collages that I analysed were among those published as book covers. This is the case with *La búsqueda de interlocutor y otras búsquedas* (1982), *Nubosidad variable* (1992) and *Agua pasada* (1993). In this artistic process of making collages, Martín Gaite also tries out her poetics. The writer creates a series of actions, such as sticking, bringing together, sewing and assembling, that are not exclusive to collages, but also recall her process of writing. The scraps, the snippets, the fragments, the splinters of mirrors are the warp and weft that Martín Gaite uses with her threads to form either a novel or a collage. In *Collages and Narrative in Carmen Martín Gaite*, I analysed in detail the collage *Retahíla con nieve en Nueva York*, dated 17 November 1980, as it allows visuals and texts to interweave and present semantic and pragmatic juxtapositions (see Figure 1).

Figure 1: *Retahíla con nieve en Nueva York*

The first juxtaposition of meaning is closely linked to the article *Retahíla con nieve en Nueva York* that headed up the lectures collected in *Fiction to Metafiction*. Martín Gaite wrote it in 1980 while she was a writer in residence at Barnard College, teaching a semester on literary theory. The second semantic juxtaposition is the *Retahíla neoyorkina* written two years later – in 1982, to be specific – and published in *Cuaderno 28* of the *Cuadernos de todo* series. If the previous 'retahíla' – a succession of events, names, actions – is made up of the narration of past and present events in the life of the author, this 'retahíla' is made up by the gaze. In *Cuaderno 28*, Martín Gaite notes the fragmented images of New York that she sees from her apartment window. From her strategic position, the writer notes down what she is looking at and the memories that are brought up by the spectacle in front of her eyes. For example, she looks at the inside of the rooms where people have their television as sole company, and that image leads her to remember her strolls around the streets of New York. The 'retahíla' of images grows as the writer compares everything that she observes from her window with the paintings of Hopper – paintings that, she believes, she comes across in each of her routes around the city. In one of them, Martín Gaite travels by bus with other women, who perhaps are going to 'meterse a un piso prestado y a sacarle calor a esos objetos, a esa llave, a esa cama donde no dormirán' ('go into a rented flat and get warmth from those objects, from that key, from that bed where they won't sleep'),[89] as though they were the unsettled woman in Hopper's *Hotel Room*.

From my point of view, this series of juxtapositions leads us to a more precise reflection about how the mechanism of repetition presents a tension in the constitution of identity. The theme of searching for an interlocutor, for example, is a topic that is associated with repetition, refraction or duplicity. By repeating *Retahíla de nieve en Nueva York*, Martín Gaite puts to the test her own writing process. I believe that these repetitions reveal a dynamic in this writing. This interplay between writing and making collages – between the visual and the literary – therefore becomes a key point in testing and searching for the text's originality. Repetition is made significant through this testing: the poetics of Martín Gaite are tested, sought and found through the artistic production of her collages and novels. In this exercise of visual and textual 'retahílas', the juxtaposition of multiple parts that is characteristic of the collage technique is recognisable. Martín Gaite superimposes a great variety of discursive features and practices – her collage is interlinked with her article and, later, with the fragment of one of her 'notebooks about everything'. The interesting thing about all of this juxtaposition between texts is the repetition seen in the permanent confrontation of time and memory.

Another collage in which Martín Gaite condenses and superimposes different discourses is the one that is the title page of the section *Fragmentos inéditos y notas fugaces* in *Cuadernos de todo* in 2002. Three years later, it was published in *Visión de Nueva York*. This collage contains various elements of Martín Gaite's poetics. I believe that the title of the collage comes from three cut-outs that appear in its centre. Put together, they read: 'La visión de lo cotidiano en la narrativa femenina' (The vision of the day-to-day in the feminine narrative) (see Figure 2).

In the background, there is a woman with her back to the viewer as she is looking with interest at what is happening outside of her window. In the top left corner, a family made up of a man, woman and child can be seen in the distance. The three are in a kind of room the depth of which means that they appear to be very far from the gaze of the woman alone at her window. Next to the family, on the left side of the collage, can be seen the handwriting of Martín

Figure 2: *La visión de lo cotidiano en la narrativa a femenina*

Gaite, who has written: 'A espaldas de los hombres y de sus pretenciosos pedestales, la mujer "ventanera" siempre ha sabido observar por su cuenta, escaparse de lo interior a lo exterior y meter dentro lo de fuera, a su modo, sin ruido ni alharacas' ('With her back to men and their pretentious pedestals, the woman in the window has always known how to observe for herself, to escape from what is inside to what is outside and to take in what is out there, in her own way, without fuss or scandal'). The collage has other cut-out and stuck-down images; however, I focus on the three elements mentioned thus far: the possible title (the vision of the day-to-day in the feminine narrative); the woman in the window; and Martín Gaite's reflection about this 'ventanera'. It is in these that we find the underlying concerns of all of the writer's work. Everything to do with the feminine gaze is written down; the woman writes from the daily spaces that have been assigned to her, and her imagination takes flight, escaping from the everyday of her life.

As well as reflecting on the lot of women in Spanish society, Martín Gaite also gave some lectures on the feminine point of view in literature. *Cuaderno 34* in her *Cuadernos de todos* series, which contains various written material from a certain time in 1984, presents segments of a paper entitled *El punto de vista femenino en la literatura*. In this text, Martín Gaite looks at how the image of woman was represented in the nineteenth-century novel, and reflects upon what were 'los sueños reales de libertad' ('the real dreams of freedom')[90] of women. She states that 'la mujer de la novela rosa no refleja ninguna de las íntimas perplejidades de la mujer de carne y hueso, ni sus anhelos indefinibles' ('the woman in the romantic novel does not reflect any of the intimate perplexities of the flesh and bone woman, nor her indefinable yearnings').[91] As well as looking at the representation in romantic novels and the nineteenth-century novel, Martín Gaite also brings the roles of the reader and the writer to the fore. If we apply this representation of women to her own writing in the 1990s, we realise that her main characters are artists: painters, writers, fashion designers. They are all constantly moving, and they travel around different geographies. They are travellers, who make their own way and whose gazes take in interior spaces but who also dream of the world bubbling away outside. They do not just remain content with this dream, but take the decision to literally leave home, just as Martín Gaite did in the 1980s when she took several trips around the United States.

The reflections about the feminine point of view are crystallised in several of her works, as in the case of *La mujer en la literatura*, published in *Pido la palabra*. In this article, Martín Gaite questions what type of woman is referred to when we talk of 'the woman' in literature. Is it that of the 'imágenes femeninas' ('feminine images')[92] that have been created and put into use by literature over the ages? Martin Gaite refers to the 'feminine images' of 'angel' or 'demon' that Sandra Gilbert and Susan Gubar develop in *The Madwoman in the Attic*. Or maybe, when talking about woman in literature, we perhaps mean the female reader and/or writer? Could there be a mix of the 'feminine images' with that of the female reader and writer? Reading Martín Gaite's works gives several answers to this questioning of the role of women in literature. In her essays, novels and collages, female characters are generally found to be writers (*El cuarto de atrás*), or painters (*Lo raro es vivir*), to give some examples, through whom Martín Gaite proposes different ways of looking at things.

In *La mirada de escritor*, published in *Pido la palabra*, Carmen Martín Gaite sees literature 'como escondite, como acceso a un tabernáculo prohibido' ('as a hiding place, as access to a forbidden trove').[93] She makes particular reference to *Retahílas*, and the passage in which Eulalia is reading a novel and her grandmother says that she pulls the face of a madwoman when she reads. For Eulalia, 'leer se convirtió progresivamente en tarea secreta y solitaria (…) leer era acceder a un terreno en el que se ingresaba con esfuerzo, emoción y destreza, terreno amenazado y siempre a conquistar, a reinventar y defender(…) la puerta de ingreso a este recinto, además de secreta debía ser empujada preferentemente de noche' ('reading progressively became a secret and solitary task (…) reading meant to enter a terrain which was accessed through force, emotion and distress, a threatened terrain, always to be conquered, reinvented and defended (…) the entry door to this zone, as well as being secret, should be preferably opened at night').[94] The hiding place is the place where fantasies are cultivated, as the main character in *El cuarto de atrás* says. You can watch from inside them, or sometimes, you can leave them and watch from outside. This is the case with David Fuente, the character in *Ritmo lento*, or with Sorpresa, the girl in *El pastel del diablo*. For Martín Gaite, 'lo mirado desde fuera tiene siempre un halo de prestigio' (what is seen from outside always has a glow of prestige).[95] Many stories, whose mysteries we always decipher, come out of what we see, and when we manage to distance ourselves from them, we watch them from outside.

The poetics of Martín Gaite centre on the gaze, as, according to her, the role of the novelist is to 'urdir historias a partir de datos fragmentarios' ('weave stories from fragmented details'),[96] that are collected through the gaze. For the writer, the outcome of the story depends on what the gaze encompasses and from where. This 'from where', she says, 'tiene mucho que ver con el 'punto de vista' (has a lot to do with the 'point of view').[97] The gaze can be from inside to outside, or from outside to inside. She believes that 'ambas miradas se complementan' ('both gazes complement each other').[98] In an analysis of her own work 'Reflexiones sobre mi obra', she states that, in *El balneario,* 'ya se entrecruzan estas dos miradas o puntos de vista' ('the two gazes and points of views had already interweaved').[99] In the first part, narrated in the first person, the main character is in a place unknown to her, which she observes from the window of her room. In the second part, narrated in the third person, Martín Gaite tells how the same character 'deja resbalar su mirada sobre el decorado archiconocido del balneario' ('lets her gaze dwell on the famous décor of the spa'). She adds that 'la mirada del intruso, del curioso, del detective, ha sido reemplazada por una mirada acostumbrada a lo que ve' ('the gaze of the outsider, the curious, the detective, has been replaced with the gaze of one accustomed to what they see').[100]

The basis of literature, Martín Gaite says, is 'la mirada distanciada ante todo aquello que provoca extrañeza' ('the detached gaze at all that causes strangeness').[101] Primarily, this gaze is presented through a stranger, who 'llega a un lugar que no conoce y trata de orientarse en él y de entender el comportamiento de sus habitantes' ('arrives in a place that they do not know and tries to orientate themselves in it and understand the behaviour of its inhabitants').[102] This is the voice of the 'intruso' ('outsider'),[103] which tells of what they have merely witnessed or have been a part of due to pure curiosity. These are novels of the witness, such as Pablo Klein in *Entre visillos,* Luisa in *Fragmentos de interior,* and, later on, Amparo Miranda in *Irse de Casa.*[104] To this gaze of the stranger, the outsider or the witness, Martín Gaite adds that 'la mirada aletargada del escritor se apuntala y complementa con la de ese 'otro' que le nace dentro y que ve las mismas cosas que él pero desde otro ángulo' ('the torpid gaze of the writer is sharpened and comple-mented by that of this 'other', which is born within it and that sees the same things, but from a different angle').[105] This, according to the writer, is 'el origen del desdoblamiento literario' ('the origin of literary refraction').[106] In this subtle web of borrowed, refracted, repeated and superimposed identities, Martín Gaite concludes her inventory with the works of painters like Hopper and Vermeer, as can be seen in another section of this book.

Martín Gaite's gaze upon herself can be seen in the collage on the cover of *Agua pasada*, made in 1992 (see Figure 3).

Figure 3: Cover of *Agua pasada*

There is a photograph of the writer sitting behind a table on which there are sheets of paper, a bottle of water, a glass and a sign that reads 'cosa por cosa' ('one at a time'). This phrase links the collage immediately with a segment from *Cuaderno 36*, also dated 1982. In this segment, the writer reflects on the workings of memory and indicates the importance of adjusting, one at a time, to daily events, to prevent these from becoming so tangled that they cannot be separated. It is also important to point out that the sign in the collage would become the title of an article by Martín Gaite published in *la Vanguardia* in 1994, according to María Vittoria Calvi's note in *Cuadernos de todo*.[107] Continuing with the analysis of the collage, the writer has her bag on the table and is looking for something. On her forehead is the word 'memoria' ('memory'). A comic-like speech bubble is coming out of her mouth, with the word 'así' ('thus'). On her throat is another speech bubble, with the word 'estímulos' ('stimuli'). If we carefully examine the cut-outs of text to the far right of the collage, we can see that it belongs to an article entitled *Un aviso: ha muerto Ignacio Aldecoa*, written by Martín Gaite in November 1969. There is also a cut-out on which we see written 'Women's Studies (Thompson Hall)', which takes us back to the time at which Martín Gaite lived in the United States. In the upper far right of the collage, there is an air mail sticker, written in red letters in English, French and Spanish. On the left corner of this sticker, we can make out a sign in capital letters that reads 'IMPORTANT!'. On the far left, starting from the centre, we can see in the background a cut-out that could be from a newspaper. This cut-out is bigger than those from the article about Aldecoa, but some of it is illegible, as it has faded to a yellowy brown in some places. Over these parts there are some dark brown cut-outs in the shape of drops of water, with white lines. On this background. we also find two signs. One, in between the water drop-shaped pieces, reads 'Nunca desde entonces' ('Never since then'). The other is almost on Martín Gaite's arm, and says 'dejados de la mano de Dios y detrás' ('left behind by the hand of God'). In the bottom left-hand corner, there is an open notebook, with a page and a half of writing, while, on the other half a page, it seems as though there are some cut-outs of text and a ladybird. Between the notebook and the table there are some words in a circle, with a blue border and seemingly written with a coloured pencil. Next to these we see a pink cut-out in the shape of a crescent moon. At the bottom of the collage, under the feet of the writer, there are four white cushions. On one of them we can make out the initials 'CMG' and the year '92'. The upper left side has a crucifix made from the dried branches of a tree. Some white flowers and a pocket watch hang from it. All of the images in the collage come from different stages in the writer's life. The reappearance of snippets about Ignacio Aldecoa take us back to the time at which Martín Gaite had just started to write, alongside other authors of her generation, as mentioned Chapter 1. The notebook that appears in the bottom right of the collage is an example of her *Cuadernos de todos*, in which she mixed images and drawings with words.

This collage that illustrated the front cover of *Agua pasada* was later published in *Visión de Nueva York*. In fact, it is the first collage in the book. Its relevance is confirmed when the reader–viewer looks at the title it is given: *Collage autorretrato (1982) de Carmen Martín Gaite* (*Self-portrait collage (1982) of Carmen Martín Gaite*). In this collage, there is a recollection of parts, segments and moments in the life of the author. There is a fascination with fragmented images. The self-portrait collage shows the fragmentation in the apprehension of the concept of the 'individual'. In this case, the writer represents herself in a range of situations, emotions, ideas, etc. This collage invites us to partake in a small private journey through time and the feelings that each segment draws upon for the viewers. In this self-portrait, there is an inclination to stop and try to order, 'one at a time', countless impressions, traces of found things that form the writer's intimate landscape. If an autobiography is a retrospective story in prose that a real person writes about their own existence according to Philippe Lejeune, in a self-portrait collage it is the positioning of fragments of images that defines the autobiographical function – that is to say, the gaze wanders and settles on certain landmarks in place and time.

These collages in *Visión de Nueva York* function as a journey because it involves us in a process of passing from one part to another. We travel with Martín Gaite through those first years of the 1980s. A change, spatial, temporal, sociological and personal, occurs along the way. There is a continuous reflection on the theme of time and its fleeting nature. In 'Martín Gaite's *Visión de Nueva York*: Collages of Public and Private Space', Debra Ochoa deems it necessary to determine whether *Visión de Nueva York* is a diary or an autobiography. In the first instance, she states that it could be classified as part of the 'genre of the I',[108] as it deals with a private tale. However, later on, she prefers to adopt the concept of 'diary writings diverse in quality and style';[109] she takes this concept from Granata de Egües, one of the first people to analyse *Visión de Nueva York*. The analysis of the collages carried out by Debra Ochoa explores the representation of private space – the house – and the presence of women in an urban space.

From my point of view, *Visión de Nueva York* is a gaze that takes place in the urban space, but with juxtapositions with private, everyday, intimate and caring spaces. With this, Martín Gaite calls upon different resources to shape a universe and a voice that evoke an 'I'. The collages analysed in this book are only a small example of how Martín Gaite's poetics deal with the fractures in different texts, such as autobiography, diaries, travel journals, essays, to name a few, and her own processes as an artist.

The trips that Martín Gaite made to New York over several years are a central experience in the composition of her novels in the 1990s, as well as of her collages. There are a series of juxtapositions by which we can perceive of *El cuento de nunca acabar* and her *Cuadernos de todo* as stories in the making. The fragmentary construction of her collages and her poetic texts are interlinked with various aspects of her work and her personal life. The collages allow us to travel through narrative geographies created by Martín Gaite, in which these pieces, these images, these moments that convert an event into a memory come to the fore. Her wanderings around the city of New York were the mould for a collection of visual texts, which interweave themselves with other texts in which Martín Gaite interrogates and comments upon her own writing process, her own poetics.

# Conclusions

The journey, the construction of space and visual elements are the three central points around which the poetics of the writer is based. *El cuento de nunca acabar* is the base of the principal poetics with which the writer creates her own terminology and displays the concepts of *el preámbulo* ('the stroll'), *los paseos interiores* ('interior wanderings'), *la novela de papeles atados* ('the novel of gathered writings'), *la geografía narrativa* ('the narrative geography'), *las conexiones significativas* ('significant connection') and the importance of the gaze *desde dentro* ('from within') or *desde fuera* ('from outside'). Presented through the characters, with particular interest in the gaze of women, these concepts would continue to develop in later works such as *Agua pasada* and would be applied in her narrative works of the 1990s. In the same period, the writer had already visited New York several times and her contact with the work of Edward Hopper led her to incorporate it into her reflections on the gaze in *Cuadernos de todo* and her *Visión de Nueva York* collages. In this way, Martín Gaite's narrative combines the collage, drawing and painting techniques.

Martín Gaite sees the journey as the centre of all storytelling, as the traveller is obliged to tell the story of how they arrived at the place from where they now recount their adventures along the way or relay what has happened since leaving a certain place. I have demonstrated that walking is an aesthetic practice with which the writer has explored the spaces of her native city (Salamanca), those of her adopted city (Madrid) and those of the city that led her to link her writing to drawing, painting, and, principally, collage (New York).

The aesthetic tool of the walk generates a whole series of actions from which Martín Gaite constructs her poetics (see Figure 4).

| | |
|---|---|
| recorrer (roam) | the city/town<br>the nooks and crannies of the premises<br>the unconscious |
| deambular (stroll) | around the town<br>down deadends<br>through the urban landscape |
| pasear (walk/pass) | your gaze over<br>    a room/gardens and railings/<br>    objects<br>    side streets<br>    the city |
| explorar (explore) | the city<br>a house/a room<br>an object |
| desplazarse (move) | around a house/from one room to another<br>to another place<br>through the   domestic<br>           urban<br>           interior<br>           narrative geography<br>around topography |
| orientarse (get your bearings) | |
| palpar (probe) | nooks and crannies/shelves/hideaways<br>the walls<br>a surface |
| hurgar (rummage) | the past<br>memories |
| viajar (travel) | with the gaze from one wall to another |
| huir (flee)<br>escapar (escape)<br>salir (leave)<br>largarse (scarper) | home |
| realizar (carry out) | journey/voyage/interior wanderings<br>route |
| contemplar (contemplate) | a landscape |
| mirar (look) | with delight/pleasure<br>far away<br>from afar/outside/inside/above |
| espiar (spy)<br>fisgar (snoop) | on people walking in the street<br>from a hideaway/window |
| punto de vista (point of view) | |
| detenerse (stop)<br>hacer una pausa (pause), hacer un nudo (tie a knot), hacer una parada (make a stop), un cruce de vías (crossroads) | |

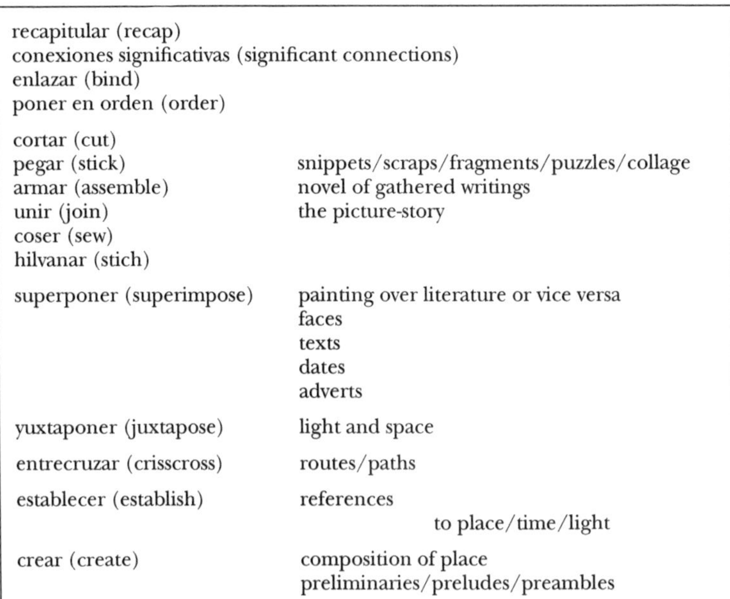

| | |
|---|---|
| recapitular (recap) | |
| conexiones significativas (significant connections) | |
| enlazar (bind) | |
| poner en orden (order) | |
| cortar (cut) | |
| pegar (stick) | snippets/scraps/fragments/puzzles/collage |
| armar (assemble) | novel of gathered writings |
| unir (join) | the picture-story |
| coser (sew) | |
| hilvanar (stich) | |
| superponer (superimpose) | painting over literature or vice versa |
| | faces |
| | texts |
| | dates |
| | adverts |
| yuxtaponer (juxtapose) | light and space |
| entrecruzar (crisscross) | routes/paths |
| establecer (establish) | references |
| | to place/time/light |
| crear (create) | composition of place |
| | preliminaries/preludes/preambles |

Figure 4: Actions as an aesthetic instrument

This series of actions becomes an aesthetic instrument with which
to explore the narrative of Martín Gaite. Describing the places that
have been visited during travels is a fundamental principle, as the
writer believes that a novel starts from the description of the place
in which the narrator finds themselves. The descriptive action gives
*referencias geográficas* ('geographic references') that work as *hitos de
lugar y de tiempo* ('place and time markers') with which Martín Gaite
builds the *preliminares* ('preliminaries') or the *preámbulos* ('preambles') of her novels.

Preceding the description, the role of the gaze is important. The
narrator must observe how the place that they are in is structured
and organised. To do this, they *recorrer* ('roam') with their gaze all
the nooks and crannies of the premises. From their chosen place,
they *mirar con placer* ('look with pleasure') at everything around
them. From the physical space that they occupy, they direct their
gaze far away, up, down, to the sides, outside, through a window or
inwards on themselves. In this way, spatial limits are dissolved. Being
in an interior space can set the imagination in motion, travelling to

other places, such as the Isla de Bergai or *el cuarto de atrás* ('the back room'). It should be stressed that, in Martín Gaite's narrative, women are the protagonists and it is they who look, spy or snoop, to use some examples of the range of actions possible with the eyes. Therefore, the prevalent *el punto de vista* ('point of view') is feminine.

The protagonists in the narrative of the 1950s and 1970s are women who inhabit interior spaces, roaming their domestic geographies in which they have deposited a series of memories of their lives as daughters, mothers and wives. In the narrative of the 1990s, the female characters leave these interior spaces and their roamings go beyond the rooms of their houses. They are women who decide to break with matrimonial and familial ties, as in the case of the characters in *Nubosidad variable* and *Lo raro es vivir*.

The action of *recorrer* ('roaming') the interior spaces, whether with the gaze or physically, is similar to that of roaming the streets of a city or town. The urban *deambular* ('strolling') is similar to that of *divagar* ('rambling'), or walking down dead ends. By extension, *pasear* ('walking') implies the movement from one place to another: not just a physical change, but an internal one, too. The term '*pasear*' is used with different meanings – for example, to 'pass' the gaze around a room, or to 'walk' down side streets or around the city. The different interpretations of '*pasear*' allow the creation of diverse geographies, as described and analysed in Chapter 3.

Martín Gaite incorporates the concepts of *geografía urbana* ('urban geography'), *geografía doméstica* ('domestic geography'), *geografía interior* ('interior geography') and *geografía narrativa* ('narrative geography') into her poetics. In the first two, space is considered as a geographic concept that contextualises and places the social relationships between men and women. For example, we might think of the nascent walks of the female characters in *Entre visillos* and compare those with the solitary wanderings that Amparo Miranda undertakes in *Irse de casa*. Natalia's walks are very different to those of Amparo and are closely linked to the socio-political situation in which both novels are set. The walks in *Entre visillos* are a journey through life in a small provincial city under Franco, while those in *Irse de casa* are a journey towards the childhood and adolescence of the protagonist. In these novels, the precise era is not specified, but we can deduce that democracy had already arrived, with the characters referring to a past period of change, and with the widening of the city streets, the disappearance of old neigh-bourhoods and the creation of new ones. Amparo Miranda and her mother battle to have their own lives, in which the memory of the man who left them is not a weight that ties them to a city in which parts of society still mark them out for not being a family made up of a father, a mother and children. The gaze of Amparo towards the city in which she grew up is a gaze from outside – from afar, as though it were the gaze of a witness. She is no longer tied to the place, and therefore decides to return to New York, where she has made another life away from the one that she lived in Spain.

Martín Gaite establishes the analogy between going out for a walk and sitting down to write. If walking in the streets of a city is what makes up the urban geography, then the narrative geography is created by the movements through a text. For Martín Gaite, writing becomes her homeland, her refuge and her space. As regards the interior geography, she adopts another simile for the act of walking. Here, she refers to *recorrer el inconsciente* ('roaming to unconscious') or *hurgar* ('rummaging') in the past and memories.

It is important to point out that the urban, domestic and interior geographies come together in the narrative geography. The text is where the writer unites the memories and the walks around different types of geography. It is here that the references to the geographic setting are vital to the creation of a *composición de lugar* ('composition of place').

Another series of actions that form part of Martín Gaite's poetics come from the use of collage. *Cortar* ('cutting'), *pegar* ('sticking') and *armar* ('assembling') are three key actions that the writer uses as much in the making of her collages as in her novels. Among the most commonly used materials are cuttings from newspapers or fragments from novels and articles by the writer, images of New York, women at the window, apartments, pictures of clouds, scraps of cloth, buttons and threads. These elements are stuck down in a collage in the same way as different bits of cloth are sewn together in a patchwork. Here, the action of *hilvanar* ('stitching') becomes not just one that is used semantically, in the field of sewing. The use goes further than that and becomes a synonym of *unir* ('joining'), *pegar* ('sticking') and even *re-anudar* ('resuming' or 'retying'). Indeed, the word '*nudo*' ('knot') implies connecting, linking or tying. This concept refers to another that also has the underlining idea of joining. I refer to the idea of the *novela de papeles atados* ('novel of gathered writings'). This takes up one of the principal poetics of the writer, establishing that a novel is made from fragments of life and that, as well as reconstructing a story (narration), it reconstructs a puzzle (or game).[1]

The *nudo* is also the starting point for writing a story. That is to say, it is the centre to which we return once all the threads of the skein have been disentangled. To translate this concept into the urban geography, the novel starts to conform to the itineraries carried out around the city, and therefore the nudo is the signage marked on the map. The writer states that 'hay una novela dentro de una ciudad (*tranche de vie*)' ('there is a novel within a city (*tranche de vie*)'.[2] The most important thing is to *enlazar* ('link') or *poner en orden* (put in order) all the images that the gaze takes in. These actions are expressed by the writer in another way: *re-capitular* ('recap') and *ordenar* ('order').

Without doubt, the journey is the centre of the narrative in the 1990s. The journeys that the characters undertake are carried out in the domestic, urban, interior and narrative geographies. Martín Gaite also uses the walk as an aesthetic practice. Her trips around cities in Spain and the streets of New York lend visual material to her novels of the 1990s. The principal poetics lie in the ideas that the visual is material for the narrative and that the narrative also overlaps with the visual. The first and only published drawings of Martín Gaite are those that appear in *Caperucita en Manhattan*. It is no accident that the novel takes place in the city most visited by the writer, in 1985 – the year in which the writer has contact with Juan Carlos Eguillor. Back then, he was doing drawings for a project called *Castillos de Manhattan*. These served as a model for those done later by Martín Gaite. It is important to emphasise the fact that the first of the thirteen drawings in a map and that, furthermore, it includes the written description of this map in the narrative voice. This is a clear example of one of the principal poetics: a novel that arises from the description of a place. In this case, it is the city of Manhattan. Martín Gaite has created her *preámbulo* ('preamble') from geographic reference in the same way that happens when Mariana describes to Sofia the place from which she is writing her a letter. In the case of *Nubosidad variable*, that is not a map for the reader to see, but it is known that Mariana has made one on squared paper, as she herself describes her own drawing. It is important to highlight that, as well as lending geographical references, it assumes a narrative idea formed as an itinerary.

The intrinsic relationship between drawing and storytelling that this uncovers is so strong that Martín Gaite creates another of her principal poetics: *el dibujo-cuento* ('the drawing-story'). This appears in *Irse de casa*, with Carolina explaining to her aunt that the drawing she has made is of a castle that acts as a refuge. In this case, the drawing is the starting place for creating a story. The same happens in *La reina de las nieves*, when Leandro paints Gerda and Kay, who are characters in the Hans Christian Andersen story *The Snow Queen*.

Among the most recurrent material in the making of the collages are cut-outs of women observing the world through a window, cuttings from newspapers or her own writings, hands that reach from clouds as though they are writing a text, scraps of cloth and thread with which she entwines the fragments of stories that will go on to form a novel. *Nubosidad variable* is the most representative in its use of collage. This *novela de papeles atados*, which tells of the reunion of two old friends, is assembled from Mariana's side of things as told in a letter; the love letters between Mariana and Guillermo; snippets from a diary; and notes that revolve around dreams and the rules on the process by which both friends have to write letters.

The making of a collage implies cutting images, newspaper articles, pieces of cloth or other materials. In sticking these materials down, the cut-outs overlap each other. In the structure of *Nubosidad variable* this process can be observed, especially in the chapter 'Persistencia de la memoria', in which three-dimensional images are created in the middle of the title and a story within a story is made. First, the grandmother tells how in one of the walls of the *refu* ('refuge') hangs Dalí's painting that shares the name of the chapter; later, Sofia and her daughter have a conversation in which the latter says that she has written a storybook that uses Dalí's painting as its title and cover. I said that three-dimensional images are created because the title of the chapter alone immediately brings to mind the visual image of Dalí's painting, which is hung on the wall and described by the grandmother; finally, in another story, we hear of the existence of another book whose title and cover have been hung one next to the other, or one above the other.

*Superponer* ('superimposing') is another of the series of actions that form part of the poetics of Martín Gaite, and comes from collage. This concept is used in her narrative by two elements overlapping and complementing each other at the same time: what came before and now. In *Lo raro es vivir* and *Irse de casa* this recurs often, in particular when the female characters are travelling around the city and begin to describe the changes happening in the visual–architectonic plans. This makes reference to the new spaces that are built upon the ruins of old buildings, for example.

In 1996, Martín Gaite is invited to present her reflections on Edward Hopper's *Hotel Room*. Her article is entitled '*El punto de vista*' ('The point of view') and is structured around the idea that the painting itself is already a novel, as just the contemplation of it suggests different questions about the woman sitting on the hotel bed, seemingly having just arrived or, maybe, about to leave. It is this doubt that forms the nexus of a whole story, according to Martín Gaite's poetics.

In the narrative of the 1990s, painting forms the basis of the relationships between characters. In *Nubosidad variable* the chance meeting between Mariana and Sofía at an art exhibition is the catalyst for the renewal of an old friendship. In *Lo raro es vivir* a painting again explains part of the relationships between characters: Águeda, the mother, was a painter and Rosario Tena gives classes in art history. Furthermore, the dialogues between the characters enable us to access the ideas of Martín Gaite in respect of the relationship between painting and literature. For the writer, there are no boundaries between the two disciplines. Painting and collage are used in narratives and, conversely, a text can serve as a model for painters, as shown by the writer when presenting the relationship between the artists of the Italian Trecento in *Lo raro es vivir*. In addition, I believe that the verbal reproduction of visual references by Martín Gaite allows the juxtaposition of images and texts, as in the case of 'Persistencia de la memoria' in *Nubosidad variable*. The perception of these characters is always to be found in relation to the visual–artistic perception.

The juxtaposition of image and texts acts as an intertextuality, with the mention of painters such as Remedios Varo, Edward Hopper and Vermeer in the novels of the 1990s enabling multiple possibilities in readings. It is no longer just a case of reading the story of two women fighting to free themselves from family and social ties, as in the case of the protagonists of *Nubosidad variable*, but of there also being a narrative that visualises one of the two inviting the other to contemplate *Rompiendo el círculo vicioso* by Remedios Varo. In itself, Martín Gaite's approach is based around the fact that it is possible to read paintings in the same way as it is to paint texts.

Taking a tour through the written and visual work of Martín Gaite and, by extension, her personal life, it is impossible not to notice the fact that the journey is the driving force behind the writer's artistic expression. Strolling around the streets and houses of Salamanca, Madrid or New York led her to create diverse types of geography that were constructed from the walks of women who lived during the Spanish Civil War, the post-war period and periods of transition and democracy.

The stories of Carmen Martín Gaite are presented like an enormous riddle that is assembled not just through the act of reading, but also through the range of visual references within. Martín Gaite may have been a writer who formed part of the *Generación de los 50* but, unlike her colleagues, she developed the use of her literary conscience, as seen in her interest in metafiction not just in the 1970s in *El cuarto de atrás*, but throughout her explorations and reflections in the 1990s. Indeed, she showed what narration and the process of creating a literary artifice meant to her in works that span nearly twenty years, as seen in *El cuento de nunca acabar*, *Cuadernos de todo* and *Visión de Nueva York*.

Carmen Martín Gaite's narrative in the 1990s is a composition in which her poetics and diverse types of geography mix with drawing, painting and collages. Her writing, therefore, is a hybrid that combines stories, ideas, lecture notes, quotes, travels and images with fragments of her life. Martín Gaite's writing unfolds a secret dialogue with other texts, discourses and fragments that are interwoven in a sea of stories. It is down to us, the readers, to journey through the places created by Martín Gaite, follow her tracks through the diverse geographies of her writing and stop to contemplate the visual references. To read Martín Gaite is to evoke the meeting with the other. Her writing is full of essays, poetry, tales, paintings and collages. Seen as such, her literature is a patchwork made from a range of materials.

# Notes

## Introduction


1   Carmen Martín Gaite, *El cuento de nunca acabar. Apuntes sobre la narración, el amor y la mentira* (Barcelona: Anagrama, 1988), p. 289.
2   Francesco Careri, *Walkscapes. El andar como práctica estética* (Barcelona: Gustavo Gili, 2002), p. 27.


## Chapter 1


1   Carme Molinero Ruiz, 'Silencio e invisibilidad: la mujer durante el primer franquismo', *Revista de Occidente*, 223 (1999), 63–82.
2   M. García Basauri, 'La sección femenina en la guerra civil española', *Historia 16*, 50 (1980), 55.
3   Geraldine M. Scanlon, *La polémica feminista en la España contemporánea: (1868–1974)* (Madrid: Akal, 1976), p. 324.
4   Josefina Rodriguez de Aldecoa, *Los Niños de la guerra* (Madrid: Anaya, 1983), pp. 17–18.
5   Alfonso Sastre, 'Poco más que anécdotas "culturales" alrededor de quince años (1950–1965)', *Triunfo*, XXVII/507 (June 1972), 81.
6   Jesús Fernández Santos, *Los bravos* (Estella: Salvat, 1971), pp. 19–20.
7   Kathleen Glenn, 'Hilos, ataduras y ruinas en la novelística de Carmen Martín Gaite', in *Novelistas Femeninas de La Postguerra Española* (Madrid: Ediciones José Porrúa, 1983), p. 35.
8   José Jurado Morales, *La trayectoria narrativa de Carmen Martín Gaite (1925–2000)* (Madrid: Gredos, 2003), p. 107.
9   Santos Sanz Villanueva, *Historia de la novela social española (1942–1975)* (Madrid: Alhambra, 1980), p. 187.
10  José Manuel Caballero Bonald, 'Coloquios Sobre Novela', *Olvidos de Granada*, 13 (1986), 166.
11  Celia Fernández and Carmen Martin Gaite, 'Entrevista Con Carmen Martin Gaite', *Anales de La Narrativa Española Contemporánea*, 4 (1979), 171.

12   Jurado Morales, *La trayectoria narrativa* , p. 58.
13   Carmen Martín Gaite, *Entre visillos* (Barcelona: Destino, 1958), p. 191.
14   Antonio Vilanova, 'Entre visillos', in *Novela y Sociedad en la España de la posguerra* (Barcelona: Lumen, Colección Palabra Critica, 1995), p. 384.
15   Sanz Villanueva, *Historia de la novela social española (1942–1975)*, p. 103.
16   Carmen Martín Gaite, *Esperando el porvenir. Homenaje a Ignacio Aldecoa* (Madrid: Siruela, 1994), p. 55.
17   Martín Gaite, *Esperando el porvenir*, pp. 55–6.
18   Juan Goytisolo, *Problemas de la novela* (Barcelona: Seix Barral, 1959), p. 28.
19   José María Castellet, 'La novela española, quince años después (1942–1957)', *Cuadernos del Congreso por la libertad de la cultura*, 33 (1958), 54.
20   Martín Gaite, *Esperando el porvenir*, p. 46.
21   Martín Gaite, *Esperando el porvenir*, p. 52.
22   Carmen Martín Gaite, *Agua pasada* (Barcelona: Anagrama, col. Argumentos, 1993), p. 35.
23   Carmen Martín Gaite, *El cuarto de atrás* (Barcelona: Destino, 1996), p. 93.
24   Martín Gaite, *El cuarto de atrás*, p. 94.
25   Martín Gaite, *Agua pasada*, p. 17.
26   Martín Gaite, *Agua pasada*, p. 18.
27   Joan Lipman Brown, *Women Writers of Contemporary Spain: Exiles in the Homeland* (Newark: University of Delaware Press; Cranbury, NJ: Associated University Presses, 1991), p. 73.
28   Carmen Martín Gaite, *Cuadernos de todo* (Barcelona: Random House–Mondadori, 2002), p. 666.
29   Martín Gaite, *Cuadernos de todo*, p. 669.
30   The concept of the heterodiegetic narrator comes from Gerard Genette's *Figures III*. This type of narrator is defined based on his position and participation in the events narrated. In this case, the narrator is a character of fiction who bears the brunt of the story, at first in the grammatical third person, and he does not intervene in the events narrated.
31   Norman Friedman, 'Point of View in Fiction: The Development of a Critical Concept', *PMLA* LXX (1955), 1170–2.
32   Carmen Martín Gaite, *Irse de casa* (Barcelona: Anagrama, col. Narrativas Hispánicas, 1998), pp. 14–15.
33   Martín Gaite, *Esperando el porvenir*, p. 88.
34   Ignacio Aldecoa, *Cuentos completos, 1949–1969* (Madrid, 1999), p. 280.
35   Martín Gaite, *Esperando el porvenir*, p. 93.
36   Martín Gaite, *Esperando el porvenir*, p. 99.
37   Martín Gaite, *Cuadernos de todo*, p. 195.
38   Joan Lipman Brown, 'One Autobiography, Twice Told: Martín Gaite's *Entre Visillos* and *El Cuarto de Atrás*', *Hispanic Journal*, 2, 7 (1986), 38.

39   Brown, 'One Autobiography, Twice Told', 40.

40   Felipe Blas Pedraza Jiménez and Milagros Rodríguez Cáceres, *Las épocas de la literatura española* (Barcelona: Ariel, 1997), p. 351.

41   Álvaro Ferray, 'La Vida Cultural: Limitaciones, Condicionantes y Desarrollo. Posfranquismo y Democracia', in Javier Paredes, *Historia Contemporánea de España (Siglo XIX–XX)*, (Madrid: Ariel, 1998), p. 1041.

42   Brown, *Women Writers of Contemporary Spain*, p. 18.

43   Santos Alonso, 'La transición: hacia una nueva novela', *Insula: revista de letras y ciencias humanas*, 512 (1989), 11.

44   María Elena Bravo, 'Ante la novela de la democracia: reflexiones sobre sus raíces', *Insula: revista de letras y ciencias humanas*, 444 (1983), 24.

45   Gonzalo Sobejano, 'Ante la novela de los años setenta', in *Historia y crítica de la literatura española, Vol. 8, Tomo 1, 1981 (Epoca contemporánea, 1939–1975 / coord. por Domingo Ynduráin)* (presented at the Historia y crítica de la literatura española, 1981), p. 22, https://dialnet.unirioja. es/servlet/articulo?codigo=592736 [accessed 4 November 2016].

46   Sobejano, 'Ante la novela de los años setenta', p. 1.

47   Darío Villanueva, 'La Novela', in *Letras Españolas* (Madrid: Ministerio de Cultura, 1987), p. 55.

48   Bravo, 'Ante la novela de la democracia', 24.

49   Sobejano, 'Ante la novela de los años setenta', p. 501.

50   Manuel Durán, '"Asi que pasen diez años", La novela española de los Setenta', *Anales de La Narrativa Española Contemporánea*, 5 (1980), 103.

51   José Luis Castillo Puche, 'Situación de la novela española actual', in *La cultura española en el posfranquismo: diez años de cine, cultura y literatura en España (1975–1985)*, 1988 (presented at the La cultura española en el posfranquismo: diez años de cine, cultura y literatura en España (1975–1985), 1988), 50, https://dialnet.unirioja.es/servlet/articulo? codigo=557587 [accessed 30 November 2016].

52   Vilanova, *Novela y sociedad en la España de la posguerra*, p. 392.

53   Carmen Martín Gaite, *El cuento de nunca acabar* (Barcelona: Anagrama, 1988), p. 243.

54   Morales, *La trayectoria narrativa de Carmen Martín Gaite (1925–2000)*, p. 251.

55   Carmen Martín Gaite, *Retahílas* (Barcelona: Destino, 1996), p. 100.

56   Martín Gaite, *El cuento de nunca acabar*, p. 181.

57   Biruté Ciplijauskaité, *La novela femenina contemporánea (1970–1985): hacia una tipología de la narración en primera persona* (Barcelona: Anthropos, 1988), p. 34.

58   Vilanova, *Novela y sociedad en la España de la posguerra*, p. 391.

59   Inmaculada de la Fuente, *Mujeres de La Posguerra* (Barcelona: Planeta Historia y Sociedad, 2002), p. 171.

60 Martín Gaite, *El cuarto de atrás*, pp. 132–3.

61 Morales, *La trayectoria narrativa de Carmen Martín Gaite (1925–2000)*, p. 195.

62 Morales, *La trayectoria narrativa de Carmen Martín Gaite (1925–2000)*, p. 196.

63 Martín Gaite, *Entre visillos*, p. 229.

64 Martín Gaite, *Entre visillos*, p. 228.

65 Carmen Martín Gaite, *Usos Amorosos de La Postguerra Española* (Barcelona: Anagrama, 2007), p. 67.

66 Catherine Davies, *Spanish Women's Writing 1849–1996* (London: Athlone Press 2000), p. 239.

67 Martín Gaite, *Cuadernos de todo*, p. 503.

68 Martín Gaite, *Cuadernos de todo*, p. 503.

69 Carmen Martín Gaite, *Visión de Nueva York* (Madrid: Siruela, 2005), p. 137.

70 Martín Gaite, *Visión de Nueva York*, p. 138.

71 Martín Gaite, *Cuadernos de todo*, p. 508.

72 Martín Gaite, *Cuadernos de todo*, p. 640.

73 Martín Gaite, *Cuadernos de todo*, p. 542.

74 Martín Gaite, *Cuadernos de todo*, p. 542.

75 Martín Gaite, *Cuadernos de todo*, p. 542.

76 Martín Gaite, *Cuadernos de todo*, p. 605.

77 Brown, *Women Writers of Contemporary Spain*, p. 72.

78 Linda Gould Levine, 'Carmen Martín Gaite's *El cuarto de atrás*: A Portrait of the Artist as Woman', in : Servodidio and Welles (eds), *From Fiction to Metafiction: Essays in Honor of Carmen Martín Gaite.* (Lincoln, Nebraska: Society of Spanish and Spanish American Studies, 1983), p. 169.

# Chapter 2

1 Carmen Martín Gaite, *El cuento de nunca acabar, Apuntes sobre la narración, el amor y la mentira* (Barcelona: Anagrama, 1988), p. 237.

2 Martín Gaite, *El cuento de nunca acabar*, p. 256.

3 Martín Gaite, *El cuento de nunca acabar*, p. 261.

4 Martín Gaite, *El cuento de nunca acabar*, p. 262.

5 Martín Gaite, *El cuento de nunca acabar*, p. 263.

6 Martín Gaite, *El cuento de nunca acabar*, pp. 270, 275 and 327.

7 Martín Gaite, *El cuento de nunca acabar*, p. 317.

8 Martín Gaite, *El cuento de nunca acabar*, pp. 318 and 328.

9 Carmen Martín Gaite, *Cuadernos de todo* (Barcelona: Random House–Mondadori, 2002), p. 9.

10   Maria-José Blanco López de Lerma, *Life-Writing in Carmen Martín Gaite's* Cuadernos de Todo *and her Novels of the 1990s* (Rochester, NY: Boydell & Brewer, 2013), p. 59.

11   de Lerma, *Life-Writing in Carmen Martín Gaite's Cuadernos de todo and her Novels of the 1990s*, p. 59.

12   Maria Vittoria Calvi, 'Presentación de los Cuadernos de todo en Salamanca', *ESPÉCULO*, 2003.

13   José María Pozuelo Yvancos, in José Teruel (ed.), '*Los Cuadernos de Todo* y la escritura del yo', in *Un Lugar Llamado Carmen Martín Gaite* (Madrid: Siruela, 2014), p. 109.

14   Pozuelo Yvancos, '*Los Cuadernos de Todo* y la escritura del yo', p. 109.

15   Pozuelo Yvancos, '*Los Cuadernos de Todo* y la escritura del yo', p. 109.

16   Pozuelo Yvancos, '*Los Cuadernos de Todo* y la escritura del yo', p. 110.

17   Martín Gaite, *Cuadernos de todo*, p. 348.

18   Martín Gaite, *Cuadernos de todo*, p. 296.

19   Martín Gaite, *Cuadernos de todo*, p. 295.

20   Francesco Careri, *Walkscapes. El andar como práctica estética* (Barcelona: Gustavo Gili, 2002), p. 10.

21   Careri, *Andar como práctica estética*, p. 25.

22   Careri, *Andar como práctica estética*, p. 19.

23   Martín Gaite, *Cuadernos de todo*, p. 241.

24   Katharina von Ankum (ed.), *Women in the Metropolis: Gender and Modernity in Weimar Culture* (Berkeley and Los Angeles: University of California Press, 1997), p. 67.

25   Martín Gaite, *Cuadernos de todo*, p. 238.

26   Biruté Ciplijauskaité, *Carmen Martín Gaite: (1925–2000)* (Madrid: Ediciones del Orto, 2000), p. 33.

27   Ciplijauskaité, *Carmen Martín Gaite*, p. 34.

28   Martín Gaite, *Cuadernos de todo*, pp. 238–9.

29   Carmen Martín Gaite, *Lo raro es vivir* (Barcelona: Anagrama, col. Compactos, 1999), p. 167.

30   Carmen Martín Gaite, *Nubosidad variable* (Barcelona: Anagrama, 1996), p. 41.

31   Carmen Martín Gaite, *La reina de las nieves* (Barcelona: Anagrama, 1994), p. 72.

32   Martín Gaite, *La reina de las nieves*, p. 195.

33   Martín Gaite, *La reina de las nieves*, p. 75.

34   Martín Gaite, *La reina de las nieves*, p. 112.

35   Martín Gaite, *Nubosidad variable*, p. 225.

36   Martín Gaite, *Nubosidad variable*, p. 310.

37   Martín Gaite, *Nubosidad variable*, p. 309.

38   Martín Gaite, *Nubosidad variable*, p. 310.

39   Martín Gaite, *La reina de las nieves*, p. 243.

40   Martín Gaite, *Nubosidad variable*, p. 244.

41  Martín Gaite, *La reina de las nieves*, p. 314.

42  Martín Gaite, *La reina de las nieves*, p. 314.

43  Martín Gaite, *Lo raro es vivir*, p. 106.

44  Martín Gaite, *Lo raro es vivir*, p. 107.

45  Martín Gaite, *Lo raro es vivir*, p. 107.

46  José Jurado Morales, *La trayectoria narrativa de Carmen Martín Gaite (1925–2000)* (2003), 251.

47  Morales, *La trayectoria narrativa de Carmen Martín Gaite (1925–2000)* (Madrid: Gredos, 2003), p. 251.

48  Martín Gaite, *El cuento de nunca acabar*, p. 218.

49  Martín Gaite, *El cuento de nunca acabar*, p. 218.

50  Martín Gaite, *El cuento de nunca acabar*, p. 219.

51  Martín Gaite, *Cuadernos de todo*, p. 636.

52  Duane Preble and Sarah Preble, *Artforms: An Introduction to the Visual Arts* (London and New York: Harper & Row, 1989), p. 454.

53  Albert E. Elsen, *Purposes of Art: An Introduction to the History and Appreciation of Art* (New York: Holt, Rinehart and Winston, 1967), p. 479.

54  Elza Adamowicz, *Surrealist Collage in Text and Image: Dissecting the Exquisite Corpse* (Cambridge: Cambridge University Press, 1998), p. 13.

55  Henri Béhar, *Littéruptures* (Lausanne: Bibliothèque Mélusine, 1988), p. 184.

56  Katherine Hoffman (ed.), *Collage: Critical Views* (Ann Arbor, Mich.: UMI Research Press, 1989), p. 5.

57  Martín Gaite, *Cuadernos de todo*, pp. 351–2.

58  Donald Kuspit, 'Collage: The Organizing Principle of Art in the Age of the Relativity of Art', in Katherine Hoffman (ed.), *Collage Critical Views* (Ann Arbor, Mich.: 4 UMI Research Press, 1989), p. 8.

59  Martín Gaite, *Cuadernos de todo*, p. 339.

60  Maria Vittoria Calvi, *Dialogo e conversazione nella narrativa di Carmen Martín Gaite* (Milano: Arcipelago Edizioni, 1990), pp. 113–14.

61  Kathleen Glenn, 'Hilos, ataduras y ruinas en la novelística de Carmen Martín Gaite', in Janet Pérez (ed.), *Novelistas Femeninas de La Postguerra Española* (Madrid: Ediciones José Porrúa, 1983), p. 41.

62  Martín Gaite, *Nubosidad variable*, p. 75.

63  Martín Gaite, *Nubosidad variable*, p. 76.

64  Martín Gaite, *Nubosidad variable*, p. 228.

65  Martín Gaite, *Nubosidad variable*, p. 267.

66  Martín Gaite, *Nubosidad variable*, p. 359.

67  Biruté Ciplijauskaité, *La novela femenina contemporánea (1970–1985): hacia una tipología de la narración en primera persona* (Barcelona: Anthropos, 1988), p. 211.

68  Carmen Martín Gaite, *Irse de casa* (Barcelona: Anagrama, col. Narrativas Hispánicas, 1998), p. 23.

69   Martín Gaite, *Irse de casa*, p. 23.
70   Martín Gaite, *Irse de casa*, p. 23.
71   Martín Gaite, *Irse de casa*, p. 320.
72   Martín Gaite, *Irse de casa*, p. 142.
73   Martín Gaite, *Irse de casa*, p. 142.
74   Miriam Schapiro, '"Femmage"', in Katherine Hoffman (ed.) *Collage Critical Views* (Ann Arbor, Mich.: UMI Research Press, 1989), p. 296.
75   Martín Gaite, *El cuento de nunca acabar*, p. 328.
76   Martín Gaite, *Cuadernos de todo*, p. 240.
77   Martín Gaite, *Cuadernos de todo*, p. 238.
78   Martín Gaite, *Cuadernos de todo*, p. 539.
79   Carmen Martín Gaite, *Agua pasada* (Barcelona: Anagrama, col. Argumentos 1993), p. 300.
80   Martín Gaite, *Cuadernos de todo*, p. 300.
81   Martín Gaite, *Cuadernos de todo*, p. 640.
82   Martín Gaite, *El cuento de nunca acabar*, p. 261.
83   Martín Gaite, *El cuento de nunca acabar*, p. 262.
84   Martín Gaite, *La reina de las nieves*, p. 235.
85   Martín Gaite, *La reina de las nieves*, p. 235.
86   Mieke Bal, *Conceptos viajeros en las humanidades. Una guía de viaje* (Murcia: CENDEAC, 2009), p. 17.
87   Bal, *Conceptos viajeros en las humanidades.* p. 22.
88   Michel de Certeau and Steven F Rendall, *The Practice of Everyday Life* (Berkeley: University of California Press, 1984), p. 127.
89   de Certeau and Rendall, *The practice of everyday life*, p. 128.
90   Carmen Martín Gaite, *Pido la palabra* (Barcelona: Anagrama, col. Argumentos, 2002), p. 193.
91   Carmen Martín Gaite, *Desde la ventana* (Madrid: Espasa Calpe, 1987), p. 201.
92   Gaite, *Desde la ventana*, p. 201.
93   Gaite, *Desde la ventana*, p. 201.
94   Martín Gaite, *Irse de casa*, p. 188.
95   Martín Gaite, *Irse de casa*, p. 188.
96   Martín Gaite, *El Cuento de nunca acabar*, p. 40.
97   Emilia Velasco Marcos, 'Las aguas y el cauce: suerte de la metanovela', *Insula: revista de letras y ciencias humanas*, 589 (enero–febrero 1996), 47.
98   Marcos, 'Las aguas y el cauce', 47.
99   Gonzalo Sobejano, 'Novela y metanovela en España', *Insula: revista de letras y ciencias humanas*, 512 (agosto–septiembre 1989), 4.
100  Morales, *La trayectoria narrativa de Carmen Martín Gaite (1925–2000)*, p. 210.
101  Sobejano, 'Novela y metanovela en España', 4.
102  Blas Matamoro, 'Carmen Martín Gaite: viaje al cuarto de Atrás', *Cuadernos hispanoamericanos*, 351 (septiembre 1979), 597.

103 Martín Gaite, *Nubosidad variable*, p. 33.

104 Martín Gaite, *Nubosidad variable*, p. 305.

105 Morales, *La trayectoria narrativa de Carmen Martín Gaite (1925–2000)*, p. 343.

106 Martín Gaite, *Nubosidad variable*, p. 20.

107 Martín Gaite, *Nubosidad variable*, p. 20.

108 Martín Gaite, *Pido la palabra*, p. 198.

109 Martín Gaite, *Nubosidad variable*, p. 22.

110 Martín Gaite, *La reina de las nieves*, p. 176.

111 Martín Gaite, *Nubosidad variable*, p. 275.

112 Morales, *La trayectoria narrativa de Carmen Martín Gaite (1925–2000)*, p. 301.

113 Morales, *La trayectoria narrativa de Carmen Martín Gaite (1925–2000)*, p. 301.

114 Mercedes Carbayo Abengózar, *Buscando un lugar entre mujeres: Buceo en la España de Carmen Martín Gaite* (Málaga: Servicio de Publicaciones de la Universidad de Málaga, 1998), p. 140.

115 Carmen Martín Gaite, *Caperucita en Manhattan* (Madrid: Siruela, 1990), p. 40.

116 Martín Gaite, *Caperucita en Manhattan*, p. 138.

117 Martín Gaite, *Caperucita en Manhattan*, p. 37.

118 Martín Gaite, *Irse de casa*, p. 10.

119 Martín Gaite, *El cuento de nunca acabar*, p. 237.

120 Martín Gaite, *Irse de casa*, p. 14.

121 Morales, *La trayectoria narrativa de Carmen Martín Gaite (1925–2000)*, p. 343.

122 Martín Gaite, *Irse de casa*, p. 34.

123 Martín Gaite, *Irse de casa*, p. 206.

124 Martín Gaite, *Irse de casa*, p. 207.

125 Martín Gaite, *Irse de casa*, p. 219.

126 Martín Gaite, *Irse de casa*, p. 219.

127 Martín Gaite, *Irse de casa*, p. 15.

128 Enric Bou, *Pintura en el aire. Arte y literatura en la modernidad* (Valencia: Pre-Textos, 2001), p. 71.

129 Martín Gaite, *Irse de casa*, p. 96.

130 Martín Gaite, *Irse de casa*, p. 96.

131 Martín Gaite, *Irse de casa*, p. 97.

## Chapter 3

1 Gaston Bachelard, *La poética del espacio* (México: Fondo de Cultura Económica, 1975), p. 34.

2   Carmen Martín Gaite, *Agua pasada* (Barcelona: Anagrama, col. Argumentos, 1993), p. 282.

3   Mercedes Jiménez González, *Carmen Martín Gaite y la narración: teoría y práctica* (New Brunswick, NJ: SLUSA, 1989), p. 61.

4   José Jurado Morales, *La trayectoria narrativa de Carmen Martín Gaite (1925–2000)* (Madrid: Gredos, 2003), pp. 276–7.

5   Morales, *La trayectoria narrativa de Carmen Martín Gaite (1925–2000)*, p. 278.

6   Morales, *La trayectoria narrativa de Carmen Martín Gaite (1925–2000)*, p. 278.

7   Carmen Martín Gaite, *Pido la palabra* (Barcelona: Anagrama, col. Argumentos, 2002), p. 287.

8   Martín Gaite, *Pido la palabra*, p. 196.

9   Carmen Martín Gaite, *El cuento de nunca acabar* (Barcelona: Anagrama, 1988), p. 275.

10  Gillian Rose, *Feminism and Geography: The Limits of Geographical Knowledge* (Cambridge: Polity Press, 1993), p. 1.

11  L. Johnson, 'Gender, genetics, and the possibility of feminist geography', *Australian Geographical Studies* 23 (1985), 161–71.

12  Gillian Rose refers to: Women and Geography Study Group of the Institute of British Geographers, *Geography and Gender: An Introduction to Feminist Geography* (London: Hutchinson, 1984).

13  Rose, *Feminism and Geography*, p. 21.

14  Rose, *Feminism and Geography*, p. 21.

15  Barbara Arneil, *Politics & Feminism* (Blackwell: Oxford; Malden, Mass.: Blackwell, 1999), p. 164.

16  Teresa de Lauretis, University of Wisconsin–Milwaukee and Center for Twentieth Century Studies (eds), *Feminist Studies, Critical Studies* (London: Macmillan, 1986), p. 12.

17  Martín Gaite, *El cuento de nunca acabar*, p. 34.

18  Martín Gaite, *El cuento de nunca acabar*, p. 33.

19  Martín Gaite, *El cuento de nunca acabar*, p. 33.

20  Martín Gaite, *Agua pasada*, p. 282.

21  Bachelard, *La poética del espacio*, p. 48.

22  Bachelard, *La poética del espacio*, p. 48.

23  Bachelard, *La poética del espacio*, p. 49.

24  Martín Gaite, *Pido la palabra*, 389.

25  Carmen Martín Gaite, *El cuarto de atrás* (1996), 187.

26  Martín Gaite, *Pido la palabra*, p. 387.

27  Martín Gaite, *Pido la palabra*, p. 387.

28  Martín Gaite, *Pido la palabra*, p. 390.

29  Martín Gaite, *Pido la palabra*, p. 390.

30  Carmen Martín Gaite, *Desde la ventana* (Madrid: Espasa Calpe, 1987), p. 12.

31  Rose, *Feminism and Geography*, p. 12.

32  Kate Millett, *Sexual Politics* (London: Virago, 1977), pp. 88–108. Chapter 6 focuses specifically on the distinction between the public and the private in feminism.

33  Carole Pateman, *The Disorder of Women: Democracy, Feminism, and Political Theory* (Cambridge: Polity Press, 1989), p. 118.

34  de Lauretis, *Feminist Studies, Critical Studies*, p. 11.

35  Emma Martinell Gifre, *El mundo de los objetos en la obra de Carmen Martín Gaite* (Cáceres: Servicio de Publicaciones de la Universidad de Extremadura, 1996), p. 11.

36  Martín Gaite, *Pido la palabra*, p. 338.

37  Carmen Martín Gaite, *Cuadernos de todo* (Barcelona: Random House–Mondadori, 2002), p. 355.

38  Carmen Martín Gaite, *Nubosidad variable* (Barcelona: Anagrama, 1996), p. 13.

39  Martín Gaite, *Nubosidad variable*, p. 12.

40  Martín Gaite, *Nubosidad variable*, p. 12.

41  Martín Gaite, *Nubosidad variable*, p. 196.

42  Martín Gaite, *Nubosidad variable*, p. 305.

43  Martín Gaite, *Nubosidad variable*, p. 22.

44  Martín Gaite, *Nubosidad variable*, p. 22.

45  Martín Gaite, *Nubosidad variable*, p. 90.

46  Bachelard, *La poética del espacio*, p. 48.

47  Bachelard, *La poética del espacio*, p. 49.

48  Bachelard, *La poética del espacio*, p. 49.

49  Martín Gaite, *Nubosidad variable*, p. 90.

50  Martín Gaite, *Nubosidad variable*, p. 140.

51  Martín Gaite, *Pido la palabra*, p. 403.

52  Martín Gaite, *Nubosidad variable*, p. 181.

53  Martín Gaite, *Nubosidad variable*, p. 403.

54  Martín Gaite, *Nubosidad variable*, pp. 178–9.

55  Carmen Martín Gaite, *Fragmentos de Interior* (Barcelona: Destino, 1986), p. 25.

56  Josefina González, 'Dibujo, Espacio y Ecofeminismo en la C. de El Cuarto de Atrás, de Carmen Martín Gaite', *Revista Canadiense de Estudios Hispánicos*, 19/1 (1994), 86.

57  Carmen Martín Gaite, *Lo raro es vivir* (Barcelona: Anagrama, col. Compactos, 1999), p. 35.

58  González, 'Dibujo, Espacio y Ecofeminismo', 86.

59  Carmen Martín Gaite, *Irse de casa* (Barcelona: Anagrama, col. Narrativas Hispánicas, 1998), p. 131.

60  Martín Gaite, *Irse de casa*, p. 210.

61  Martín Gaite, *Irse de casa*, pp. 210–11.

62  Martín Gaite, *Irse de casa*, p. 212.

63　Martín Gaite, *Nubosidad variable*, p. 195.

64　Bachelard, *La poética del espacio*, p. 178.

65　Martín Gaite, *Irse de casa*, p. 212.

66　Martín Gaite, *Irse de casa*, p. 27.

67　Martín Gaite, *Pido la palabra*, p. 327.

68　Martín Gaite, *El cuarto de atrás*, p. 126.

69　Carmen Martín Gaite, *El balneario* (Barcelona: Destino, 1977).

70　Martín Gaite, *Pido la palabra*, p. 248.

71　Martín Gaite, *Pido la palabra*, pp. 331–2.

72　Gaston Bachelard, *La poética de la ensoñación* (México: Fondo de Cultura Económica, 1982), p. 25.

73　Bachelard, *La poética de la ensoñación*, p. 24.

74　Bachelard, *La poética de la ensoñación*, p. 36.

75　Bachelard, *La poética de la ensoñación*, p. 226.

76　Bachelard, *La poética de la ensoñación*, p. 20.

77　Bachelard, *La poética de la ensoñación*, p. 23.

78　Bachelard, *La poética de la ensoñación*, p. 30.

79　Bachelard, *La poética de la ensoñación*, p. 32.

80　Gaston Bachelard and Ernestina de Champourcin, *El Aire y los sueños: ensayo sobre la imaginación del movimiento* (México: Fondo de Cultura Económica, 1958), p. 307.

81　Bachelard and Champourcin, *El Aire y los sueños*, p. 308.

82　Martín Gaite, *El cuento de nunca acabar*, p. 188.

83　Martín Gaite, *El cuento de nunca acabar*, p. 81.

84　Martín Gaite, *El cuento de nunca acabar*, p. 81.

85　Martín Gaite, *El cuento de nunca acabar*, p. 81.

86　Martín Gaite, *El cuarto de atrás*, p. 180.

87　Martín Gaite, *El cuarto de atrás*, p. 185.

88　Martín Gaite, *El cuarto de atrás*, p. 187.

89　Martín Gaite, *El cuarto de atrás*, p. 187.

90　Martín Gaite, *El cuarto de atrás*, p. 188.

91　Martín Gaite, *El cuarto de atrás*, p. 195.

92　Gaite, *Desde la ventana*, p. 37.

93　Martín Gaite, *Pido la palabra*, p. 200.

94　Carmen Martín Gaite, *Entre visillos* (Barcelona: Destino, 1958), p. 174.

95　Carmen Martín Gaite, *Las ataduras; relatos* (Barcelona: Destino, 1960), p. 108.

96　Martín Gaite, *Nubosidad variable*, p. 112.

97　Martín Gaite, *Nubosidad variable*, p. 112.

98　Martín Gaite, *Nubosidad variable*, p. 113.

99　Martín Gaite, *Nubosidad variable*, p. 113.

100　Uxó González Carlos, 'La Recuperación de la memoria en La reina de las nieves de Carmen Martín Gaite', *Donaire*, 13 (1999), 43.

101  Emma Martinell Gifre, *El mundo de los objetos en la obra de Carmen Martín Gaite*, 117.

102  Martín Gaite, *Nubosidad variable*, p. 348.

103  Martín Gaite, *Nubosidad variable*, p. 354.

104  Martín Gaite, *Nubosidad variable*, p. 360.

105  Martín Gaite, *Nubosidad variable*, p. 360.

106  Martín Gaite, *Nubosidad variable*, p. 355.

107  Carmen Martín Gaite, *La reina de las nieves* (Barcelona: Anagrama, 1994), p. 305.

108  Martín Gaite, *Irse de casa*, p. 54.

109  Martín Gaite, *Irse de casa*, p. 56.

110  Martín Gaite, *Irse de casa*, p. 27.

111  Martín Gaite, *El cuento de nunca acabar*, p. 275.

112  Martín Gaite, *Pido la palabra*, p. 389.

113  Martín Gaite, *Pido la palabra*, p. 389.

114  Martín Gaite, *Pido la palabra*, p. 391.

115  Martín Gaite, *El cuarto de atrás*, p. 91.

116  Martín Gaite, *Pido la palabra*, p. 138.

117  Martín Gaite, *Pido la palabra*, p. 138.

118  Martín Gaite, *Cuadernos de todo*, p. 495.

119  Martín Gaite, *Cuadernos de todo*, p. 495.

120  Michel de Certeau and Steven F Rendall, *The practice of everyday life* (Los Angeles: University of California Press, 1984), p. 95.

121  Martín Gaite, *La reina de las nieves*, p. 176.

122  Martín Gaite, *La reina de las nieves*, p. 176.

123  Martín Gaite, *La reina de las nieves*, p. 172.

124  Martín Gaite, *La reina de las nieves*, p. 177.

125  Martín Gaite, *Desde la ventana*, p. 37.

126  Iñaki Torre Fica, '"La Mujer ventanera" en La Poesía de Carmen Martín Gaite', 19 *Espéculo: Revista de Estudios Literarios* (2001), 18.

127  Martín Gaite, *La reina de las nieves*, p. 244.

128  Martín Gaite, *La reina de las nieves*, p. 242.

129  Martín Gaite, *La reina de las nieves*, p. 243.

130  Martín Gaite, *La reina de las nieves*, pp. 243–4.

131  Martín Gaite, *Irse de casa*, p. 188.

132  Martín Gaite, *Nubosidad variable*, p. 347.

133  Martín Gaite, *Lo raro es vivir*, p. 169.

134  Martín Gaite, *Lo raro es vivir*, p. 169.

135  Martín Gaite, *Lo raro es vivir*, p. 169.

136  Martín Gaite, *Lo raro es vivir*, p. 170.

137  Martín Gaite, *Irse de casa*, p. 170.

138  Biruté Ciplijauskaité, *Carmen Martín Gaite: (1925–2000)* (Madrid: Ediciones del Orto, 2000), p. 62.

139  Martín Gaite, *Irse de casa*, p. 11.

140 Martín Gaite, *Nubosidad variable*, p. 388.
141 Martín Gaite, *Irse de casa*, p. 16.
142 Martín Gaite, *Irse de casa*, p. 14.
143 Martín Gaite, *Irse de casa*, p. 15.
144 Martín Gaite, *Irse de casa*, p. 33.
145 Martín Gaite, *Irse de casa*, p. 15.
146 Martín Gaite, *Irse de casa*, p. 142.
147 Martín Gaite, *Irse de casa*, p. 142.
148 Martín Gaite, *Nubosidad variable*, p. 42.
149 Martín Gaite, *El cuento de nunca acabar*, p. 270.
150 Martín Gaite, *El cuento de nunca acabar*, p. 270.
151 Carmen Martín Gaite, *Retahílas* (1996), pp. 33–4.
152 Martín Gaite, *Nubosidad variable*, p. 130.
153 Martín Gaite, *Nubosidad variable*, p. 130.
154 Martín Gaite, *Nubosidad variable*, p. 375.
155 Martín Gaite, *Nubosidad variable*, p. 346.
156 Martín Gaite, *Nubosidad variable*, p. 139.
157 Martín Gaite, *Nubosidad variable*, p. 150.
158 Martín Gaite, *Nubosidad variable*, p. 150.
159 Martín Gaite, *Nubosidad variable*, p. 255.
160 Martín Gaite, *Cuadernos de todo*, p. 629.
161 Martín Gaite, *Nubosidad variable*, p. 314.
162 Martín Gaite, *Nubosidad variable*, p. 314.
163 Martín Gaite, *Nubosidad variable*, p. 314.
164 Martín Gaite, *El cuento de nunca acabar*, p. 275.
165 Joan Lipman Brown, *Women Writers of Contemporary Spain: Exiles in the Homeland* (Newark: University of Delaware Press; Cranbury, NJ: Associated Univerties Press, 1991), p. 72.

# Chapter 4

1   Kathleen M. Glenn, 'Collage, Textile and Palimpsest: Carmen Martín Gaite's Nubosidad variable', *Romance Languages Annual*, 5 (1993), 409.
2   Carmen Martín Gaite, *Pido la palabra* (Barcelona: Anagrama, col. Argumentos, 2002), p. 147.
3   Martín Gaite, *Pido la palabra*, p. 147.
4   Martín Gaite, *Pido la palabra*, p. 147.
5   Martín Gaite, *Pido la palabra*, p. 147.
6   Carmen Martín Gaite, *Caperucita en Manhattan* (Madrid: Siruela, 1990), pp. 14–15.
7   Martín Gaite, *Caperucita en Manhattan*, p. 31.
8   Martín Gaite, *Caperucita en Manhattan*, p. 31.
9   Martín Gaite, *Caperucita en Manhattan*, pp. 31–2.

10  Martín Gaite, *Caperucita en Manhattan*, p. 32.

11  Martín Gaite, *Caperucita en Manhattan*, p. 32.

12  Martín Gaite, *Caperucita en Manhattan*, p. 32.

13  Martín Gaite, *Caperucita en Manhattan*, p. 205.

14  Martín Gaite, *Caperucita en Manhattan*, p. 35.

15  Juan Senís Fernández, Marta Sanjuán Álvarez and Eva Villar Secanella, 'Carmiña and the City: Visiones de Nueva York En La Obra Gráfica de Carmen Martín Gaite', *Hispanófila*, 175/1 (2016), 247.

16  Fernández, Álvarez and Secanella, 'Carmiña and the City', 247.

17  Martín Gaite, *Pido la palabra*, p. 387.

18  Martín Gaite, *Pido la palabra*, p. 387.

19  Martín Gaite, *Pido la palabra*, p. 393.

20  Martín Gaite, *Pido la palabra*, p. 395.

21  Martín Gaite, *Pido la palabra*, p. 395.

22  Carmen Martín Gaite, *El cuarto de atrás* (Barcelona: Destino, 1996), p. 22.

23  Martín Gaite, *El cuarto de atrás*, pp. 11–12.

24  Carmen Martín Gaite, *Nubosidad variable* (Barcelona: Anagrama, col. Compactos, 1996), pp. 21–2.

25  Carmen Martín Gaite, *El cuento de nunca acabar* (Barcelona: Anagrama, 1988), p. 275.

26  Martín Gaite, *El cuento de nunca acabar*, p. 34.

27  Carmen Martín Gaite, *Irse de casa* (Barcelona: Anagrama, col. Narrativas Hispánicas, 1998), p. 250.

28  Martín Gaite, *Irse de casa*, p. 254.

29  Carmen Martín Gaite, *La reina de las nieves* (Barcelona: Anagarama, 1994), p. 97.

30  Martín Gaite, *La reina de las nieves*, p. 97.

31  Martín Gaite, *La reina de las nieves*, p. 98.

32  Carmen Martín Gaite, *Lo raro es vivir* (Barcelona: Anagrama, col. Compactos, 1999), p. 44.

33  Martín Gaite, *Lo raro es vivir*, p. 45.

34  Martín Gaite, *Lo raro es vivir*, p. 45.

35  Martín Gaite, *Lo raro es vivir*, p. 46.

36  Martín Gaite, *Lo raro es vivir*, p. 85.

37  Martín Gaite, *Lo raro es vivir*, p. 86.

38  Martín Gaite, *Lo raro es vivir*, p. 86.

39  Yi-fu Tuan, *Space and Place: The Perspective of Experience* (Minneapolis: University of Minnesota Press, 1977), p. 77.

40  Italo Calvino and Aurora Bernárdez, *Colección de arena* (Madrid: Siruela, 2001), p. 54.

41  Martín Gaite, *Nubosidad variable*, p. 56.

42  Martín Gaite, *Lo raro es vivir*, p. 92.

43  Martín Gaite, *Lo raro es vivir*, p. 91.

44　Martín Gaite, *Lo raro es vivir*, p. 91.

45　Martín Gaite, *Lo raro es vivir*, p. 96.

46　Martín Gaite, *Lo raro es vivir*, p. 96.

47　Martín Gaite, *Lo raro es vivir*, p. 96.

48　Martín Gaite, *Lo raro es vivir*, p. 97.

49　Martín Gaite, *La reina de las nieves*, p. 224.

50　Carmen Martín Gaite, *Desde la ventana* (Madrid: Espasa Calpe, 1987), p. 35.

51　Martín Gaite, *Desde la ventana*, p. 35.

52　Martín Gaite, *Desde la ventana*, p. 136.

53　Martín Gaite, *Desde la ventana*, p. 37.

54　Martín Gaite, *Desde la ventana*, p. 133.

55　Martín Gaite, *Desde la ventana*, p. 133.

56　Martín Gaite, *Desde la ventana*, p. 133.

57　Martín Gaite, *Desde la ventana*, p. 134.

58　Carmen Martín Gaite, 'El Punto de vista', *Fundación Colección Thyssen-Bornemisza* (14 dic. 1996) (1997), p. 7.

59　Martín Gaite, 'El Punto de vista', p. 8.

60　Martín Gaite, 'El Punto de vista', p. 6.

61　Martín Gaite, 'El Punto de vista', p. 17.

62　Martín Gaite, 'El Punto de vista', p. 17.

63　Martín Gaite, 'El Punto de vista', p. 8.

64　Juan Senís Fernández, 'Amistades de ida y vuelta a través del texto', *Espéculo*, 43 (2009), *https://pendientedemigracion.ucm.es/info/especulo/cmgaite/senis.htm*.

65　Senís Fernández, 'Amistades de ida y vuelta a través del texto', 2.

66　Senís Fernández, 'Amistades de ida y vuelta a través del texto', 2.

67　Senís Fernández, 'Amistades de ida y vuelta a través del texto', 2.

68　Martín Gaite 'El Punto de vista', p. 7.

69　Martín Gaite 'El Punto de vista', p. 8.

70　Martín Gaite 'El Punto de vista', p. 19.

71　Martín Gaite 'El Punto de vista', p. 19.

72　Martín Gaite 'El Punto de vista', p. 20.

73　Martín Gaite 'El Punto de vista', p. 20.

74　Martín Gaite 'El Punto de vista', p. 22.

75　Martín Gaite 'El Punto de vista', p. 23.

76　Martín Gaite 'El Punto de vista', p. 23.

77　Enric Bou, *Pintura en el aire: arte y literatura en la Modernidad* (Valencia: Pre-Textos, 2001), p. 31.

78　Martín Gaite, *Lo raro es vivir*, p. 176.

79　Martín Gaite, *Lo raro es vivir*, p. 183.

80　Martín Gaite, *Lo raro es vivir*, p. 183.

81　Martín Gaite, *Nubosidad variable*, pp. 140–1.

82　Martín Gaite, *La reina de las nieves*, p. 123.

83  Martín Gaite, *La reina de las nieves*, p. 123.
84  Martín Gaite, *Lo raro es vivir*, p. 47.
85  Martín Gaite, *Lo raro es vivir*, p. 183.
86  Martín Gaite, *Lo raro es vivir*, p. 86.
87  Martín Gaite, *Nubosidad variable*, p. 195.
88  Carmen Martín Gaite, *Visión de Nueva York* (Madrid: Siruela, 2005), p. 33.
89  Carmen Martín Gaite, *Cuadernos de todo* (Barcelona: Random House–Mondadori, 2002), p. 532.
90  Martín Gaite, *Cuadernos de todo*, p. 605.
91  Martín Gaite, *Cuadernos de todo*, p. 606.
92  Martín Gaite, *Pido la palabra*, p. 326.
93  Martín Gaite, *Pido la palabra*, p. 196.
94  Carmen Martín Gaite, *Retahílas* (Barcelona: Destino, 1996), p. 198.
95  Martín Gaite, *El cuento de nunca acabar*, p. 199.
96  Martín Gaite, *El cuento de nunca acabar*, p. 202.
97  Martín Gaite, *El cuento de nunca acabar*, p. 196.
98  Martín Gaite, *El cuento de nunca acabar*, p. 202.
99  Martín Gaite, *Pido la palabra*, p. 248.
100  Martín Gaite, *Pido la palabra*, p. 249.
101  Martín Gaite, *Pido la palabra*, p. 204.
102  Martín Gaite, *Pido la palabra*, p. 204.
103  Martín Gaite, *Pido la palabra*, p. 204.
104  Martín Gaite, *Pido la palabra*, p. 205.
105  Martín Gaite, *Pido la palabra*, p. 206.
106  Martín Gaite, *Pido la palabra*, p. 206.
107  Martín Gaite, *Cuadernos de todo*, p. 640.
108  Debra J. Ochoa, 'Martín Gaite's Visión de Nueva York: Collages of Public and Private Space', in Marian Womack and Jennifer Wood (eds), *Beyond the Back Room* (Oxford; New York: Peter Lang, 2011), p. 85.
109  Ochoa, 'Martín Gaite's Visión de Nueva York', p. 86.

## Conclusion

1  Carmen Martín Gaite, *Cuadernos de todo* (Barcelona: Random House-Mondadori, 2002), p. 411.
2  Martín Gaite, *Cuadernos de todo*, p. 669.

# Bibliography

## Works authored by Carmen Martín Gaite


Martín Gaite, Carmen, 'El silencio da miedo', in *Agua pasada* (Barcelona: Anagrama, col. Argumentos, 1993), pp. 300–2.

Martín Gaite, Carmen, 'El punto de vista', in *Fundación Colección Thyssen-Bornemisza* (14 dic. 1996) (1997), pp. 5–23.

Martín Gaite, Carmen, 'La mirada del escritor', in *Pido la palabra* (Barcelona: Anagrama, col. Argumentos, 2002), pp. 192–208.

Martín Gaite, Carmen, *Entre visillos* (Barcelona: Destino, 1958).

Martín Gaite, Carmen, *Las ataduras* (Barcelona: Destino, 1960).

Martín Gaite, Carmen, *Ritmo lento* (Barcelona: Destino, 1963).

Martín Gaite, Carmen, *El proceso de Macanaz: Historia de un empapelamiento* (Madrid: Moneda y Crédito, 1970).

Martín Gaite, Carmen, 'Prólogo' in Jesús Fernández Santos, *Los bravos* (Navarra: Salvat, 1971), pp. 16–22.

Martín Gaite, Carmen, *Usos amorosos del dieciocho en España* (Madrid: Siglo XXI, 1972).

Martín Gaite, Carmen, *La búsqueda de interlocutor y otras búsquedas* (Madrid: Nostromo, 1973).

Martín Gaite, Carmen, *Retahílas* (Barcelona: Destino, 1974).

Martín Gaite, Carmen, *Fragmentos de interior* (Barcelona: Destino, 1976).

Martín Gaite, Carmen, *El balneario* (Barcelona: Destino, 1977).

Martín Gaite, Carmen, *El cuarto de atrás* (Barcelona: Destino, 1978).

Martín Gaite, Carmen, *El castillo de las tres murallas* (Barcelona: Lumen, 1981).

Martín Gaite, Carmen, El cuento de nunca acabar. Apuntes sobre la narración, el amor y la mentira (Madrid: Trieste, 1983).

Martín Gaite, Carmen, *El pastel del diablo* (Barcelona: Lumen, 1985).

Martín Gaite, Carmen, *Desde la ventana* (Madrid: Espasa Calpe, 1987).

Martín Gaite, Carmen, *El cuento de nunca acabar. Apuntes sobre la narración, el amor y la mentira* (Barcelona: Anagrama, 1988).

Martín Gaite, Carmen, *Caperucita en Manhattan* (Madrid: Siruela, 1990).

Martín Gaite, Carmen, *Agua pasada* (Barcelona: Anagrama, col. Argumentos, 1993).

Martín Gaite, Carmen, *Después de todo. Poesía a rachas* (ed. umentada) (Madrid: Hiperión, 1993).

Martín Gaite, Carmen, *Cuentos completos y un monólogo (a Palo seco)* (ed. aumentada) (Barcelona: Anagrama, 1994).

Martín Gaite, Carmen, *Esperando el porvenir. Homenaje a Ignacio Aldecoa* (Madrid: Siruela, 1994).

Martín Gaite, Carmen, *La reina de las nieves* (Barcelona: Anagrama, 1994), p. 97.

Martín Gaite, Carmen, *Hilo a la cometa. La visión, la memoria y el sueño* (Madrid: Espasa–Calpe, 1995).

Martín Gaite, Carmen, *El cuarto de atrás* (Barcelona: Destino, 1996).

Martín Gaite, Carmen, *Nubosidad variable* (Barcelona: Anagrama, 1996).

Martín Gaite, Carmen, *Retahílas* (Barcelona: Destino, 1996).

Martín Gaite, Carmen, *La reina de las nieves* (Barcelona: Anagrama, col. Compactos, 1997).

Martín Gaite, Carmen, *Irse de casa* (Barcelona: Anagrama, col. Narrativas Hispánicas, 1998).

Martín Gaite, Carmen, *Cuéntame* (Madrid: Espasa–Calpe, col. Austral, 1999).

Martín Gaite, Carmen, *Desde la ventana*, 3rd ed. (Madrid: Espasa–Calpe, 1999).

Martín Gaite, Carmen, *La hermana pequeña* (Barcelona: Anagrama, col. Narrativas Hispánicas, 1999).

Martín Gaite, Carmen, *Lo raro es vivir* (Barcelona: Anagrama, col. Compactos, 1999).

Martín Gaite, Carmen, *Nubosidad variable*, 6th ed. (Barcelona: Anagrama, col. Compactos, 2000).

Martín Gaite, Carmen, *Usos amorosos de la postguerra española*, 7th ed. (Barcelona: Anagrama, col. Compactos, 2000).

Martín Gaite, Carmen, *Dos cuentos maravillosos*, 5th ed. (Madrid: Siruela, 2001).

Martín Gaite, Carmen, *Los parentescos* (Barcelona: Anagrama, col. Narrativas Hispánicas, 2001).

Martín Gaite, Carmen, *Cuadernos de todo* (Barcelona: Random House–Mondadori, 2002).

Martín Gaite, Carmen, *Pido la palabra* (Barcelona: Anagrama, col. Argumentos, 2002).

Martín Gaite, Carmen, *Visión de Nueva York* (Madrid: Siruela, 2005).

Martín Gaite, Carmen, *Tirando del hilo: artículos, 1949–2000*, José Teruel (ed.) (Madrid: Siruela, 2006).

## Bibliography on Carmen Martín Gaite


Alemany Bay, Carmen, *La novelística de Carmen Martín Gaite*. 1st edn (Salamanca: Diputación de Salamanca, 1990).

Andreu, Alicia G., 'La Sección Femenina de la Falange en la obra de Carmen Martin Gaite: la popularidad de las novelas rosa en la posguerra española', *Revista De Estudios Hispánicos*, 36/1 (2002), 145–52.

Bautista Botello, Ester, 'Collages and Narrative in Carmen Martín Gaite', in Marian Womack and Jennifer Wood (eds), *Beyond the Back Room* (Oxford–New York: Peter Lang, 2011), pp. 11–34.

Bautista Botello, Ester, 'El punto de vista literario y visual: Hooper y Martín Gaite', *Espéculo: Revista de Estudios Literarios*, Carmen Martín Gaite. Nuevas perspectivas, 52 (enero–junio 2014), 70–80.

Bermejo, José María, 'Carmen Martín Gaite: una crónica de la soledad', *Cuadernos Hispanoamericanos*, 350 (agosto, 1979), 437–9.

Brown, Joan Lipman, 'Martín Gaite's short stories. 1953–1974: the writer's workshops', in Mirella Servodidio and Marcia L. Welles (eds), *From Fiction to Metafiction: Essays in Honor of Carmen Martín Gaite* (Lincoln, Nebraska: Society of Spanish and Spanish American Studies, 1983), pp. 39–48.

Brown, Joan Lipman, 'One Autobiography, Twice Told: Martín Gaite's *Entre visillos* and *El cuarto de atrás*', *Hispanic Journal* 7 (1986), 37–47.

Brown, Joan Lipman, 'Carmen Martín Gaite: Reaffirming the Pact between Reader and Writer', in *Women Writers of Contemporary Spain. Exiles in the Homeland* (London and Toronto: University of Delaware Press, 1991).

Brown, Joan Lipman, 'Women Writers of Spain: An Historical Perspective', in *Women Writers of Contemporary Spain. Exiles in the Homeland* (London and Toronto: University of Delaware Press, 1991).

Brown, Joan Lipman, *Women Writers of Contemporary Spain: Exiles in the Homeland* (Newark: University of Delaware Press; Cranbury, NJ: Associated University Presses, 1991).

Calvi, María Vittoria, *Dialogo e conversazione nella narrativa di Carmen Martín Gaite* (Milano: Arcipelago Edizioni, 1990).

Calvi, María Vittoria, 'Ritratto di scrittore in un interno: Da *Fragmentos de interior* a *El cuarto de atrás*' in María Vittoria Calvi (ed.), *Dialogo e conversazione nella narrativa di Carmen Martín Gaite* (Milano: Arcipelago Edizioni, 1990), pp. 113–48.

Calvi, Maria Vittoria, 'Poética del lugar y actitud autobiográfica en Carmen Martín Gaite', in Teruel José and Valcárcel Carmen (eds), *Un lugar llamado Carmen Martín Gaite* (Madrid: Siruela, 2014), pp. 124–37.

Calvi, Maria Vittoria, 'Presentación de los Cuadernos de todo en Salamanca', *ESPÉCULO*, 2003.

Cantavella, Juan, *Semblanzas entrevistas: Carmen Martín Gaite, Narciso Yepes, Manuel Gutiérrez Mellado* (Madrid: PPC, 1995).

Carbayo Abengózar, Mercede*s*, *Buscando un lugar entre mujeres: Buceo en la España de Carmen Martín Gaite* (Málaga: Servicio de Publicaciones de la Universidad de Málaga, 1998).

Casorrán Marín, María José, *Estudio crítico de El cuarto de atrás* (Biblioteca Estudios, Zaragoza: Mira Editores, 2006).

Ciplijauskaité, Biruté, *La novela femenina contemporánea (1970–1985) Hacia una tipología de la narración en primera persona* (Barcelona: Anthropos, 1994).

Ciplijauskaité, Biruté, *Carmen Martin Gaite (1925–2000)* (Madrid: Ediciones del Orto, 2000).

Cruz-Cámara, Nuria, *Metaficción e intertextualidad en la narrativa de Los Noventa de Carmen Martín Gaite* (Buffalo: State University of New York, 1999).

Cruz-Cámara, Nuria, 'Chicas raras en dos novelas de Carmen Martin Gaite y Carmen Laforet', *Hispanófila*, 139 (2003), 97.

Cruz-Cámara, Nuria, 'La re-Creación del romanticismo en *La reina de las nieves* de Martin Gaite', *Symposium*, 57/2 (2003), 81.

Cruz-Cámara, Nuria, 'Utopia y critica social: los espacios del "romance" en "*La reina de las nieves*" de Carmen Martin Gaite', *Revista Hispánica Moderna: Boletín Del Instituto De Las Españas*, 58/1 (2005), 119.

Cruz-Cámara, Nuria, *El laberinto intertextual de Carmen Martín Gaite: un estudio de sus novelas de los noventa* (Newark: Juan de la Cuesta Hispanic monographs, 2008).

Davies, Catherine, 'Writing from Within, with her Own Voice: Carmen Martín Gaite' (1925), *Spanish Women's Writing 1849–1996* (London: Athlone Press, 1998), pp. 228–46.

de la Fuente, Inmaculada, *Mujeres de la posguerra. De Carmen Laforet a Rosa Chacel: Historia de una generación* (Barcelona: Planeta Historia y Sociedad, 2002).

de Lerma, María-José Blanco López, *Life-Writing in Carmen Martín Gaite's* Cuadernos de Todo *and her Novels of the 1990s* (Rochester, NY: Boydell & Brewer, 2013).

El Saffar, Ruth, 'Redeeming Loss: Reflections on Carmen Martín Gaite's *The Back Room*', *Revista de Estudios Hispánicos*, XX/1 (enero de 1986), 1–14.

Encinar, Ángeles and Kathleen M. Glenn, 'Ventanas al yo y al mundo americano en *Los Cuadernos de todo* de Carmen Martín Gaite', *Un lugar llamado Carmen Martín Gaite* (Madrid: Siruela, 2014), pp. 94–108.

Fernández, Celia, 'Entrevista a Carmen Martín Gaite', *ALEC*, 4 (1979), 165–72.

Gamallo, I. C. A., 'El Cuarto de atrás de Carmen Martin Gaite o La ambigüedad de lo Fantástico', *Confluencia*, 22/1 (2006), 67–82.

García, Adrián M., *Silence in the Novels of Carmen Martín Gaite* (New York: Peter Lang Publishing, 2000).

Garlinger, Patrick Paul, 'Corresponding with Carmen Martin Gaite: The Death of the Letter Writer', *Revista De Estudios Hispánicos*, 36/1 (2002), 191–5.

Glenn, Kathleen M., 'Hilos, ataduras y ruinas en la novelística de Carmen Martín Gaite', in Janet Pérez (ed), *Novelistas femeninas de la postguerra española* (Madrid: Ediciones José Porrúa, 1983, pp. 33–45.

Glenn, Kathleen M., 'Collage, Textile and Palimpsest: Carmen Martín Gaite's *Nubosidad variable*', *Romance Languages Annual*, 5 (1993), 408–13.

Granata de Egües, Gladis, 'La literatura y la vida: los cuadernos de Carmen Martín Gaite', *Revista de literaturas modernas*, 36 (2006), 123–36.

Hernández Álvarez, María Vicenta, 'Un rincón para leer con la ventana abierta. Los Cuadernos de todo de Carmen Martín Gaite', *Cauce*, 36 (2014), pp. 95–116.

Illán Martín, Magdalena, 'Las mujeres en el espacio públcio de la creatividad en la España de Posguerra: Carmen Laffón y Carmen Martín Gaite', in Esperanza Bosch Fiol (Coord.), *Los feminismos como herramientas de cambio social* (España: Universitat de les Illes Balears, 2006), pp. 189–205.

Jiménez Corretjer, Zoé, *El fantástico femenino en España y América: Martín Gaite, Rodoreda, Garro y Peri Rossi* (San Juan: Editorial de la Universidad de Puerto Rico, 2001).

Jiménez González, Mercedes, *Carmen Martín Gaite y la narración: teoría y práctica* (New Brunswick, NJ: SLUSA, 1989).

Jurado Morales, José, 'Mundo interior versus sociedad posmoderna o una lectura de *Los parentescos* de Carmen Martín Gaite', *Revista De Estudios Hispánicos*, 36/1 (2002), 205–9.

Jurado Morales, José, *La trayectoria narrativa de Carmen Martín Gaite (1925–2000)* (Madrid: Gredos, 2003).

Levine, Linda Gould, 'Carmen Martín Gaite's *El cuarto de atrás*: A Portrait of the Artist as Woman', in Servodidio and Welles (eds), *From Fiction to Metafiction: Essays in Honor of Carmen Martín Gaite* (Lincoln, Nebraska: Society of Spanish and Spanish American Studies, 1983), 161–72.

Lluch Villalba, Ma. Ángeles, *Los cuentos de Carmen Martín Gaite. Temas y técnicas de una escritora de los años cincuenta* (Pamplona: Ediciones de la Universidad de Navarra, col. Anejos de RILCE, 2000).

Martinell Gifre, Emma (ed), *Carmen Martín Gaite* (Madrid: Ediciones de Cultura Hispánica, 1993).

Martinell Gifre, Emma, *El mundo de los objetos en la obra de Carmen Martín Gaite* (Cáceres: Servicio de Publicaciones de la Universidad de Extremadura, 1996).

Martinell Gifre, Emma, *Al encuentro de Carmen Martín Gaite. Homenajes y bibliografía* (Barcelona: Departamento de Filología de la Universidad de Barcelona, 1997).

Martínez Rodríguez, María del Mar, *El lenguaje del auto-descubrimiento en la narrativa de Merce Rodoreda y Carmen Martin Gaite* (Madison, Wis: University of Wisconsin Press, 1988).

Matamoro, Blas, 'Carmen Martín Gaite: viaje al cuarto de Atrás', *Cuadernos Hispanoamericanos*, 351 (septiembre 1979), 581–605.

Ochoa, Debra J., 'Martín Gaite's *Visión de Nueva York*: Collages of Public and Private Space', in Marian Womack and Jennifer Wood (eds), *Beyond the Back Room* (Oxford–New York: Peter Lang, 2011), pp. 81–97.

Ordóñez, Elizabeth Jane, *Voices of their own: Contemporary Spanish Narrative by Women* (Plainsboro, NJ: Associated University Presses, 1991).

Paatz, Annette, 'Medio Siglo al servicio de la narración: estudios recientes sobre la obra de Carmen Martín Gaite (1925–2000)', in *Iberoamericana. América Latina, España, Portugal: Ensayos sobre letras, historia y sociedad* in Instituto Ibero-Americano de Berlín, el Instituto de Estudios Iberoamericanos de Hamburgo y la Editorial Iberoamericana/ Vervuert, 17 (2005), 177–82.

Parker, Margaret, 'Revisiting Spain as Liberation from the Past in *Irse de casa* and *A Woman Unknown: Voices from a Spanish Life*', *South Central Review* 18:1/2 (2001), 114–26.

Pérez, Janet (ed), *Novelistas femeninas de la postguerra española* (Madrid: Porrúa Turanzas, 1983).

Pérez, Janet, *Contemporary Women Writers of Spain* (Boston: Twayne Publishers, 1988).

Pittarello, Elide, '*El cuento de nunca acabar* y *Visión de Nueva York. Notas en forma de collage*', in Florencio de la Rosa, Ignacio Arroyo *et al.*, *Geométrica explosion*, pp. 351–72, seen at http://www.mediosiglo.es/docs/ Pittarello_cuento_nunca_acabar.pdf

Pittarello, Elide. 'Visión de Nueva York de Carmen Martín Gaite: el ojo, la mano, la voz', in José Teruel (ed.), *Un Lugar Llamado Carmen Martín Gaite* (Madrid: Siruela, 2014), pp. 154–74.

Pozuelo Yvancos, José María. '*Los Cuadernos de todo* y la escritura del yo', in José Teruel (ed.), *Un Lugar Llamado Carmen Martín Gaite* (Madrid: Siruela, 2014), pp. 109–23.

Puente Samaniego, Pilar de la, *La narrativa breve de Carmen Martín Gaite* (Salamanca: Plaza Universitaria Ediciones, 1994).

Rodríguez Álvarez, Josefina, *Los niños de la guerra* (Madrid: Ediciones Generales Anaya, 1983).

Rodríguez Magda, Rosa María, *Modelo Frankenstein, (El) 'De la diferencia a la cultura postmoderna'* (Madrid: Tecnos, 1997).

Rolón-Collazo, Lissette, *Figuraciones. Mujeres en Carmen Martín Gaite, revistas femeninas Y ¡Hola!* (Madrid: Iberoamericana, 2002).

Senís Fernández, Juan, 'Más allá del diario: los "Cuadernos de todo", de Carmen Martín Gaite', in *El diario como forma narrativa: IX Simposio*

*Internacional sobre Narrativa Hispánica Contemporánea, El Puerto de Santa María, Noviembre 2001* (Fundación Luis Goytisolo, 2002). pp. 61–72.

Senís Fernández, Juan, 'Amistades de ida y vuelta a través del texto', *Espéculo*, 43 (2009): *https://pendientedemigracion.ucm.es/info/especulo/cmgaite/senis.htm*

Senís Fernández, Juan, 'Du collage à l'album: Hybridité discursive et générique dans *Visión de Nueva York* de Carmen Martín Gaite', *Babel*, 33 | 2016. URL: http://babel.revues.org/4428; DOI: 10.4000/babel.4428

Senís Fernández, Juan, Marta Sanjuán Álvarez and Eva Villar Secanella, 'Carmiña and the city: Visiones de Nueva York en la obra gráfica de Carmen Martín Gaite', *Hispanófila* 175/1 (2015), 247–61.

Servodidio, Mirella, and Marcia Welles (eds), *From Fiction to Metafiction: Essays in Honor of Carmen Martín Gaite* (Lincoln, Nebraska: Society of Spanish and Spanish–American Studies, 1983).

Sieburth, Stephanie, 'The Conversation I Never Had with Carmen Martin Gaite', *Revista De Estudios Hispánicos*, 36/1 (2002), 227.

Sotelo Vázquez, Adolfo, 'Introducción', in Carmen Martin Gaite, *Retahílas*, (Barcelona: Destino, col. Clásicos Contemporáneos Comentados, 1996), pp. xlvii–lxv.

Spires, Robert C., 'Intertextuality in *El Cuarto De Atrás*', in Servodidio and Welles (eds), *From Fiction to Metafiction: Essays in Honor of Carmen Martín Gaite* (Lincoln, Nebraska: Society of Spanish and Spanish–American Studies, 1983), pp. 139–48.

Spires, Robert C., *Beyond the Metafictional Mode. Directions in the Modern Spanish Novel* (Lexington: University Press of Kentucky, 1984).

Talbot, Lynn K., 'Female Archetypes in Carmen Martín Gaite's *Entre Visillos*', *ALEC*, 12 (1987), 79–94.

Teruel, José and Carmen Valcárcel, *Un lugar llamado Carmen Martín Gaite* (Madrid: Siruela, 2014).

Torre Fica, Iñaki '"La mujer ventanera" en la Poesía de Carmen Martín Gaite', *Espéculo. Revista de Estudios Literarios: http://www.ucm.es/info/especulo/numero19/ventana.html* (2001; accessed 19 April 2002).

Uxó González, Carlos, 'La recuperación de la memoria en *La reina de las nieves* de Carmen Martín Gaite', *Donaire*, 13 (1999), 39–46.

Vilanova, Antonio, 'El balneario', in *Novela y Sociedad en la España de la posguerra* (Barcelona: Lumen, Colección Palabra Critica, 1995), pp. 379–82.

Vilanova, Antonio, 'Entre visillos', in *Novela y Sociedad en la España de la posguerra* (Barcelona: Lumen, Colección Palabra Critica, 1995), pp. 382–6.

Vilanova, Antonio, 'Carmen Martín Gaite y la teoría de la novela dentro de la novela', in *Acta Románica Basiliensia*, 4 (1994): 15–29.

Zanetta, María Alejandra, 'Carmen Martín Gaite y Remedios Varo: Trayecto hacia el interior a través de la literature y la pintura', *ALEC*, 27:2 (2002), 279–309.

Zatlin, Phyllis, 'Women Novelists in Democratic Spain: Freedom to Express the Female Perspective', *Anales de la Literatura Española Contemporánea*, 12 (1987), 29–44.

Zecchi, Barbara, 'Inconsciente generico, feminismo y Nubosidad variable de Carmen Martin Gaite', *Arbor* 182/720 (2006), 527.

## General bibliography

Acton, Mary, *Learning to Look at Paintings* (London: Routledge, 1997).

Adamowicz, Elza, *Surrealist Collage in Text and Image: Dissecting the Exquisite Corpse* (Cambridge: Cambridge University Press, 1998).

Alcalde, Carmen, *Mujeres en el Franquismo: Exiliadas, nacionalistas y opositoras* (Barcelona: Flor del Viento, 1996).

Alonso, Santos, 'Novela en la transición, transición en la novela (1975–1980)', in *Nueva Estafeta*, 31/32 (1981), 86–91.

Alonso, Santos, 'La transición: hacia una nueva novella', *Ínsula* 512/513 (agosto–septiembre 1989), 11–12.

Alter, Robert, *Partial Magic: The Novel as a Self-Conscious Genre* (Berkeley: University of California Press, 1975).

Amell, Samuel, 'El cine y la novela española de la postguerra', *Actas del X Congreso de la Asociación Internacional de Hispanistas*, 2 (1989), 1593–600.

Amorós, Celia, *Tiempo de feminismo: sobre feminismo, proyecto ilustrado y post-modernidad* (Madrid: Ediciones Cátedra, 1997).

Ankum, Katharina von (ed.), *Women in the Metropolis: Gender and Modernity in Weimar Culture* (Berkeley and Los Angeles: University of California Press, 1997).

Aragon, Louis, *Los colages* (Madrid: Síntesis, 2001).

Ardener, Shirley, 'Ground Rules and Social Maps for Women: An Introduction', in Shirley Ardener, *Women and Space: Ground Rules and Social Maps* (London: Oxford University Women's Studies Committee, 1981), pp. 30–55.

Arneil, Barbara, *Politics and Feminism* (Oxford: Blackwell, 1999).

Bachelard, Gaston, *El aire y los sueños: ensayo sobre la imaginación del movimiento*, 1943, trans. Ernestina de Champourcin, 1st edn (México: Fondo de Cultura Económica, 1980).

Bachelard, Gaston, *La poética de la ensoñación*, 1960, trans. Ida Vitale (México: Fondo de Cultura Económica, 1982).

Bachelard, Gaston, *La poética del espacio*, trans. Ernestina de Champourcin, 2nd edn (México: Fondo de Cultura Económica, 1975).

Bachelard, Gaston and Ernestina de Champourcin, *El Aire y los sueños: ensayo sobre la imaginación del movimiento* (México: Fondo de Cultura Económica, 1958), p. 30.

Bal, Mieke. *Conceptos viajeros en las humanidades. Una guía de viaje* (Murcia: CENDEAC, 2009).

Ballarín Domingo, Pilar, María Teresa Gallego Méndez and Isabel Martínez, *Los estudios de las mujeres en las Universidades españolas, 1975–1991: Libro Blanco* (Madrid: Instituto de la Mujer, 1995).

Barrero Pérez, Oscar, *La novella existencial española de posguerra* (Madrid: Gredos, 1987).

Barrero Pérez, Oscar, *Historia de la literatura española contemporánea (1939–1990)* (Madrid: Istmo, 1992).

Basanta, Ángel, 'Autobiografías noveladas y novelas autobiográficas', *Ínsula* 589–90 (enero-febrero 1996), 7–9.

Béhar, Henri, *Littéruptures. Lausanne: L'Age d'homme* (Lausanne: Bibliothèque Mélusine, 1988).

Benjamin, Walter, 'The Work of Art in the Age of Mechanical Reproduction', in Hannah Arendt (ed.), *Illuminations* (New York: Schocken Books, 1969).

Benjamin, Walter, *Baudelaire: Un Poeta en el esplendor del Capitalismo* (Madrid: Taurus, 1972).

Bieder, Maryellen, 'Gender and Language: The Womanly Woman and Manly Writing', in Lou Charnon-Deutsch and Jo Labanyi (eds), *Culture and Gender in Nineteenth-Century Spain* (Oxford: Clarendon Press, 1995), 98–119.

Bordo, Susan R., *The Flight to Objectivity: Essays on Cartesianism and Culture* (Albany: SUNY Press, 1987).

Bou, Enric, *Pintura en el aire. Arte y literatura en la modernidad* (Valencia: Pre-Textos, 2001).

Bowlby, Sophia et al., *Geography and Gender. An Introduction to Feminist Geography.* (London: Hutchinson in association with The Explorations in Feminism Collective, 1984).

Buckley, Ramón, *Problemas formales en la novela española contemporánea* (Barcelona: Península, 1973).

Buckley, Ramón, *La doble transición. Política y literature en la España de los años setenta.* (Madrid: Siglo XXI, 1996).

Bravo, María Elena, 'Ante la novela de la democracia: reflexiones sobre sus raíces', *Ínsula* 444–5 (noviembre–diciembre 1983), 1, 24–5.

Buck-Morss, Susan, 'The Flaneur, the Sandwichman and the Whore: The Politics of Loitering', *New German Critique*, 39 (1986), 99–140.

Caballé, Anna, and Tania Pleitez, *Lo mío es escribir. Vida escrita por las mujeres 1* (Barcelona: Lumen, 2004).

Caballero Bonald, José Manuel, 'Coloquios sobre novela', *Olvidos de Granada*, 13 (1986), 160–72.

Calvino, Italo and Aurora Bernárdez, *Colección de arena* (Madrid: Siruela, 2001).

Campbell, Federico, *Conversaciones con escritores* (México: Consejo Nacional para la Cultura y las Artes–Fondo Editorial Tierra Adentro, 2004).

Careri, Francesco, *Walkscapes. El andar como práctica estética* (Barcelona: Gustavo Gili, 2002).

Castellet, José María, 'La novela española, quince años después, 1942– 1975', *Cuadernos del Congreso por la libertad de la cultura*, 33 (1958), 43–55.

Castillo-Puche, José Luis, 'Situación de la novela española actual', in Samuel Amell and Salvador García Castañeda (eds), *La cultura española en el posfranquismo: diez años de cine, cultura y literatura en España (1975–1985)* (Madrid: Playor, 1988).

Chadwick, Whitney, *Women, Art, and Society* (London: Thames & Hudson, 1996).

Charnon-Deutsch, Lou, *Gender and Representation: Women in Spanish Realist Fiction* (Amsterdam: John Benjamins, 1990).

Cruz, Anne J., Rosilie Hernández-Pecoraro and Joyce Tolliver, *Disciplines on the Line: Feminist Research on Spanish, Latin American, and U.S. Latina Women.* Juan de la Cuesta Hispanic monographs (Newark, NJ: Juan de la Cuesta, 2004).

Davies, Catherine, *Contemporary Feminist Fiction in Spain: The Work of Montserrat Roig and Rosa Montero* (Oxford: Berg, 1994).

de Certeau, Michel, *The Practice of Everyday Life* (Los Angeles: University of California Press, 1984).

de Lauretis, Teresa, 'Feminist Studies/Critical Studies: Issues, Terms and Contexts', in *Feminist Studies/Critical Studies* (London: Macmillan, 1986), pp.1–19.

D'Souza, Aruna, and Tom McDonough, *The Invisible Flaneuse? Gender, Public Space and Visual Culture in Nineteenth-Century Paris* (Manchester: Manchester University Press, 2006).

Durán, Manuel, '"Así que pasen diez años": la novela española de los setenta', *Anales de la Narrativa Española Contemporánea*, V (1980), 91–106.

Elsen, Albert E., *Purposes of Art* (New York: Holt, Rinehart and Winston, 1967).

Ewen, Elizabeth, and Stewart Ewen, *Channels of Desire: Mass Images and the Shaping of American Consciousness* (New York: McGraw-Hill, 1982).

Fernández, Luis Miguel, *El neorrealismo en la narración española de los años cincuenta* (Santiago de Compostela: Servicio de Publicacións e Intercambio Científico da Universidade de Santiago de Compostela, 1992).

Ferrary, Álvaro, 'La vida cultural: limitaciones, condicionantes y desarrollo. Posfranquismo y democracia', in Javier Paredes (Coord.), *Historia contemporánea de España (siglo XIX –XX)* (Madrid: Ariel, 1998), 1035–49.

Felski, Rita, 'Feminism, Postmodernism, and the Critique of Modernity', *Cultural Critique* 13 (Autumn 1989), 33–56.

Folguera, Pilar, 'Las mujeres en la España Contemporánea', *Historia de las mujeres en España* (España: Síntesis, 1997), 417–20.

Fowler, Alastair, *Kinds of Literature. An Introduction to the Theory of Genres and Modes.* (Cambridge: Harvard University Press, 1982).

Friedberg, Anne, 'Les Flaneurs Du Mal (L): Cinema and the Postmodern Condition', *PMLA*, 106/3 (May 1991), 419–23.

Friedman, Norman, 'Point of View in Fiction: The Development of a Critical Concept', *PMLA*, LXX (1955), 1160–84.

García, María Antonia, 'Los estudios de Género en España (un balance)', *Revista Complutense de Educación*, 10/2 (1999), 167–87.

García Basauri, Mercedes, 'La Sección Femenina en la guerra civil española', *Historia 16* 50 (Junio 1980), 45–56.

García Berrio, Antonio, and Teresa Hernández Fernández, *'Ut Poesis Pictura'. Poética del arte visual* (Madrid: Tecnos, 1988).

Garlinger, Patrick Paul, *Confessions of the Letter Closet Epistolary Fiction and Queer Desire in Modern Spain* (Minneapolis: University of Minnesota Press, 2005).

Genette, Gerard, *Figuras III* (Barcelona: Lumen, 1989).

Gil Casado, Pablo, *La novela social española, 1920–1973* (Barcelona: Seix Barral, 1973).

Gilbert, Sandra M, and Susan Gubar, *La loca del desván. La escritora y la imaginación literaria del siglo XI*, trans. Carmen Martínez Gimeno (Madrid: Cátedra, col. Feminismos, 1998).

Gleber, Anke, 'Female Flanerie and the *Symphony of the City*', in Katharina von Ankum (ed.), Women *in the Metropolis: Gender and Modernity in Weimar Culture* (Berkeley and Los Angeles: University of California Press, 1997), pp. 67–88.

Godsland, Shelley, and Nickianne Moody, *Reading the Popular in Contemporary Spanish Texts* (Newark: University of Delaware Press, 2004).

Golding, John, *Cubism: A History and an Analysis 1907–1914* (Cambridge: Harvard University Press, 1988).

Gómez Redondo, Fernando, *La crítica literaria del siglo XX* (Madrid: EDAF, 1996).

González, Josefina, 'Dibujo, Espacio y Ecofeminismo en la C. de El Cuarto de Atrás, de Carmen Martín Gaite', *Revista Canadiense de Estudios Hispánicos*, 19/1 (1994), 86.

González Castro, Francisco, *Las relaciones insólitas: literatura fantástica española del siglo XX* (Madrid: Pliegos, 1996).

Goytisolo, Juan, *Problemas de la novela* (Barcelona: Seix Barral, 1959).

Haraway, Donna, *Simians, Cyborgs and Women: The Reinvention of Nature* (London: Free Association Books, 1991).

Herzberger, David, 'The Spanish Novel and Its Critics: 1936–1986', *ALEC*, 13 (1988), 13–24.

Hoffman, Katherine (ed.), *Collage Critical Views* (Ann Arbor: UMI Research Press, 1989).

hooks, bell, *Feminist Theory: From Margin to Center* (Boston: South End Press, 1984).

Irigaray, Luce, 'Interview with Luce Irigaray', in M.-F. Hans and G. Lapouge (eds), *Les Femmes, La Pornographie et L'Érotisme* (Paris: Seuil, 1978).

Irigaray, Luce, *Speculum of the Other Woman*, trans. Gillian C. Gill (Ithaca: Cornell University Press, 1985).

Joeres, Ruth-Ellen B., and Elizabeth Mittman, *The Politics of the Essay: Feminist Perspectives* (Bloomington: Indiana University Press, 1993).

Johnson, Louise, 'Gender, Genetics, and the Possibility of Feminist Geography', *Australian Geographical Studies*, 23 (1985), 161–71.

Johnson, Roberta, 'Carmen de Burgos and Spanish Modernism', *South Central Review* 18/1–2 (Spring–Summer, 2001), 66–77.

Kirkpatrick, Susan, and Jaqueline Cruz, *Mujer, modernismo y vanguardia en España: 1898–1931* (Madrid: Cátedra, 2003).

Kuspit, Donald B., 'Collage: The Organizing Principle of Art in the Age of the Relativity of Art', in Katherine Hoffman (ed.), *Collage Critical Views* (Ann Arbor: UMI Research Press, 1989), pp. 39–57.

Kymlicka, Will, *Multicultural Citizenship* (Oxford: Clarendon Press, 1995).

Labanyi, Jo, *Gender and Modernization in the Spanish Realist Novel* (Oxford and New York: Oxford University Press, 2000).

Lee, Rensselaer, *Uc Pictura Poesis. La teoría humanística de la pintura* (Madrid: Cátedra, 1982).

Lejeune, Philippe, 'De la autobiografía al diario: historia de una deriva', in Ma. Pilar Saiz Cerreda y Rosalía Baena (eds), RILCE 28.1 *Monográfico. Identidad y representación en el discurso autobiográfico* (2012), pp. 82–8.

Litvak, Lily, *Imágenes y textos. Estudios sobre literatura y pintura 1849–1936* (The Netherlands: Rodopi, 1998).

Magny, Claude-Edmonde, *L'Age du roman américain* (París: Seuil, 1947).

Massey, Doreen, *Space, Place and Gender* (Cambridge: Polity Press, 1994).

Mechthild, Albert (ed.), *Vencer no es convencer: literature e ideología del fascismo español* (Frankfurt and Madrid: Vervuert e Iberoamericana, 1998).

Miller, Nancy K., 'Arachnologies: The Woman, the Text, and the Critic', in Nancy K. Miller (ed.), *The Poetics of Gender* (New York: Columbia University Press, 1986), pp. 270–95.

Millett, Kate, *Sexual Politics* (London: Virago, 1977).

Mirzoeff, Nicholas, *The Visual Culture Reader* (London: Routledge, 1998).

Moi, Toril, *Sexual/Textual Politics: Feminist Literary Theory* (London: Methuen, 1985).

Moi, Toril, *Teoría literaria feminista*, trans. Amaia Bárcena (Madrid: Cátedra, 1999).

Molinero, Carme, 'Silencio e invisibilidad: la mujer durante el primer franquismo', in *Ideología y cultura en la España de los vencedores (1939–1945)*, *Monográfico de Revista de Occidente*, 223 (1999), 63–82.

Montero Díaz, Julio, 'El franquismo: planteamiento general', in Javier Paredes (coord.), *Historia contemporánea de España (siglo XIX–XX)* (Madrid: Ariel, 1998), pp. 639–62.

Nava, Mica, 'Modernity's Disavowal: Women, the City, and the Department Store', in *Modern Times: Reflections in a Centruy of English Modernity* (London and New York: Routledge, 1996).

Navajas, Gonzalo, *Teoría y práctica de la novela española posmoderna* (Barcelona: Edicions del Mall, 1987).

Nord, Deborah Epstein, *Walking the Victorian Streets: Women, Representation and the City* (Ithaca, New York and London: Cornell University Press, 1995).

Ordóñez, Elizabeth J., 'Reading Contemporary Spanish Narrative by Women', *ALEC*, 7/2 (1982), 237–51.

Ordóñez, Elizabeth J., 'Inscribing Difference: "L'Ecriture Feminine" and New Narrative by Women', *ALEC*, 12 (1987), 45–58.

Ordóñez, Elizabeth J., *Voices of Their Own: Contemporary Spanish Narrative of Women* (London and Toronto: Associated University Presses, 1991).

Orozco Díaz, Emilio, *Temas del barroco de poesía y pintura* (Granada: Universidad de Granada, 1989).

Paredes Nuñez, Juan, *5 narradores de posguerra* (Granada: Universidad de Granada, 1987).

Parsons, Deborah, 'Flaneur or Flaneuse? Mythologies of Modernity', *New Formations*, 38 (1999), 91–5.

Pateman, Carole, *The Disorder of Women: Democracy, Feminism and Political Theory* (Cambridge: Polity Press, 1989).

Pedraza Jiménez, Felipe Blas, *Las épocas de la literatura española* (Barcelona: Ariel, 1997).

Pignatari, Decio, 'Semiótica del montaje', *Acta Poética*, 6 (1986), 71–80.

Pollock, Griselda, 'Modernity and the Spaces of Femininity', in *Vision and Difference: Femininity, Feminism and the Histories of Art* (London and New York: Routledge, 1988), pp. 50–90.

Postigo, Marta, 'Mujer, Feminismo y Modernidad: Atrapadas entre lo público y lo privado', *Thémata. Revista de Filosofía*, 39 (2007), 281–6.

Praz, Mario, *Mnemosyne: The Parallel between Literature and the Visual Arts* (London: Oxford University Press, 1970).

Preble, Duane, and Sarah Preble, *Artforms* (London and New York: Harper & Row, 1989).

Prieto, Char, Cuatro *décadas, cuatro autoras: la forja de la novela feminina española en los albores del nuevo milenio* (New Orleans: University Press of the South, 2003).

Rappaport, Erika, '"The Halls of Temptation": Gender, Politics, and the Construction of the Department Store in Late Victorian London', *Journal of British Studies*, 35/1 (1996), 58–83.

Rey Hazas, Antonio, *Mostrar con propiedad un desatino: la novela española contemporánea* (Madrid: Eneida, 2004).

Rodríguez, Josefina, *Los niños de la Guerra* (Madrid: Anaya, 1983).

Rodríguez Magda, Rosa María, *El modelo Frankenstein. De la diferencia a la cultura post* (Madrid: Tecnos, 1997).

Roig, Montserrat, *¿Tiempo de mujer?* (Barcelona: Plaza y Janés, 1980).

Roig, Montserrat, *Mujeres en busca de un nuevo humanismo* (Barcelona: Salvat, 1985).

Rose, Gillian, *Feminism and Geography: The Limits of Geographical Knowledge* (Cambridge: Polity Press, 1993).

Sanz Villanueva, Santos, *Tendencias de la novela española actual (1950–1970)* (Madrid: Ediciones de Bolsillo, 1972).

Sanz Villanueva, Santos, *Historia de la novela social española (1942–1975)* (Madrid: Alhambra, 1980).

Sanz Villanueva, Santos, *Historia de la Literatura Española* (Barcelona: Ariel, 1984).

Scanlon, Geraldine, *La polémica feminista en la España contemporánea 1868–1974* (Madrid: Akal, 1986).

Scanlon, Geraldine, 'Emilia Pardo Bazán (1851–1921)', in Rosa María Capel (coord.), *Mujeres para la historia. Figuras destacadas del primer feminismo* (Madrid: Abada, 2004), pp. 140–75.

Schapiro, Miriam. 'Femmage', in Katherine Hoffman (ed.), *Collage in the Twentieth Century: An Overview* (Ann Arbor: UMI Research Press, 1989), pp. 295–315.

Segre, Cesare, *Principios de análisis del Texto Literario* (Barcelona, Crítica, 1985).

Showalter, Elaine, 'Piecing and Writing', in Nancy K. Miller (ed.), *The Poetics of Gender* (New York: Columbia University Press, 1986), pp. 222–47.

Sobejano, Gonzalo, *Novela española de nuestro tiempo (en busca del pueblo perdido)* (Madrid: Prensa Española, 1975).

Sobejano, Gonzalo, 'Ante la novela de los años setenta', *Ínsula* 396–7 (noviembre–diciembre 1979), 1 and 22.

Sobejano, Gonzalo, 'La novela poemática y sus alrededores', *Ínsula* 464–5 (julio–agosto 1985), 1 and 26.

Sobejano, Gonzalo, 'Novela y metanovela en España', *Ínsula* 512–13 (agosto–septiembre 1989), 4–6.

Soldevila Durante, Ignacio, *La novela desde 1936* (Madrid: Alambra, 1980).

Soler, Esteban, 'Narradores españoles del medio siglo', in *Miscellanea di Studi Ispanici Universidad de Pisa* (1971–1973), 217–370.

Soria Olmedo, Andrés, 'Cubismo y Creacionismo: Matices del Gris', *Boletín de la Fundación García Lorca*, 9 (1991), 39–49.

Spain, Daphne, *Gendered Spaces* (Chapel Hill and London: University of North Carolina Press, 1992).

Steiner, Wendy, *The Colors of Rethoric: Problems in the Relation between Literature and Painting* (Chicago: University of Chicago Press, 1982).

Tester, Keith (ed.), *The Flâneur* (London: Routledge, 1994).

Tuan, Yi-Fu, *Space and Place* (Minneapolis: University of Minnesota Press, 1977).

Velasco Marcos, Emilia, 'Las aguas y el cauce: Suerte de la metanovela', *Insula*, 589–90 (enero–febrero 1996), 40–7.

Vilanova, Antonio, *Novela y sociedad en la España de la posguerra* (Barcelona: Lumen, 1995).

Vilarós, Teresa M., *El mono del desencanto. Una crítica cultural de la transición española (1973–1993)* (Madrid: Siglo XXI, 1998).

Villanueva, Darío, 'La novela', in *Letras españolas* (Madrid: Ministerio de Cultura, 1987), pp. 19–64.

Vinci, Leonardo Da, Paragone, *A Comparison of the Arts* (New York: Oxford University Press, 1949).

Waugh, Patricia, *Metafiction: The Theory and Practice as Self-Conscious Fiction* (London: Methuen, 1984).

Weisman, Leslie Kanes, *Discrimination by Design: A Feminist Critique of the Man-Made Environment* (Chicago: University of Illinois Press, 1992).

Wescher, Herta, *Collage* (New York: Harry N. Abrams, 1968).

Wilson, Elizabeth, 'The Invisible *Flaneur*', in *The Contradictions of Culture: Cities, Culture, Women* (London: SAGE, 2001), pp. 72–89.

Wilson, Elizabeth, 'The Invisible *Flaneur*: Afterword', in *The Contradictions of Culture: Cities, Culture, Women* (London: SAGE Publications, 2001), pp. 90–4.

Wilson, Elizabeth, *The Sphinx in the City: Urban Life, the Control of Disorder, and Women* (Berkeley and Los Angeles: University of California Press, 1991).

Wilson, Elizabeth, *Adorned in Dreams: Fashion and Modernity* (Berkeley: University of California Press, 1987).

Wolff, Janet, 'The Invisible *Flaneuse*: Women and the Literature of Modernity', in *Feminine Sentences: Essays on Women and Culture* (Cambridge: Polity Press, 1990), pp. 34–50.

Wolff, Janet, 'Feminism and Modernity', in *Feminine Sentences: Essays on Women and Culture* (Cambridge: Polity Press, 1990), pp. 51–66.

Women and Geography Study Group of the IBG, *Geography and Gender: An Introduction to Feminist Geography* (London: Hutchinson in association with the Explorations in Feminism Collective, 1984).

Woolf, Virginia, *Un cuarto propio*, trans. María-Milagros Rivera Garretas (Madrid: horas y HORAS la editorial, 2003).

Zambrano, María, *Algunos lugares de la pintura* (Madrid: Espasa-Calpe, 1991).

# Index